Marriage and Divorce
in the Bible and the Church

Marriage & DIV*O*RCE

in the Bible and the Church

Alex R. G. Deasley

Beacon Hill Press of Kansas City
Kansas City, Missouri

Copyright 2000
by Beacon Hill Press of Kansas City

ISBN 083-411-7630

Printed in the
United States of America

Cover Design: Kevin Williamson

Index: Katie Roat

Library of Congress Cataloging-in-Publication Data

Deasley, Alex R. G.
    Marriage and divorce in the Bible and the church / Alex R. G. Deasley.
        p. cm.
    Includes bibliographical references and index.
    ISBN 0-8341-1763-0
        1. Marriage—Biblical teaching. 2. Divorce—Biblical teaching. 3. Church of the
Nazarene—Doctrines. I. Title.
    BS680.M35 D43 2000
    241'.63—dc21   99-087528

10 9 8 7 6 5 4 3 2

To Joyce
with my love now and always

Contents

Preface

THIS BOOK had its beginnings in a paper for a denominational committee on divorce, which eventually formed the basis of legislation presented to the General Assembly of the Church of the Nazarene in June 1993. The book is much longer than the original paper, not only because it attempts to explore more fully the biblical teaching on marriage as well as divorce, but also because it endeavors to address some of the problems encountered at the pastoral and personal levels.

I have tried to make the book accessible to two main audiences: first, to pastors and others of theological bent who wish to know the exegetical and theological bases on which the interpretation rests. For their sakes, I have included a considerable number of footnotes to spell out some points of argument more fully, as well as to indicate where further information might be found. However, I have also tried to write for the informed and inquiring layperson (of whom there are many), who, without being concerned with technical details, wishes to have access to a considered statement of biblical teaching. I have tried to write in such a way that it will be possible for such readers to follow the drift of the argument without troubling with the notes at all. How far I have succeeded is not for me to say, especially since, at some points, the biblical teaching calls for effort: but this, at the least, is what I have attempted.

I have many debts. The subject has been of interest to me for many years, and I owe much to those with whom I have discussed it, not least those who have responded to earlier pieces I have written. My debts to other writers are indicated in the footnotes. If, by oversight, I have failed to do this, I apologize to those concerned. I also owe much to the committee referred to above, and not least its adviser, Dr. Jerald D. Johnson, who encouraged me to put my work in published form. But my greatest debt is to my wife, Joyce, not only because she toiled over successive drafts at the word processor, but also for other reasons "too deep for words." To her the book is gratefully dedicated.

Introduction

THE TITLE OF THIS BOOK is a sufficient indication of its substance and purpose. Both the choice of components and their order are intentional and together hint (to say no more) at the measure of the task facing both writer and readers. Thus, it would have been easier to write a book about divorce, treating marriage as little more than the necessary presupposition of divorce. Besides making the biblical teaching about divorce harder to grasp, it would have also risked misrepresenting the biblical emphasis, which is on marriage, not divorce.

The second pair of components, the Bible and the Church, likewise is chosen deliberately. Again, it would have been much easier to write an academic treatise about what the Bible teaches, leaving the practical application to take care of itself. The Church not only stands under the judgment of the Word of God but also desperately needs to know what to say to an age when the lives of individuals, families, and society as a whole are being disrupted by divorce on a scale unprecedented in modern times. It is indispensably necessary, therefore, for the biblical guidelines to be brought to bear on the Church and the contemporary scene in which the Church bears its witness.

Accordingly, what will be attempted is first an examination of the biblical design or ideal for marriage; that is, what it was intended to be and, by God's grace, can be. Second, we shall look at those passages in both Old and New Testaments that speak, directly or indirectly, of divorce. Next, we shall inquire if and how the gospel, with its promise of forgiveness through grace, enters into the understanding of this issue. Finally, we shall seek to bring all of this to bear on the area of contemporary church life, asking what should be the Church's message to and treatment of those who are contemplating divorce or are already divorced.

The biblical evidence begins with the creation accounts in Gen. 1 and 2 and continues through both Testaments to the close of the New Testament period. Many different customs and patterns of life are covered by such a span; and many different types of literature and speech (narrative, law, wisdom saying) are used to convey the biblical message. It is important to read these sensitively so as to avoid, for example, misreading a general principle as an absolute law. Many of the differences of interpretation regarding marriage and divorce arise because of this very thing.

With these considerations in mind, we may now turn to our first topic: the biblical ideal of marriage.

Abbreviations

AB	*Anchor Bible*
ACW	*Ancient Christian Writers*
ANF	*Ante-Nicene Fathers*
BJRL	*Bulletin of John Rylands University Library*
CBQ	*Catholic Biblical Quarterly*
CRINT	*Compendia Rerum Iudicairum ad Novum Testamentum*
EBC	*Expositor's Bible Commentary*
ET	English Translation
IC	*Interpretation Commentaries*
ICC	*International Critical Commentary*
IDB	*Interpreter's Dictionary of the Bible*
JBL	*Journal of Biblical Literature*
JLA	*Journal Law Annual*
JSNT	*Journal for the Study of the New Testament*
MT	Massoretic Text
NCB	*New Century Bible*
NICNT	*New International Commentary on the New Testament*
NICOT	*New International Commentary on the Old Testament*
NIDNTT	*New International Dictionary of New Testament Theology*
NPNF	*Nicene and Post-Nicene Fathers*
NTS	*New Testament Studies*
OTL	*Old Testament Library*
TCGNT	*Textual Commentary on the Greek New Testament*
TDNT	*Theological Dictionary of the New Testament*
TNTC	*Tyndale New Testament Commentary*
TS	*Theological Studies*
WBC	*Word Biblical Commentary*
WC	*Westminster Commentaries*

1 ⁓ The Biblical Ideal of Marriage

IN CONSIDERING the biblical ideal of marriage it is important to define the word "ideal." The term may be used in at least two distinguishable senses. On the one hand, it may denote that which exists only in idea but has no existence in reality. In this sense it indicates not only the unreal but also the unrealizable, as when we say of someone's plans or proposals, "They seem rather idealistic." On the other hand, the word may denote an existing thing as the type or standard for imitation, as when we say, "Let that be your ideal." The assumption in this case is that the ideal, far from being unattainable, is perfectly capable of realization.

Here we are concerned to set forth the biblical picture or image of marriage. As we proceed, we shall note that it is presented, not as something attainable only by an exalted few, but rather as the pattern to be followed by all. The real expectation is to achieve it, even though it takes effort and cost and, above all, the assistance of divine grace.

The Ideal of Marriage in the Old Testament

We may begin by reviewing the ideal of marriage in the Old Testament.

1. The Creation Ideal (Gen. 2:18-24)

The verses indicated clearly stand together as a unit. Verse 18 expresses God's concern to find a "helper suitable" for the man, and verse 20 notes the failure of the first attempt: "But for Adam no suitable helper was found." A second attempt is then made, which is successful (v. 23); and a comment is made indicating that the success achieved is the reason people marry (v. 24).

The passage may be said to consist of two pieces of narrative (vv. 19-20 and 21-23) describing the attempts to provide Adam with a "suitable helper," the narratives being encased in two sayings (vv. 18, 24). We shall consider these four components in order.

13

First, the opening states the problem: "It is not good for the man to be alone" (v. 18*a*). This is of fundamental importance in defining the problem to which marriage is presented as the solution, namely, the problem of the man's aloneness. But aloneness in what sense? William A. Heth replies, "Man's aloneness in Genesis 2:18 is not his 'loneliness' but his 'helplessness,' his inability, apart from the woman, to carry out God's creation directives to perpetuate and multiply the race and to cultivate and govern the earth (Gen. 1:26-28)."[1] This is sound as far as it goes, even though it may not bring the point into full focus. This takes place in verse 18*b:* "I will make a helper suitable for him." This rendering does not do full justice to the original Hebrew. Thus, the word translated "helper" *(ēzer)*, whose meaning can vary according to context, may carry the sense of "strength" (e.g., Deut. 33:26, 29). Similarly, "suitable" may not be the most apt rendering of the Hebrew *kənegdō* (which occurs only here in the Bible). It is used more frequently in later Hebrew and carries the meaning "equal."

Accordingly, R. David Freedman concludes: "I believe the customary translation of these words, despite its near universal adoption, is wrong. That is not what the words are intended to convey. They should be translated to mean approximately 'a power equal to man.' That is, when God concluded that He would create another creature so that man would not be alone, He decided to make 'a power equal to him,' someone whose strength was equal to man's. Woman was not intended to be merely man's helper. She was to be instead his partner."[2]

The heart of the biblical ideal of marriage is partnership. To appeal to the creation mandate of Gen. 1:26-28 to exclude the idea of companionship from the creation understanding of marriage is as misguided as to interpret companionship from a wholly 20th-century perspective. Claus Westermann says judiciously: "The majority of interpreters . . . have stressed correctly that the meaning is not just

---

1. Cf. William A. Heth, "Divorce, but No Remarriage," in H. Wayne House, ed., *Divorce and Remarriage: Four Christian Views* (Downers Grove, Ill.: InterVarsity Press, 1990), 78.

2. R. David Freedman, "Woman, a Power Equal to Man," *Biblical Archaeology Review* (Jan.-Feb. 1983): 56. Freedman goes on to affirm that this rendering is justified not only philologically but also by the contexts, distant and remote of the position of woman in the Old Testament (58). Walter C. Kaiser comments on Freedman's rendering, "This translation may now be the preferred one," *Towards Old Testament Ethics,* in *Academie Books* (Grand Rapids: Zondervan, 1983), 154 n. 6, cf. also 182 n. 1.

help at work . . . nor is it concerned merely with the begetting of descendants; . . . it means support in a broad sense. . . . The man is created by God in such a way that he needs the help of a partner; hence mutual help is an essential part of human existence."[3]

Adam, then, is lacking in regard to partnership, and the Lord God sees such a situation as "not good." This leads to the second part of the unit, namely the first attempt to provide Adam with partnership (Gen. 2:19-20). The search begins, appropriately enough, with other existing creatures—animals and birds—whom God created from the ground as He did the man himself (vv. 7, 19). As sharing a common origin, they might be likely to provide man with partnership. God therefore brings them to the man for naming. In the thought of the ancient world, including the Old Testament, a name was not merely a label as it is today but a description of character. To know the name was to know the nature. Adam was not merely labeling his fellow creatures but getting to know what they were like and, in particular, whether they could provide the partnership he lacked. The result of the exercise was frustration. "For Adam no suitable helper was found" (v. 20).

The third component in the unit is verses 21-23, in which the narrative of the creation of the woman is recorded. Man's plight will be resolved only by a special act of creation in which the man's partner is fashioned out of the man himself. Almost all translations read that God took one of the man's ribs for the purpose, closing up the place with flesh. But the Hebrew word *tsēlāʻ* in all of its other occurrences in the Hebrew Bible is rendered "side," and no good reason has been shown for not retaining that rendering here. If this means that the part of man from which woman was made is therefore unspecified, it more importantly indicates figuratively the nature of the relationship man lacked, namely, one to stand alongside him. Wenham comments, "Here the ideal of marriage as it was understood in ancient Israel is being portrayed, a relationship characterized by harmony and intimacy between partners."[4]

---

3. Claus Westermann, *Genesis 1—11: A Commentary,* English translation John Scullion (Minneapolis: Augsburg Publishing House, 1984), 227. Cf. S. R. Driver, "It is not enough to place man in the garden: further provision is yet required for the proper development of his nature, and satisfaction of its needs: a *help,* who may in various ways assist him, and who may at the same time prove a companion, able to interchange thought with him, and be in other respects his intellectual equal, is still needed" (*The Book of Genesis,* in *Westminster Commentaries,* 8th ed. [London: Methuen, 1911], 41).

4. Gordon J. Wenham, *Genesis 1—15,* in *Word Biblical Commentary* (Waco, Tex.: Word Books, 1987), 69.

The success of this second attempt to find a partner for the man is indicated by the poetic exclamation into which he breaks when God brings the woman to him:

This is now bone of my bones
and flesh of my flesh;
She shall be called "woman,"
for she was taken out of man (v. 23).

The meaning of the second half of the verse seems clear enough. In the same way that Adam came to "name" or know the birds and beasts and found them wanting as possible partners, so he "names" or comes to know the woman and finds her to be just like himself. This similarity is expressed in the name he gives her that bears a similar assonance to his own in Hebrew as in English: "woman" means "wife of man." The expression affirms positively what the earlier part of the narrative has indicated negatively; that is, the only being who can give man the partnership he needs is one who is like him.

The first half of verse 23 has given rise to more discussion. On the face of it, it might well seem to be a statement regarding the origin of woman and so bear the same meaning as the second half of the verse. Scholars who take this view regard the expression as a traditional formula of relationship.[5] The English equivalent would be, "This is my flesh and blood."[6] However, this is not the only possibility. Brueggemann points out that the terms "bone" and "flesh" may denote "strength" and "frailty" and that rather than being a formula of blood relationship, a formula using this expression may be a formula of covenant commitment.[7] If this is sound, then the man, on seeing the woman, is stirred to make a commitment of enduring loyalty to her: "She will be mine for better or worse." In Brueggemann's words: "A relation is affirmed which is unaffected by changing circumstances. It is a formula of constancy, of abiding loyalty which in the first place has nothing to do with biological derivation,

---

5. Cf. Wenham, "a poetic formulation of the traditional kinship formula" (ibid., 70).

6. For other examples of the Old Testament usage, see Gen. 29:14; Judg. 9:2; 2 Sam. 5:1; 19:12-13. In each of them the Hebrew reads literally "bone and flesh."

7. So when the northern tribes came to David at Hebron saying, "We are your bone and flesh" (2 Sam. 5:1), their meaning is: "We will be with you through thick and thin"; and the result is that David concludes a covenant with them (v. 3). Cf. Walter Brueggemann, "Of the Same Flesh and Bone," *Catholic Biblical Quarterly* 32, No. 4 (October 1970): 532-42.

as it is often interpreted."[8] In short, the partnership between man and woman, grounded initially in her being derived from him, is transcended by his spontaneous response of lifelong loyalty to her. As such it prepares the way for verse 24.

The fourth and final element in the unit—the saying in verse 24—is clearly linked to what goes before by this causal formula: "For this reason . . ." The saying is regarded as a statement of Adam's by some commentators, but this is improbable since it presupposes factors that have had no place in the narrative thus far, for example, parents and children. It is more probably to be seen as a comment of the narrator who, by implication, is telling the story. It indicates the point and purpose of the entire unit, namely, to explain why a man will leave the closest relationship he has known—with his father and mother—and bind himself to his wife.[9] How then is this radical rearrangement of preference explained by the preceding narrative?

One would expect a restatement and recapitulation of the main points contained in the narrative, and this, in fact, is what we find. First, reference is made to the covenantal aspect of marriage. As we have seen, it is the man's encounter with the woman, in contrast with his encounter with the beasts and birds, that prompts him to vow himself to her forever: "This is now bone of my bones and flesh of my flesh" (v. 23*a*). The covenantal overtone is underscored by the use of verbs that are standard stock in covenantal contexts in the Old Testament: to "leave" (Hebrew *'āzab)* and to "cleave" or "be united to" (Hebrew *dābaq).* The former is used repeatedly with reference to Israel's "leaving" or "forsaking" the covenant with God (Deut. 29:25; 1 Kings 19:10; Jer. 22:9; etc.), while the latter is used with similar frequency for maintaining the covenant stipulations (Deut. 11:22; 30:20). Gen. 2:24 affirms that it is the discovery of partnership with his wife that prompts a man to leave his parents and enter into a covenant with his wife. This implies not only that the awareness of complementarity is the basis of marriage but also that marriage is more than a temporary or makeshift agreement. It takes the form of a solemn covenant.

The second point, again drawing upon the earlier narrative, expresses the basis and consequence of such covenant unity: the two

---

8. Brueggemann, "Of the Same Flesh and Bone," 535.

9. Cf. Wenham, "This is not a continuation of the man's remarks in v. 23 but a comment of the narrator, applying the principles of the first marriage to every marriage" (*Genesis 1—15,* 70).

will become "one flesh." The narrative determines the meaning of the expression. The condition of man in his solitude was "not good" (v. 18), and his solitude could be cured only when a partner was created for him from his own flesh. It is precisely because his partner was created from his flesh that the two become one flesh in marriage. For what is happening is that his flesh is returning to him—yet in an unimaginably richer form: one who can share his life and labor. What the narrator is saying in verse 24 is that in potential, this is what happens in every marriage; and it is precisely because of this perceived potential that "a man will leave his father and mother and be united to his wife."

In addition the expression "one flesh" in the context of marriage also carries overtones of sexual union. It means that sexual union is the ultimate measure of mutual knowledge that binds the marriage partners together. It is no accident that the verb used in Hebrew to refer to the sex act is the verb "to know" (*yāḏaʻ* as in Gen. 4:1: "Now the man knew his wife Eve, and she conceived and bore Cain," NRSV). But the knowledge is far more than physical. In the words of D. S. Bailey: "Although the union in 'one flesh' is a physical union established by sexual intercourse . . . it involves at the same time the whole being and affects the personality at the deepest level. It is a union of the entire man and the entire woman. In it they become a new and distinct unity."[10]

---

10. Derrick Sherwin Bailey, *The Mystery of Love and Marriage* (New York: Harper, 1950), 44. Note may be taken here of yet another interpretation of the one-flesh relationship: viz. kinship. Wenham writes, "Just as blood relations are one's flesh and bone, so marriage creates a similar kinship between man and wife. They become related to each other as a brother is related to a sister. The laws in Lev. 18 and 20, and possibly Deut. 24:1-4, illustrate the application of this kinship-of-spouses principle to the situation following the divorce or death of one of the parties. Since a woman becomes at marriage a sister to her husband's brothers, a daughter to her father-in-law and so on, she cannot normally marry any of them should her first husband die or divorce her. . . . The kinships established by marriage are therefore not terminated by death or divorce" (*Genesis 1—15,* 71). On this basis Heth and Wenham argue that "a binding, perhaps even metaphysical relationship results when a man and woman leave their respective families, cleave to one another and consummate their marriage" (W. A. Heth and G. J. Wenham, *Jesus and Divorce* [Nashville: Thomas Nelson, 1985], 112). Interpreting Deut. 24:1-4 on this same principle, they conclude: "The passage seems to imply that to seek a divorce is to try to break a relationship with one's wife that in reality cannot be broken. Just as we cannot 'divorce' our children from being our own blood relations no matter how disreputable they may be, so a man cannot 'divorce' his wife who is his own flesh and blood through marriage. Thus Deut. 24:1-4 understands the 'one flesh'

Westermann sums up the overall intent of the saying when he says that "the significance of the verse lies in this, that in contrast to the established institutions and partly in opposition to them, it points to the basic power of love between man and woman."[11] To this, one would simply want to add that the love is covenanted love and that the relationship is divinely instituted inasmuch as it was God who made the woman and brought her to the man (Gen. 2:22).

---

bond of marriage to survive legal or customary divorce" (ibid., 110). Deut. 24:1-4 will be dealt with more fully in chap. 2. Whether it is sound to draw conclusions about the impossibility of divorce from Lev. 18 is questionable. The relationships within which marriage is forbidden are psychic rather than metaphysical. Thus, the prohibition against marrying one's father's wife (Lev. 18:7-8) "means that between the father and his wives the feeling of shame has been abolished; they form a psychic unity, and the women have thereby entered into one particular intimate relationship with the father's sons which cannot be reconciled with the different intimate relationship of being the son's wife" (Kenneth Grayston, "Marriage," in *A Theological Word Book of the Bible,* ed. Alan Richardson [New York: Macmillan, 1969], 139). It is also worth noting that the penalties vary, which one would hardly expect if moral issues were at stake, as the view of Heth and Wenham implies. If Gen. 2:24 has been interpreted correctly above, then the points emphasized are the complementarity of man and woman and their union in a covenant that is permanent because it is created and blessed by God. It is this aspect that Jesus appears to fasten on in Matt. 19:6 when, having quoted Gen. 2:24, He adds, "Therefore what God has joined together, let man not separate." The same may be said of other views that speak of marriage as the creation of some *tertium quid.* Cf. Otto Piper, who finds three ideas in the concept of "one flesh": "(1) Sexual intercourse establishes an inner union between the two persons concerned. (2) That union is a 'unity of the flesh' (i.e., it affects the vital wills of those persons). (3) This union can never be dissolved" (*The Biblical View of Sex and Marriage* [New York: Scribner's, 1960], 22). He concludes: "Jesus contended that, in the last analysis a marriage relationship could not really be dissolved because it rested on an indestructible ontological basis; it could only be disregarded. Therefore, his rejection of divorce is absolute" (151). Against this one may set Bailey's conclusion: "The sexual act certainly establishes the 'one flesh' *henosis,* and brings about an ontological change both in the man and woman themselves and in their relation. Neither can ever be again as they were before they came together; each does something to the other that is ineffaceable. But while intercourse has indelible personal consequences and initiates a new and unique relation, it does not effect an indissoluble union. There are, for instance, certain false states of 'one flesh' that are by their nature ephemeral, such as that resulting from fornication. It has already been shown that a union in 'one flesh' is valid or false according to the character of the sexual act by which it was established, and that the latter is determined by the intention of the parties and by the context of their intercourse. What is true of the initiation of the relation must also hold good in regard to its continuance" (Bailey, *Mystery of Love and Marriage,* 78-79). It is hazardous to import metaphysical categories to interpret what is essentially a personal relationship. In particular, it is hazardous to make such categories the basis of absolute conclusions. It is one thing to say that marriage is permanent and binding because it is a covenantal relationship provided and sealed by God. It is another thing to say that it is indestructible.

11. Westermann, *Genesis 1—11,* 233.

Marriage as God intended it to be and created it to be is thus a union of two like persons who, in covenantal commitment, find oneness in a partnership that engages their whole beings. Because they become one flesh, marriage is monogamous. Because it is a covenantal relationship divinely ordained, it is permanent and lifelong. Nor does the ideal change with the Fall. As we have seen, Gen. 2:24 is written to explain not only the marriage of the first pair but also all marriages since then; and the saying makes clear that the first marriage is the pattern and design for all marriages after it.

2. Marriage in the Teaching of the Prophets and the Wisdom Literature

A second area where we may look for evidence of the Old Testament view of marriage is the writings of the prophets and in wisdom books such as Proverbs and Job.

Special caution is needed in handling this material on two counts. First, in much of it, marriage is being used metaphorically to describe the religious relationship between God and Israel. It is the latter that is of first concern, and care must be taken to avoid making the illustration—marriage—the baseline for understanding the religious relationship, rather than the reverse. A second caution is that in many contexts, the emphasis falls on the negative side of marriage, namely, on Israel's unfaithfulness to God. We shall be examining these passages more fully in terms of their primary concern with marital breakdown in a later chapter on divorce. However, even from their negative aspect, it is possible to draw inferences regarding the positive view of marriage that is implied.

We may begin with the wider and more general considerations and, from these, move inward to the more specific points of emphasis. First, marriage is regarded as a desirable state, which brings satisfaction and fulfillment, and as such is an apt image for God's relation to His people. Prov. 18:22 declares that "he who finds a wife finds what is good and receives favor from the LORD." In Isa. 62:4-5 it is said prophetically of Judah, returned from exile: "No longer will they call you Deserted, or name your land Desolate. But you will be called Hephzibah,[12] and your land Beulah;[13] for the LORD will take delight in you, and your land will be married. As a young man marries

---

12. *"Hephzibah* means *my delight is in her"* (NIV margin).
13. *"Beulah* means *married"* (NIV margin).

a maiden, so will your sons marry you; as a bridegroom rejoices over his bride, so will your God rejoice over you."

This basic perception of marriage as a desirable thing is elaborated in several specific considerations. To begin with, it is stressed that marriage is covenantal. Thus, after an allusion to the Noachian covenant, there follows a declaration by God to the exiles: "Though the mountains be shaken and the hills be removed, yet my unfailing love for you will not be shaken nor my covenant of peace be removed, says the LORD, who has compassion on you" (Isa. 54:10). Ezekiel speaks in a similar vein: "I gave you my solemn oath and entered into a covenant with you, declares the Sovereign LORD, and you became mine" (16:8, cf. also vv. 59-63).

The distinctiveness of this emphasis is of great significance in underlining the lofty view of marriage presupposed. The notion of a god as the husband of the land where he was worshiped was common enough in the nature religions of the ancient Near East and was enacted in such sordid forms as ritual prostitution, but the Old Testament use of the image is worlds away from this. As Robertson Smith says of the use of marriage imagery by Hosea: "Instead of rejecting the current symbolism he appropriates it; but he does so in a way that lifts it wholly out of the sphere of nature religion and makes it the vehicle of the profoundest spiritual truths. Jehovah is the husband of his nation. But the essential basis of the marriage relation is not physical, but moral. It is a relation of inmost affection and lays upon the spouse a duty of conjugal fidelity that the popular religion daily violated. The betrothal of Jehovah to Israel is but another aspect of the covenant already spoken of; it is a betrothal 'in righteousness and in judgment, in kindness and in love,' a betrothal that demands the true knowledge of Jehovah" (Hos. 2:19-20).[14] Or as the verses partially quoted read in full: "I will betroth you to me forever; I will betroth you in righteousness and justice, in love and compassion. I will betroth you in faithfulness, and you will acknowledge the LORD" (2:19-20). That is to say, marriage is grounded, not in a casual alliance based on ephemeral attraction or passing convenience, but on covenant commitment implying faithfulness and permanence.

But another point of significance is contained in the use of the imagery of marriage to describe the relation of God with His people,

---

14. W. Robertson Smith, *The Prophets of Israel* (London: Adam and Charles Black, 1897), 174-75. Robertson Smith's entire treatment of the emergence of the marriage imagery in Israelite religion is worth consulting (170-80).

namely, that at the heart of both lies a personal relationship. It is important to avoid reading modern views of romantic love into an ancient document. Yet it is impossible to do justice to the Old Testament data while omitting the dimension of commitment based not only on verbal or written contract but also on affection and love. We have already heard the note in Isa. 54:9-10. It is sounded also by the Preacher: "Enjoy life with your wife, whom you love" (Eccles. 9:9)— perhaps the more significant for being placed against the backdrop of his customary astringency.

It is in the prophecy of Hosea that the note resounds most strongly, nowhere more so than in the Lord's command to the prophet to redeem his faithless wife: "The LORD said to me, 'Go, show your love to your wife again, though she is loved by another and is an adulteress. Love her as the LORD loves the Israelites, though they turn to other gods'" (3:1). In the words of Robertson Smith: "The argument of this prophecy is an argument of the heart, not of the head. His whole revelation of Jehovah is the revelation of a love that can be conceived under human analogies and whose workings are to be understood not by abstract reasonings but by the sympathy of a heart that has sounded the depths of human affection and knows in its own experience what love demands of its object."[15] As Pierre Grelot observes, no husband would have acted that way; and what we are witnessing here is the emergence of a new dimension of conjugal love: personalization of the bond between man and woman going beyond the view of fertility and continuance of the family.[16] Or to put it in different terms, what is being brought into focus with a sharpness and clarity never achieved before is the motive behind God's choice of Israel, what Eichrodt has called "the quite irrational power of love as the ultimate basis of the covenant relationship."[17]

A final point embodied in employment of marriage imagery to

---

15. Ibid., 177.

16. Pierre Grelot, "The Institution of Marriage: Its Evolution in the Old Testament," in *The Future of Marriage as Institution,* ed. F. Böckle (New York: Herder and Herder, 1970), 46.

17. W. Eichrodt, *Theology of the Old Testament* (Philadelphia: Westminster, 1961), 1:251. See Eichrodt's entire treatment of this theme in which he notes the relative absence of the language of emotion to describe the covenant until Hosea (250-51). Note especially his statement, "The transition from the idea of the covenant to the conception of the marriage between Yahweh and Israel was made easier by the element of contractual obligation common to both, but it needed the shattering experience of the prophet, whose whole being was committed to Yahweh's service, to make the marriage-bond the supreme demonstration of God's attitude to Israel" (251).

describe the relationship of God with His people is that marriage is monogamous and therefore exclusive. The Book of Proverbs warns more than once against the lures of the prostitute and the adulteress (chaps. 5 and 6; cf. Job 31:9-12). It is but one step from this to the conclusion that marriage is permanent and binding, a point likewise implicit in the idea of the covenant itself. Hence the prophetic denunciations of Israel's departure from the Lord to serve other gods in terms of marital infidelity. Further than this we cannot press without crossing from the idea of marriage to that of divorce, which will be best dealt with separately.

The Ideal of Marriage in the New Testament

We may now turn to the New Testament in search of the picture of marriage presented there. Our procedure will be the same as in our study of the Old Testament data, namely, to uncover the *normative* understanding of marriage. This may well differ considerably from the *average* picture of marriage and, still more, from *exceptional* marriages described or referred to. The yardstick we are using is marriage *as it ought to be and can be.* Departures from the norm will be considered in a later chapter.

In pursuing this search, we find ourselves directed to two main sources: the teaching of Jesus and the teaching of Paul. We shall treat them in that order.

1. Marriage in the Teaching of Jesus

Jesus made frequent use of the imagery of marriage in His teaching. He compared himself to a bridegroom, thereby implicitly comparing His ministry to a wedding feast (Mark 2:19) or a time of joy. Several of His parables employ the same image, such as the parable of the marriage feast (Matt. 22:1-10) and the parable of the ten virgins (25:1-13). Such language was common in Jewish teaching about the future, which envisaged the coming of the Messiah as being the occasion for a great banquet. As such, Jesus' teaching—and its implications for His understanding of His ministry—would have been readily intelligible to His listeners.

Teaching of that kind underscores a favorable view of marriage, inasmuch as it sees it as an occasion of joy, and still more, as an appropriate symbol for the coming of the Messiah. For more specific indicators of Jesus' evaluation of marriage, however, we must go to four particular passages in which He dealt directly with marriage as an institution.

The first is Mark 10:2-12. The narrative falls into two parts. The first part (vv. 2-9) recounts an exchange on the subject between Jesus and the Pharisees; while the second (vv. 10-12) consists of a summarizing statement made in private to the disciples.

According to verse 2, the episode began when "some Pharisees came and tested him by asking, 'Is it lawful for a man to divorce his wife?'" Such an inquiry would have been a test question indeed, for a number of reasons. For one thing, divorce was permitted in Judaism at that time,[18] even if there were differences of opinion about the grounds on which it might be sought.[19] For Jesus to have replied negatively would not merely have set Him apart from the acknowledged and respected teachers of the law but have had the further advantage—or so His questioners thought—of setting Him in opposition to the Mosaic Law itself.[20] (From the development of the debate one may infer that the Pharisees' next move would have been to appeal to Moses against Jesus' expected negative reply. This would imply that Jesus' opposition to divorce had become common knowledge. Jesus, however, sensing where the argument was headed, forestalled the Pharisees by appealing to Moses first.)

The Pharisees duly quote the Mosaic directive of Deut. 24:1, that if a man puts away his wife, he must give her a divorce certificate. Jesus, with stunning daring, sweeps this aside as a departure from God's will, made only because of human hard-heartedness. God's true design for marriage, according to Jesus, was seen at creation. Jesus makes His point by juxtaposing two statements from the creation narratives: first, from Gen. 1:27, God "made them male and female" (Mark 10:6); and second, from Gen. 2:24, "For this reason a man will leave his father and mother and be united to his wife, and the two will become one flesh" (Mark 10:7-8). Jesus' understanding of these texts is shown both in the way in which He links them as well as in His comments on them. In Gen. 2:24, "for this reason" refers back to Adam's discovery that the woman is a true partner for

---

18. The Pharisees' question is clearly based on that assumption. For an account of the Jewish attitude to divorce at the time of Jesus, see George F. Moore, *Judaism in the First Centuries of the Christian Era* (Cambridge, Mass.: Harvard University Press, 1950), 2:122-26.

19. Ibid., 123-24. Jeremias argues that since Philo and Josephus know only the Hillelite view, it must have prevailed in the first half of the first century A.D. See Joachim Jeremias, *Jerusalem in the Time of Jesus* (London: SCM Press, 1974), 370.

20. That there may have been other considerations at work also will be shown when we return later to the teaching of this passage about divorce.

him. In Mark 10:6, it refers to the quotation that God "made them male and female" (Gen. 1:27), a statement that means—in Hugh Anderson's words—that "in creating two sexes God declared His intention that *one* man is for *one* woman."[21] It is for this reason that a man will leave his parents and be united to his wife, namely—to quote Anderson again—that "the union between one man and one woman in marriage was ordained by God to transcend all other human ties and relationships."[22] From this, Jesus draws the conclusion: "So they are no longer two, but one"; to which He appends the directive: "Therefore what God has joined together, let man not separate" (Mark 10:8*b*-9). It will suffice to say at this point that verses 10-12, which brand divorce and remarriage by either spouse as adultery, confirm and reinforce Jesus' insistence that God's design for marriage is that it be lifelong and permanent.

The truths about Jesus' view of marriage conveyed in this account may be summarized as follows. First, marriage is a divine ordinance. It was the climax of God's activity "at the beginning of creation" (Mark 10:6). The initiative throughout was His. Second, marriage is a complementarity of male and female. It is not merely that it is the male and female sexes that together reflect the image of God (Gen. 1:27) but also that God makes one woman for one man (2:21-22), and in this exclusive union fulfillment is found (v. 23). "They are no longer two, but one" (Mark 10:8*b*). Third, this union is binding and permanent. It is so, not because the two have joined themselves together, but because God has joined them together. And what God has joined together it is not for man to separate. Fourth, such a marriage ideal is not unattainable. Whatever the law may have accepted by way of divorce not only is in conflict with God's will but also was given because of human hardness of heart. The implication is that hardness of heart need no longer prevail to thwart God's intention at the beginning. If one asks how this is so, the answer is that with Jesus has come the power of the Kingdom, or reign of God, making possible Kingdom behavior. As David Catchpole has expressed it: "The one scheme which can set Moses aside and argue from creation is eschatology: Jesus presupposes that the end time has already come. The declaration regarding divorce belongs to the

---

21. Hugh Anderson, *The Gospel of Mark,* in *New Century Bible* (Greenwood, S.C.: Attic Press, 1976), 242.
22. Ibid.

central concerns of the mission of Jesus. Participation in the present age alone is the hallmark of exclusion from the Kingdom."[23]

The second passage (Matt. 5:31-32) deals directly with divorce rather than marriage. However, in defining the limits of the former, implications are made for the latter, and it is these that will be considered here. The saying stands as one of a series, sometimes known as antitheses, in an early part of the Sermon on the Mount (vv. 21-48) in which Jesus defines His attitude to the law in contrast with that of teachers of old as well as of His hearers.[24] The law of Deut. 24:1-4, which in truth (as will be seen later) places certain limits on divorce, had been taken as legislation making divorce legally permissible, provided certain formalities were observed. This Jesus resoundingly sets aside, using the rabbinic formula "I say to you," commonly employed to state the true meaning.[25] That meaning is indicated by His declaration that divorce and remarriage are tantamount to adultery. In short, without here quoting or alluding to the creation narratives, Jesus in effect is returning to the creation ideal that marriage is lifelong and permanent.

The third passage in which Jesus addresses the subject of marriage specifically is Matt. 19:3-12. As in Mark 10:2-12, the primary concern of this passage is with divorce rather than marriage. Nevertheless, some important implications for the meaning of marriage are contained in it, and it is to these that we shall confine ourselves here.

The episode begins like its Marcan counterpart, with a test question: "Is it lawful for a man to divorce his wife for any and every rea-

---

23. David R. Catchpole, "The Synoptic Divorce Material as a Traditio-Historical Problem," in *Bulletin of the John Rylands Library* 57 (1974-75): 125.

24. It is sometimes said that Jesus is here *overthrowing* the Law of Moses. This, however, would be strange following the claim that He had not come to abolish the Law but to fulfill it (v. 17). Moreover, it rests on a misperception of what is taking place in the antitheses. Some quote the Old Testament words at the expense of the sense (e.g., No Old Testament law enjoins hatred of one's enemies [v. 43]). However, this was what the teachers of the Law taught and what their followers "heard" (note the use of the term "heard" in 5:21, 27, 33, 38, 43). David Daube shows that rabbinic formulae underlie the passage (*The New Testament and Rabbinic Judaism* [London: Athlone Press, 1956], 55-62); hence it is not the Law as such but the current understanding of it that Jesus is setting aside. Cf. David Hill, "The main point is that in none of these passages is there an intention to annul the demands of the Law, but only to carry them to their ultimate meaning, to intensify them, or to reinterpret them in a higher key. This is the true fulfillment of the Law, not its destruction" (*The Gospel of Matthew*, in NCB [Greenwood, S.C.: Attic Press, 1978], 120).

25. Daube, *New Testament and Rabbinic Judaism*, 55-62.

son?" (Matt. 19:3). The words "for any and every reason," which constitute an addition to the parallel in Mark 10:2, refer to a dispute between the parties of Shammai and Hillel in Judaism (which will be more fully explained later) as to whether divorce was justified only for a few, weighty reasons (as Shammai held) or for more or less any reason at all (as was held by Hillel). In short, the test for Jesus is about which side He is on in a rabbinical dispute between conservatives and liberals. Jesus responds, as in the Marcan account, by sweeping aside legal hairsplitting and returning to the design of creation. As in Mark, He links Gen. 1:27 and 2:24 and concludes with identically the same comments: "So they are no longer two, but one. Therefore what God has joined together, let man not separate" (Matt. 19:6).

Jesus' interrogators then raise the question of the permission to divorce granted by Moses (Deut. 24:1). As in Mark, Jesus dismisses this as a temporary concession occasioned by hardness of heart and no part of God's original design. He reinforces His earlier order against separating those whom God has joined with the assertion that if a man divorces his wife and marries another woman, he commits adultery (Matt. 19:9).

Clearly then, Jesus makes the same points about marriage in Matt. 19:3-9 as were found in Mark 10:2-12: it is a divine ordinance; it is an exclusive union; it is binding and permanent; and—presumably for the same reason given in Mark—the creation ideal is not unattainable, inasmuch as, because of Christ's coming, hardness of heart can be done away.

There remains the fourth passage in which Jesus addresses—again implicitly—the question of marriage. Luke 16:18 reads, "Anyone who divorces his wife and marries another woman commits adultery, and the man who marries a divorced woman commits adultery." The saying is virtually without context. The preceding verse refers to the permanence of the law; and if this constitutes the context, then the point of the saying is that the law has abiding validity.[26] However that may be, the implication of the saying for marriage is clear enough that inasmuch as divorce and remarriage, and even marriage to a divorced woman, constitute adultery, marriage is permanent and lifelong.

---

26. For this and other possibilities, see R. H. Stein, "Divorce," in *Dictionary of Jesus and the Gospels,* ed. Joel B. Green and Scot McKnight (Downers Grove, Ill.: InterVarsity Press, 1992), 198.

It is not difficult to sense the general direction of Jesus' teaching about marriage. Much of it is set in the context of controversy, controversy with those who in greater or lesser degree had departed from the creation ideal. Jesus' response is to return to that ideal, affirming that in God's design and intention, marriage is a divine ordinance in which one man and one woman in union not only reflect the image of God but also find fulfillment in common partnership. As a divinely created and confirmed union, it is permanent and lifelong; it is not for man to undo what God has done. Any declension from this results from human hardness of heart; and if there has been such in the past, the coming of Christ in grace and power has made attainable the original ideal as set forth at creation.

2. Marriage in the Teaching of Paul

As with the teaching of Jesus about marriage, so with the teaching of Paul: nowhere does he treat the subject in a direct and comprehensive way. We are largely confined to drawing inferences from passages where his specific theme is other than marriage itself. Care must be taken to avoid converting a secondary theme, or even an illustration, into a primary topic and forcing from it information it was never intended to yield or deducing conclusions from the absence of evidence, when the author's intention was simply to maintain silence on that issue.

Nowhere do these dangers array themselves more formidably than in the interpretation of 1 Cor. 7. One need only set down some quotations from it to see how Paul has come to be credited with a distinctly jaundiced view of marriage, which served as the fountainhead of asceticism within Christianity. "It is good for a man not to marry" (v. 1). "Now to the unmarried and the widows I say: It is good for them to stay unmarried, as I am. But if they cannot control themselves, they should marry, for it is better to marry than to burn with passion" (vv. 8-9). "Are you married? Do not seek a divorce. Are you unmarried? Do not look for a wife. But if you do marry, you have not sinned" (vv. 27-28a). "From now on those who have wives should live as if they had none" (v. 29b). "A woman is bound to her husband as long as he lives. But if her husband dies, she is free to marry anyone she wishes, but he must belong to the Lord. In my judgment, she is happier if she stays as she is—and I think that I too have the Spirit of God" (vv. 39-40).

What is to be said of this apparently grudging approval of marriage, so far removed from the creation ideal or the positive depiction underlying the view of the Old Testament prophets? Clearly, the first matter to be determined is the angle of Paul's approach. Other of his treatments might readily be misread also if attention were not given to this question. For example, one might infer from 1 Thess. 4:3-8 that Paul's sole concern with marriage was the avoidance of immorality or from Rom. 7:1-6 that marriage was a form of bondage comparable to the law of sin.

In addressing this issue in 1 Corinthians, it is necessary to try to pinpoint the situation Paul was confronting both as to its substance and its mood. In the light of the available evidence, it seems not inaccurate to describe Paul's correspondents in Corinth as superspiritual, overheated adventists. As to the substance of the problem, Gordon Fee has argued cogently that "the key issue between Paul and them . . . has to do with the Corinthian understanding of what it means to be 'spiritual' *(pneumatikos)*."[27] He points (among other things) to their preoccupation with "wisdom" and "knowledge," their experience of Spirit inspiration, and above all their emphasis on the gift of tongues.[28] But other factors also played a role. Typical of the Greek milieu that had produced them, their mentality was influenced by dualism, leading them not only to prize the spiritual but to disparage the material, including the physical body. "Despite their continuing existence in the body, the Corinthians consider themselves to be the 'spiritual ones,' already as the angels. Hence, since from their perspective the body is eschatologically insignificant (cf. 6:13; 15:12), neither does it have present significance. This attitude toward corporeal existence is at least in part responsible for such things as the denial of a future bodily resurrection (15:12) and both the affirmation of sexual immorality and the denial of sexual relations within marriage (6:12-20 and 7:1-6)."[29] For these reasons they regarded themselves as "spiritual," all the while harboring doubts about any who did not share their views and experiences—including Paul (14:37; cf. 7:40).

So much for the "superspiritual" aspect. But another tributary also seems to have fed into the stream, not altogether unrelated to dualism. This was the notion that since the Spirit was the mark of

---

27. Gordon D. Fee, *The First Epistle to the Corinthians,* in *The New International Commentary on the New Testament* (Grand Rapids: Wm. B. Eerdmans Publishing Co., 1988), 6.

28. Ibid., 10-11.

29. Ibid., 12.

the Age to Come and was self-evidently at work in them in their "wisdom" and "prophecy" and "speaking in tongues," this could only mean that for them the Age to Come had already arrived. As Paul says to them—with sarcasm: "Already you have all you want! Already you have become rich! You have become kings—and that without us!" (4:8). To borrow a common expression, they viewed their present existence in terms of what has been labeled "overrealized eschatology" or in Fee's expression "spiritualized eschatology."[30]

When 1 Cor. 7 is read against such a background, it assumes quite a different appearance. The thoughts expressed in the quotations listed above, that the unmarried state is "good" and is not to be avoided by all, that marriage is not a sin, and so on, are apparently not written *by* one who had doubts about marriage but rather *to* those who did. Indeed, it would appear that those having doubts about the propriety of marriage included not merely persons seeking to avoid it, as well as abstain from sexual relations within it, but also, it seems, those who thought they would be thoroughly spiritual only if they divorced their mates altogether (vv. 10-11). In a word, the central theme in 1 Cor. 7 is not marriage at all but celibacy, and it is only as a corrective to the exaggerated views of the Corinthians about celibacy that Paul discusses marriage.[31]

Another point of substance that conditions the view of marriage in 1 Cor. 7 from Paul's side is his view of the current situation and its implications for married Christians. In giving advice about "virgins" (probably young women engaged to be married)[32] Paul refers to "the present crisis" (v. 26), the "many troubles in this life" (v. 28*b*) that will face those who marry, that "the time is short" (v. 29), "for this world in its present form is passing away" (v. 31*b*).

Interpreters are divided as to the crisis (with its attendant tribulations) that Paul has in mind. F. F. Bruce writes the following: "This dis-

---

30. Ibid.

31. For a thorough and well-documented account of how celibacy was viewed in the ancient world in Greco-Roman as well as in Jewish thought, see Craig S. Keener, *And Marries Another* (Peabody, Mass.: Hendrickson Publishers, 1991), 68-78. It is doubtful whether celibacy in the Corinthian church is to be traced to any of the specific sources Keener mentions and much more likely that it derived from the general Hellenistic mind-set referred to earlier. See Helmut Koester, *Introduction to the New Testament,* vol. 1, *History, Culture and Religion of the Hellenistic Age* (Philadelphia: Fortress Press, 1984), 141-44.

32. The meaning of the term is disputed. For a good survey of the main possibilities, together with the reasons for supporting the understanding adopted here, see Fee, *First Epistle to the Corinthians,* in NICNT, 325-27.

tress is the time of increasing tribulation, heralding the end of the age, of which signs had already manifested themselves. . . . This time would be particularly harassing for those with family responsibilities. . . . The whole discussion of marriage in this chapter is influenced by Paul's eschatological awareness in addition to his pastoral concern."[33] Gordon Fee, on the other hand, while conceding the eschatological backdrop, sees "not a reference to eschatological woes as such, but to real affliction in the present life, probably enhanced by the ordeal that they are currently experiencing."[34] It is unnecessary for us to make a decision between these explanations. The point for our concern is that Paul's teaching on marriage in 1 Cor. 7 is conditioned by stressful circumstances in the Corinthian situation.[35] In different circumstances, his advice might well be different.

This leads from the question of substance to that of mood, which, again, is very important. The same words can bear opposite meanings depending on the tone in which they are spoken. For our concern, this is true in two respects. First, it is important with regard to the Epistle as a whole. What was the tone of the relations between Paul and the Corinthians? Without going into exhaustive detail,[36] it is clear that relations were strained. Earlier problems had prompted Paul to write to them in a letter now lost to us (5:9); the letter we know as 1 Corinthians appears to have been in response to their reply to his previous letter (16:15-17). Apparently, some had questioned his authority as apostle (e.g., 9:1-3), as well as his message, which lacked the aura of "wisdom" by which the Corinthians set such store (e.g., 2:1-5; 3:1-4). Indeed, they questioned whether he was really "spiritual" at all (4:1-4).

Paul replies to all of this with vigor, using all the weapons in his rhetorical armory, including interrogation, raillery, and sometimes sarcasm. Two sections, however, are of markedly different tone: 7:1-40 and 11:2-16. Fee, who draws attention to this phenomenon fre-

---

33. F. F. Bruce, *1 and 2 Corinthians,* in NCB (Greenwood, S.C.: Attic Press, 1985), 74. Similarly, C. K. Barrett, *The First Epistle to the Corinthians,* in *Black's New Testament Commentaries* (London: Adam and Charles Black, 1973), 176-77.

34. Fee, *First Epistle to the Corinthians,* in NICNT, 333. Cf. 329. His whole treatment of verses 26-35 should be consulted (324-48).

35. Fee makes the point repeatedly that while, in verses 25-38, Paul counsels the unmarried to remain so, the grounds of this advice are not anything morally objectionable in marriage but rather difficulties rooted in the pressures of their current situation (328, 330, 348). Moreover, what Paul says, he says by way of advice—and good advice, as he believes—not by divine command (v. 25; cf. Fee, 328, 333, 348).

36. For a full treatment see Fee, *First Epistle to the Corinthians,* in NICNT, 4-15.

quently,[37] thinks this may be because these sections deal with issues raised by the Corinthians in their reply to Paul's original letter.[38] But this can hardly be the explanation, since some of the most combative sections (e.g., chapters 8—10 and 12—14) were also raised by the Corinthians.

Another factor 7:1-40 and 11:2-16 have in common is that both involve women in significant ways. The command against divorce in 7:10-11 is addressed to the wife first, so this may imply that it was "superspiritual" women who were setting the pace in Corinth in terms of divorce. Similarly, 11:2-16 seems to be directed to women who were conducting themselves in worship in a way Paul thought unbecoming.[39] Paul may have been anxious to instruct rather than debate; in particular, he may have been anxious to avoid seeming to demean women in a society in which that was the rule rather than the exception.[40]

This leads directly to a second way in which an understanding of the mood of 1 Cor. 7 conditions its interpretation. Reference has already been made to the letter the Corinthians wrote to Paul in response to his to them. Chapter 7 makes the first reference to it: "Now for the matters you wrote about" (v. 1*a*).[41] It appears that one of Paul's techniques for dealing with the explosive situation was to quote their words in a way that gave them a sense that accorded with his mind rather than theirs. For example, if verse 1*b* is an instance of this phenomenon, as is widely agreed, the words "It is good for a man not to marry" would have meant widely different things to Paul from what they would to the Corinthians.[42] The Corinthians would have meant, "It is best for a man not to marry";

---

37. Ibid., 10, 266-67, 491.

38. This requires the hypothesis that the subject of 11:2-16, namely, the conduct of women in worship, was raised by the Corinthians in their letter to Paul. Fee is prepared to make this assumption (ibid., 491-92). The subject of 7:1-40 was certainly raised by them in their letter, of which more anon.

39. See R. Scroggs, "Paul and the Eschatological Women," *Journal of the American Academy of Religion* 40 (1972): 283-303.

40. Cf. "The women of the upper classes—mothers, wives and daughters—were expected, both in Greek and in Roman tradition, to be modest and unobtrusive and to lead uneventful and unexciting lives" (John E. Stambaugh and David L. Balch, *The New Testament in Its Social Environment,* in Library of Early Christianity [Philadelphia: Westminster Press, 1986], 111).

41. The same formula (whose literal translation is "Now concerning") recurs at 7:25; 8:1; 12:1; 16:1, 12. In all cases, it seems to refer to matters raised by the Corinthians.

42. For a review of the various options, see Keener, *And Marries Another,* 78-79.

whereas Paul would have meant, "It is not a bad thing to remain unmarried." It is important to keep Paul's technique in mind and avoid reading into it what was not intended.

Against this somewhat lengthy background statement, we may now seek the positive view of marriage that underlies what is really a discussion with those who were advocates of celibacy. Two items stand out sharply. First, in marriage each partner is devoted to the good of the other. The point is made very strikingly. With regard to the sexual relationship Paul writes: "The wife's body does not belong to her alone but also to her husband. In the same way, the husband's body does not belong to him alone but also to his wife" (v. 4). Such mutual obligation was not unknown in Jewish marriage contracts,[43] nor, indeed, in Hellenistic Greek marriage contracts.[44] Roman marriage contracts were a different story.[45] The context of Paul's statement is the danger of abstinence as an occasion of immorality (vv. 2-3). Even so, there is an insistence on mutual consent where abstinence is to be practiced as a spiritual discipline (vv. 5-6), which in effect gives veto power to each partner.[46]

Still more striking is the reason Paul gives for advising against marriage "because of the present crisis" (v. 26). This is that "a married man is concerned about the affairs of this world—how he can please his wife. . . . a married woman is concerned about the affairs of this world—how she can please her husband" (vv. 33, 34c). In a passage where Paul makes a negative recommendation about marriage, he does so because of the lofty view of marriage that he holds; that is, the partners are so dedicated to pleasing each other that this will create tensions with their service to the Lord in times of stress

---

43. See Ben Witherington III, *Women in the Ministry of Jesus* (Cambridge, England: University Press, 1991), 2-6.

44. Keener, *And Marries Another,* 79-80.

45. Ibid., 79.

46. J. J. von Allmen makes the point that, whereas in Judaism, procreation was the ultimate justification for marriage inasmuch as a wife's barrenness after 10 years of marriage was a valid ground for divorce, Paul's view is different. "It is in fact noteworthy that the apostle does not even see a direct connection between the sexual act and procreation (cf. Eph. 5:22ff; 1 Cor. 7:1-9). This act seems rather, according to him, to find its meaning and its virtue in its capacity to unite the couple . . . for St. Paul it is not firstly the desire to have children which justifies physical encounter on the part of the couple. For the woman is not a medium for the man which allows him to reproduce himself and thus live on in a son, nor is the man a means for the woman to find her fulfillment in motherhood. Once the pair have given themselves to each other (1 Cor. 7:3-4), they are not to exploit one another, even in an obliquely religious manner" (*Pauline Teaching on Marriage* [London: Faith Press, ET 1963], 68-69).

such as the Corinthians are experiencing. Mutual care and concern is a primary mark of Christian marriage as Paul understands it.

Thus Paul's insistence on mutuality within marriage seems to rest squarely on Gen. 2:24, even if he does not quote it at this point.[47] If, later in 1 Cor. 7, Paul will find it possible to advise against marriage, he recognizes that marriage is a gift (Greek *charisma*) from God (v. 7). "So, by marrying, they will be truer to themselves, . . . truer still to their heritage and more faithful to their destiny, than by imposing upon themselves a celibacy which would canker their very being (1 Cor. 7:9). Their desire to quit their isolation and to find deep within themselves a sense of want, and suffering from that want, like the sharp longing of Adam when numbering the beasts of paradise (cf. Gen. 2:20*b*), comes from God. It is he who gives birth in them to that prayer to which marriage will be the fulfillment."[48]

The second feature that stands out conspicuously in the positive view of marriage underlying 1 Cor. 7 is its permanence. Paul's comprehensive teaching on divorce will be examined later. Suffice it to say that the baseline to which he brings it is the command of Jesus: "A wife must not separate from her husband. . . . And a husband must not divorce his wife" (vv. 10*b*, 11*b*). No reasoning, however specious or spiritual, can justify the separating of what God has joined together. In God's design, marriage is lifelong and permanent.

The other context in which Paul treats marriage in an extended way is Eph. 5:22-33. This passage constitutes part of one of the "household codes"[49] found in various passages of the New Testament Epistles. The codes were ethical in content, concerned to spell out appropriate Christian behavior. The code addressed to wives and

---

47. He has just quoted it in 1 Cor. 6:16.
48. Von Allmen, *Pauline Teaching on Marriage*, 23.
49. "Household codes" is one translation of the German "Haustafeln" (literally "house-tables"), which has come to be used of the lists of directions to members of households, such as husbands and wives, parents and children, masters and slaves. Cf. Col. 3:18—4:1; 1 Tim. 2:8-15; Titus 2:1-10; 1 Pet. 2:18—3:7. Each directive consists of three parts: the member addressed, the behavior enjoined, and the motive for conforming to it. The behavior is usually submission and the motive subordination to the Lordship of Christ. There is no need for us to consider the origin of this form. Some scholars think it has roots in Hellenism; others in Judaism. Reviews may be found in R. P. Martin, appendix to "Virtue, Blameless," in *The New International Dictionary of New Testament Theology*, ed. Colin Brown (Grand Rapids: Zondervan, 1979), 3:928-32; and Ben Witherington III, *Women in the Earliest Churches* (Cambridge, England: University Press, 1988), 42-47. Witherington concludes that the early Christians, possibly Paul, gave it its form, drawing chiefly on Jewish and Old Testament materials (47).

husbands in Eph. 5:22-33 presents certain preliminary problems that must be resolved before we can deduce its contribution to the biblical ideal of marriage.

The passage consists essentially of a comparison between the relationship of husband and wife in marriage with the relationship of Christ and the Church viewed as Christ's bride. The interpretative problem consists in determining the limits of the analogy. For example, Christ's role as Head of the Church is explicated by the phrase "he is the Savior" of the Body (v. 23). Is there also a sense in which this is true of the husband as head of the wife? Again, in verses 26-27 the illustration takes on a life of its own, describing how Christ sanctifies and cleanses the Church; and after an injunction to husbands to love their wives as their own bodies, the comment is added, "This is a profound mystery—but I am talking about Christ and the church" (v. 32).

This has led some interpreters to conclude that the Christ-Church imagery is primary and the application to marriage secondary, but this can hardly be so when the passage stands as part of a household code. It is nearer the truth to say that Paul draws upon the absolute relationship between Christ and the Church to illustrate the relative relationship between husbands and wives.[50] That is to say, Christ is Lord and Savior of the Church in a way that the husband is not lord and savior of his wife.[51] Moreover, there are aspects of the marriage relationship that are not illustrated by the Christ-Church image. It is noteworthy that the role and responsibility of husbands is given much more space than that of wives, and the degree of reciprocity required of wives is given much less attention both in terms of length and content. No mention is made of the love of the Church for Christ or of wives for husbands. This does not mean there is no place for it in either relationship. It simply means

---

50. Cf. Witherington, *Women in the Earliest Churches*, 54-55.

51. F. F. Bruce observes, "As in 1 Cor. 11:3-15 the argument depends on an oscillation between the literal and figurative senses of 'head,' so in the present argument from analogy different senses of the word are involved. For when Christ is said to be 'head of the church,' that involves the correlative figure of the church as his body (Eph. 1:22-23; 4:15-16; cf. Col. 1:18; 2:19)—a correlative which is absent from the husband-wife relationship." He adds in a footnote, "When the husband is said to be head of the wife, it is not implied that the wife is his body. Even v. 29 does not say this" (*The Epistles to the Colossians, to Philemon, and to the Ephesians,* in NICNT [Grand Rapids: Wm. B. Eerdmans Publishing Co., 1984], 384-85).

that within the writer's purpose and intention, it does not enter into consideration.

This leads directly to a second preliminary consideration, namely, the character of marriage presupposed in the passage. It is evident from the household code as a whole that the society to which it is addressed is patriarchal in structure, including within it not only the submission of wives to husbands but also the institution of slavery. To what degree is Paul's teaching here applicable to our own very differently structured society?[52] The clue to this is to be found in the distinctive features of Paul's instruction here, which not only diverge from the societal practice of his own day but could have no other effect than to correct it. First, there is his insistence that submission is not merely for wives, children, and slaves, nor is it merely the appropriate attitude for all Christians toward Christ: it is the appropriate attitude for all Christians toward each other "Submit to one another out of reverence for Christ" (v. 21).[53] This does not mean that in the household code, we are to conclude that all-round submission is intended: of husbands to wives, parents to children, masters to slaves.[54] But it does mean that within the Christian community, there was a mutual submissiveness at work that could not but modify the exercise of authority as it was commonly practiced in pagan families. Second, it is noteworthy that "Wives, submit to your husbands" (v. 22) is balanced not with "Husbands, rule your wives" but rather "Husbands, love your wives" (v. 25), and the love in question is to be of the quality of Christ's when He gave himself up for the Church. Love of this kind could not but have a transforming effect on the meaning of submission, making it impossible for it to

---

52. I may refer to an article in which I attempted to show how the underlying principles of this passage rather than their specific form are applicable today. See Alex Deasley, "God's Will for the Family: Marital and Family Relationships in Ephesians," *The Preacher's Magazine* 54, No. 4 (June, July, August 1979): 21-25, 58.

53. There has been some discussion as to whether verse 21 belongs with verses 15-20 or with the household code in verses 22-33. It almost certainly belongs with both. R. P. Martin notes that the preceding verses (especially 19-20) deal with worship in which women had been instructed to be submissive to their husbands (see 1 Cor. 14:34 where the same verb is used) (*Ephesians, Colossians, and Philemon,* in Interpretation Commentaries [Atlanta: John Knox Press, 1991], 67-68). At the same time, the Greek text for verse 22 contains no verb, and it is probable that (as in NIV) the verb "submit" is to be carried forward from verse 21. F. F. Bruce comments: "It is more closely attached to what follows, supplying the unexpressed verb in verse 22" (*Epistles to the Colossians, Philemon, and Ephesians,* 383).

54. Cf. Bruce, "While the household code is introduced by a plea for mutual submissiveness, the submissiveness enjoined in the code itself is not mutual" (ibid.).

mean "blind obedience, docile servility, and unthinking subservience."[55]

In short, while the patriarchal structure is retained, as it could not but be in the circumstances of the time,[56] yet a powerful Christian leaven is implanted within it that would not only transform its fabric and functioning[57] but culminate in its eventual overthrow as being inconsistent with the principles and spirit of the gospel.[58] It is in light of these principles and that spirit that this passage must be interpreted and applied today.

A third preliminary consideration that helps to illuminate the passage as a whole concerns the question of why Paul uses the relation of Christ and the Church to illustrate the marriage relationship. A leading theme of the Ephesian Epistle is unity. One thinks readily of specific aspects such as unity of Jews and Gentiles in Christ (2:14-

---

55. R. P. Martin, *Ephesians, Colossians, and Philemon,* 69. In the same context Martin quotes comparative views from the contemporary world and also shows how the use of the term "submissive" in other New Testament contexts suggests that it "cannot carry the sense of degrading servility" (70).

56. Cf. C. L. Mitton, "He (Paul) recognizes that the marriage relationship has been transformed for real Christians . . . But Paul seems to have been aware of another responsibility besides that of explaining to Christians the radical change which Christ brings into all human relationships, including marriage. As a wise pastor he had to try to see to it that the new freedom and status to the Christian woman within her own home and marriage relationship was not so practiced as to create dangerous misunderstandings and resentments among pagan neighbors. Such behavior on the part of Christian women would have prevented their neighbors from hearing sympathetically the message of the gospel. Paul said of himself that he was ready to endure any deprivation rather than put an obstacle in the way of the gospel of Christ (1 Cor. 9:12), and for this reason, if no other, he asked wives not to provoke antagonism to the gospel by insubordination to their husbands (*Ephesians,* in NCB [Greenwood, S.C.: Attic Press, 1976], 197-98). R. P. Martin goes so far as to suggest that the house codes may have been designed for that purpose ("Virtue, Blameless," 931-32).

57. Cf. Andrew T. Lincoln, "The writer of Ephesians brings a distinctive vision of marriage to the process, and, although the roles and duties of believers who shared this vision would from the outside have been hard to distinguish from those in other marriages, the internal ethos and dynamic of such marriages would have felt quite different. To have fulfilled one's role and carried out one's duties under the guidelines of mutual submission, and as a wife to have subordinated oneself voluntarily to a husband who cherishes one with a self-sacrificial love, would have been to experience a very different reality than that suggested by the traditional discussions of household management" (*Ephesians,* in WBC [Dallas: Word Books, 1990], 42:391).

58. Cf. Walther Guenther, "Though the New Testament essentially looks on marriage from the man's standpoint, the Greek and the Old Testament traditions are so transcended that the man's special rights fall away, and throughout the New Testament the shared life of husband and wife stands in the foreground (1 Corinthians 7:3, Ephesians 5:21-33, Colossians 3:18-19)" ("Marriage, New Testament," in NIDNTT, 2:579).

22), unity within the Body of Christ (4:1-6), and unity within the family (5:21-33). J. Paul Sampley has shown that such passages follow the same pattern: the particular situation calling for unity among believers is addressed; then Christ as the agent of unity is described; and, finally, a return is made to the situation of believers.[59] What is happening in 5:21-33 is—in Sampley's words—that "the Haustafel (household code) provides the author an opportunity to develop an idealized picture of the unity that must pertain in the smallest units of the Christian community, the family. The unity that husband and wife are to manifest has as its paradigm the close relationship that exists between Christ and his church."[60]

With this groundwork laid, we may now seek to construct the picture of marriage that emerges from the letter to the Ephesians. The first thing to be said is that by the very act of comparing the relation between husband and wife to that between Christ and the Church, the Epistle exalts marriage to the highest possible level. In the pagan world of the first century, marriage was effectively a contractual agreement like any other contract, unaccompanied by any legal or religious ceremony. In Eph. 5:21-33 it becomes a sacred thing, embodying qualitatively the same elements as obtain between the Redeemer and the Church: self-giving, sacrificial love, intimate union. As Pheme Perkins has put it, "It participates in and reflects the new reality of grace which is at the heart of salvation."[61]

Second, self-giving love is the engine of the Christian marriage relationship. "Husbands, love your wives, just as Christ loved the church and gave himself up for her" (v. 25). The self-giving referred to is that of the Cross, and Paul continues by drawing out the intent of that supreme act of self-giving: the purification of the Church to be a fit partner for Christ (vv. 26-27). There the analogy fails, but it resumes in verse 28a: "In this same way, husbands ought to love their wives as their own bodies." Andrew Lincoln is entirely right when he says: "A contemporary appropriation of Ephesians will build on this passage's own introductory exhortation (v. 21) and see

---

59. J. Paul Sampley, *And the Two Shall Become One Flesh,* in Society for New Testament Studies Series (Cambridge, England: University Press, 1971), 16:103-8, 150. In chap. 6, Sampley argues that this pattern is followed throughout the Epistle, while in pages 150-53 he shows how it is maintained in 5:21-33.

60. Ibid., 152.

61. Quoted in Lincoln, *Ephesians,* 363. Lincoln observes later that "the use of 'sacred marriage' imagery . . . about human marriage appears to be the distinctive contribution of Ephesians" (391).

a mutual loving submission as the way in which the unity of the marriage relationship is demonstrated. . . . Both husband and wife can look to Christ as the model for the sacrificial kind of love required (cf. 5:2). In this way submission and love can be seen as two sides of the same coin—selfless service of one's marriage partner."[62]

Such self-giving love is grounded in the union that is the quintessence of marriage. This is the third characteristic of marriage underlined here. Verses 28b and following say boldly: "He who loves his wife loves himself. After all, no one ever hated his own body, but he feeds and cares for it, just as Christ does the church." Two Old Testament passages lie behind these statements. The first is Lev. 19:18: "Love your neighbor as yourself." The second, as quoted in verse 31, is Gen. 2:24: "For this reason a man will leave his father and mother and be united to his wife, and the two will become one flesh." These two statements are cross-cultivated so that the self receiving the love that is to set the standard for how one loves one's neighbor is none other than the wife with whom one is joined in the one-flesh relationship of marriage. The Ephesian passage concludes on the high note: "Each one of you also must love his wife as he loves himself" (v. 33a).

The distinction is sometimes made between love as an act of will and love as an emotion. The inference is that the former—active concern for the good of one's neighbor—is what is enjoined in the biblical command. Witherington maintains that the same is true here. "That Paul can command love suggests that he is talking about loving actions, not feelings, and particularly self-sacrificial actions analogous to Christ's actions for the Church. Actions can be commanded; feelings cannot."[63] As a generalization, the point is doubtless well made. It is doubtful, however, whether the two can be disengaged in this context where Christ's love for the Church is the paradigm. If anything, the meaning of love is being deepened here,[64] and the leaving of parents and being joined to one's wife assumes a new intensity of meaning as it is compared to the self-sacrifice of Christ out of love for the Church.

---

62. Ibid., 393.

63. Witherington, *Women in the Earliest Churches,* 61.

64. The language of emotion is not absent from the context. In verse 29, the opposite of love is hate; while in 4:32 kindness, compassion, and forgiveness are enjoined as the due response to the forgiveness of God. The parallel passage to the latter in Col. 3:12-14 contains a still greater concentration of attitudes and emotions in the form of commands.

Conclusion

We may now attempt to draw together the main constituents of the biblical understanding of marriage disclosed by our survey of the biblical data. At least three seem to be indicated.

First, the dominant image used to convey the meaning of marriage is that of covenant. Covenant is the basic frame of reference within which marriage is presented and interpreted. From Gen. 2:24, where the covenantal language of "cleaving" is found, to the quotation of that same verse in Eph. 5:31, the covenant idea as the pattern of marriage is predominant. Central to the understanding of covenant is the mutual commitment of male and female, with God standing as witness to the uniting of the two whom He made for each other (Mal. 2:14).

Second, just as the distinctive character of any covenant resides in the subject matter of the covenant, so the distinctive character of the marriage covenant lies in the biblical understanding of marriage. The heart of this is oneness: "A man will leave his father and mother and be united to his wife, and they will become one flesh" (Gen. 2:24). Certainly this implies physical union, but it goes far beyond this so that it can be compared to the union of Christ and the Church and expresses itself in the mutual submissiveness and care that are prompted and sustained by love (Eph. 5:21-31).

Third, while the implication of any covenant is fidelity, it is possible for covenants to be broken. This is no less true of the marriage covenant. Indeed, much of the Old Testament teaching on marriage is derived from settings in which the covenant has been broken. Here again, however, the meaning of the breaking of a marriage covenant rests upon the biblical meaning of marriage. Marriage is not simply a legal contract that may be torn up when either or both parties break its terms or simply tire of keeping them. On the contrary, as a commitment to one-flesh union, the marriage covenant is a commitment to lifelong fidelity. As such, it should not be broken. This, as we have already seen and shall see even more fully in chapter 3, is the repeated insistence of Jesus, sustained by the apostle Paul. The biblical design for marriage is that it be permanent. Yet while the marriage covenant should not be broken, it may be.[65] If a

---

65. For an extended discussion of various perspectives on this point, see n. 10 above.

relationship can be created, it can be destroyed, though this is not to be determined by the keeping of a legal scorecard.[66]

However, this is to deviate from the primary purpose of this chapter, which is to uncover the biblical view of marriage. The picture of marriage as God designed it to be and as it ought to be has shown remarkable consistency. Not all of the elements we have found in our survey—divine institution, covenant, monogamy, union, permanence, equality, self-giving—are present in every context, nor need they be. It is remarkable that even when the view of marriage has had to be excavated from an essentially negative context or has become intertwined with societal structures that obscure and even distort its pristine form, enough has remained intact for the creation ideal to be visible. It remains not only visible but also permanently relevant to all who acknowledge as Lord Him who said, "What God has joined together, let man not separate" (Mark 10:9; Matt. 19:6b).

---

66. Cf. David Atkinson, "Not every act of the will which threatens the heart of marriage necessarily destroys it. Breaches of the covenant can be forgiven and healed . . . However, where the will becomes so determined in its abandonment of the marriage relationship, by the refusal or spurning of forgiveness, for example, so that reconciliation and restoration become human impossibilities or where the 'one flesh' is severed beyond healing by the habitual breach of the internal meaning of the covenant relationship then the question of civil divorce . . . arises" (*To Have and to Hold: The Marriage Covenant and the Discipline of Divorce* [Grand Rapids: Wm. B. Eerdmans Publishing Co., 1981], 137).

2 ～ The Old Testament Teaching on Divorce

AGAINST THE BACKGROUND of the biblical ideal of marriage, set forth in chapter 1, we may turn now to the teaching of the Bible regarding divorce. We will follow the same plan as in chapter 1, dealing first with the Old Testament evidence and, in the next chapter, with the teaching of the New Testament. Our purpose is to examine those passages that clearly address the issue of divorce or are frequently regarded as doing so.

The Background of the Biblical Teaching on Divorce

Before examining the biblical divorce passages we will consider a prior question. If it has been accurately shown in chapter 1 that in the divine plan and intention marriage was intended to be permanent and lifelong, how does divorce come to be present in the biblical story at all? The question is framed carefully to avoid prejudging the issue. For example it is not suggested that divorce is *instituted* in the Bible or that it is *approved*. But it is certainly *recorded* and *referred to* in both testaments. The prior question then is, Within what frame of reference is divorce spoken of? Determining this provides the backdrop against which the biblical material regarding divorce is to be evaluated.

Two factors provide the background to divorce as it is treated in the Bible. The first is a catastrophic lapse from the creation ideal of marriage in all of its aspects. The subjugation of women, strife between partners, polygamy, infidelity, and divorce became common features of the biblical history. The result is that by the New Testament period, divorce had become an accepted institution within Judaism.

The point is sufficiently clear so that extensive documentation is unnecessary. It is not merely that there are individual instances of decline, such as the polygamy of Lamech (Gen. 4:19) or the strife that erupts from the preference of Jacob for Rachel over Leah (Gen. 29:14—30:13), but rather that the whole institution of marriage is debased as, in a patriarchal society, women become chattel for

43

whom family heads will bargain as over merchandise in a bazaar. During that time a woman became primarily a sexual creature with childbearing as her chief function. Since such high value was placed upon offspring, polygamy readily became commonplace. Wives were obtained by marriage payment to the father of the bride (Gen. 34:11-12; 1 Sam. 18:25) and, in consequence, became the possession of their husbands (2 Sam. 3:13-16).[1] Since this made the chief actor in marriage the husband, it follows that the marriage law was formulated from his point of view and with his interests in mind. While he could divorce his wife in certain circumstances (Deut. 24:1), his wife had no right to divorce him. And whereas a husband was guilty of adultery only when he had intercourse with a married or betrothed woman (Deut. 22:22-29), intercourse with any man other than her husband made a wife an adulteress. In other words, while a wife could commit adultery against her husband, a husband could not commit adultery against his wife but only against another woman's husband or husband-to-be.

The picture must not be overdrawn. It is true, as has frequently been pointed out, that—in the words of Helmut Thielicke—"the personal sense of belonging to each, which is evident in the order of creation, is constantly breaking into the general tendency to regard the wife as an object, as a mere piece of property. One might even say that the human element repeatedly asserts itself and transcends the legal ordinance."[2] Thielicke goes on to cite Jacob's courtship of

---

1. If Millar Burrows is right, the *mohar* or bride-price in Israelite marriage is not to be understood as a purchase payment but rather as a gift or compensation for loss of a family member. "The gift established a bond not merely by creating good will or a sense of obligation but by actually conveying something of the life of the giver to the recipient . . . From this point of view a gift serves to establish something comparable to a blood-covenant between giver and recipient, and the bond is made complete when there is a fair exchange and compensation" (*The Basis of Israelite Marriage* [New Haven, Conn.: American Oriental Society, 1938], 12-13). He goes on to admit that "the principle of compensation, far from being contrary to the fundamental conception involved in marriage by purchase, is closely related to it if not identical . . . With the emergence of private property, moreover, it would not be surprising if the relation between husband and wife came to be thought of in terms of ownership" (14-15). A similar view is maintained by E. Neufeld (though with some additional features): "Purchase price and compensation are not necessarily and in all applications conceptions which differ from each other, and it is suggested that in this particular application they are fundamentally identical" (*Ancient Hebrew Marriage Laws* [London: Longmans, Green, and Co., 1944], 98).

2. Helmut Thielicke, *The Ethics of Sex*, ET John W. Doberstein (New York: Harper and Row, 1964), 106. The same point is made by Geoffrey W. Bromiley, *God and Marriage* (Grand Rapids: Wm. B. Eerdmans Publishing Co., 1980), 9-10.

Rachel (Gen. 29), the love of Shechem for Dinah (Gen. 34:1-4), and of Paltiel for Michal (2 Sam. 3:15-16).

It should also be noted that if there are laws that speak of women as so much property, then there are others that, in some measure at least, protect the wife's status as a person. Thus, although she was the possession of her husband, she might not be sold into slavery (Deut. 21:14). Again, if a man took a second wife, he must provide his first wife with "food, clothing and marital rights," and if he failed to do so, she had the right to go free (Exod. 21:10-11). The links with her father's household, built into the marriage by the bride-price, guaranteed the married woman at least some degree of assurance that the laws protecting her would be observed.

By the time of the New Testament, marriage in Judaism had both stabilized in some respects and also decayed in comparison with Israelite practice. The status of women showed little change. Even if Judaism was not monolithic, it is safe to say that in every major area of life women were regarded as inferiors. The woman's place was in the home, where her duties included grinding meal, baking, washing, and cooking (Ket. 5,5). Whatever assurance she may have derived from knowing that her position was secured by her right to the marriage payment and to the stipulation in the marriage contract that she receive a portion of her husband's goods if he divorced her or died (Ket. 4,7), the fact remained that she could be dismissed—and for the most frivolous of reasons, at least according to some rulings.[3]

On the other hand, while polygamy remained legally possible, in practice it was rare. As George F. Moore observes: "The Gospels and the whole Tannaite literature evidently suppose a practically monogamous society. The great mass of the people, indeed, lived in circumstances which precluded polygamy."[4]

The inferior position of women in the home and specifically in

---

3. "The School of Shammai say: A man may not divorce his wife unless he has found unchastity in her, for it is written, 'Because he hath found in her *indecency* in *anything*.' And the School of Hillel say: . . . 'even if she spoiled a dish for him.' R. Akiba says: 'Even if he found another fairer than she'" (Gitt. 9-10). Jeremias observes that, since Philo and Josephus appear to know only the Hillelite point of view, "It appears that this must have been the prevailing view in the first half of the first century A.D." (*Jerusalem in the Time of Jesus,* 370).

4. Moore, *Judaism in the First Centuries of the Christian Era,* 2:122. A. Oepke observes pointedly, "In Judaism, the real evil was successive polygamy." Art. *gune, Theological Dictionary of the New Testament,* 1:784.

the sphere of marriage is all the evidence needed to demonstrate their inferiority in the area of religion and in the life of society at large. Ten men were the required quorum for a meeting of the synagogue; nine men and one woman would not suffice. Synagogue schools were for boys, not girls. In the towns, and supremely in Jerusalem, any woman who ventured outside without being veiled to the point of being unrecognizable could be divorced without benefit of the marriage payment (Ket. 7,6).

Doubtless it is possible to quote illustrations to the contrary, but when the evidence is weighed, it is difficult to resist Witherington's conclusion that "a low view of women was common, perhaps even predominant, before, during and after Jesus' era . . . there was no monolithic entity, rabbinic Judaism, in Tannaitic times and . . . various opinions were held about women and their roles, though it appears that by the first century of the Christian era a negative assessment was predominant among the rabbis."[5] The evidence of the New Testament supports this estimate (e.g., John 4:27). Whatever shafts of light illuminate the scene, there can be little doubt of the prevailing gloom.

Clearly, we have traveled—descended—a long way from the ideal of Gen. 2:24. When we inquire not merely *what* had happened but *why* it had happened, we are led to the second factor in the biblical background to divorce. Between the exalted picture of Gen. 2 and the degradation of chapter 4 with its record of the first murder and the first instance of polygamy, there stands in chapter 3 the account of the disobedience and the Fall.

This is not the place to examine the Fall narrative in detail or to explore all of its theological ramifications. Suffice it to say that the import of the narrative seems to make clear that a decisive—and catastrophic—decline took place in the relationship between the man and the woman, on the one hand, and God, on the other, as well as between the man and the woman themselves.

As to the former, Eichrodt is surely correct in affirming, against claims to the contrary,[6] that Gen. 3 "speaks of a decisive event, by which God's plan for Man in his creation was frustrated, and human

---

5. Witherington, *Women in the Ministry of Jesus,* 10. The entire first chapter, "Women and Their Roles in Palestine," is a balanced account of the overall picture. Other treatments, with slightly different assessments, are Moore, *Judaism in the First Centuries of the Christian Era,* 2:119-31, and Jeremias, *Jerusalem in the Time of Jesus,* chap. 18.

6. See Westermann who denies that temporal succession—"before the Fall," "after the Fall"—is a factor in the narrative, which he interprets existentially (*Genesis 1—11,* 275-78, esp. 276).

history came to be stamped with the brand of enmity toward God. This event has the character of a 'Fall,' that is, of a falling out of the line of development willed by God, and, as the subsequent narrative shows, exerts a determining influence on the spiritual attitude of all men."[7] The subtlety of the temptation, laced as it is with insinuation and innuendo; the pathos of the "revelation" that comes to the man and his wife, "they realized they were naked" (Gen. 3:7); the divine remonstration (vv. 11-13); and the eventual expulsion from the garden (vv. 22-24)—all combine to show that beneath the artless simplicity of the story there lies a battle of titanic dimensions, fraught with cosmic consequences.[8] In the words of von Rad: "Man has stepped outside the state of dependence, he has refused obedience and willed to make himself independent. The guiding principle of his life is no longer obedience, but his autonomous knowing and willing, and thus he has really ceased to understand himself as creature."[9]

The dislocation of the relationship between creatures and Creator was impossible without a concomitant dislocation of the relationship between the man and the woman. Each became victim to individual pain, though within the bond of marriage no pain remains individual very long but is soon referred to the other partner.[10] The pain of the woman in childbirth and the frustration of man in his battle to wrest food from the soil (3:16-19) are a far cry from the commandment—with blessing—to "be fruitful and increase in number," to "fill the earth and subdue it" (1:28), to "work" the garden and "take care of it" (2:15). Instead their lives are set in a context of anguish and anxiety, culminating in death (3:19).

---

7. W. Eichrodt, *Theology of the Old Testament,* 2:406. Cf. T. C. Vriezen, *An Outline of Old Testament Theology* (Oxford: Basil Blackwell, 1958), 210-11. For a rebuttal of the view that the Fall figures nowhere in the rest of the Old Testament, emerging into the light only in early Judaism, Eichrodt's entire treatment should be consulted (Eichrodt, *Theology of the Old Testament,* 2:400-413).

8. For sensitive exegeses of the nuances of language of the chapter, see the commentaries, such as Victor P. Hamilton, *Genesis Chapters 1—17,* in *The New International Commentary on the Old Testament* (Grand Rapids: Wm. B. Eerdmans Publishing Co., 1990), 186-212, and Gordon J. Wenham, *Genesis 1—15,* in WBC, 72-91.

9. Gerhard von Rad, *Genesis, a Commentary,* in *Old Testament Library* (Philadelphia: Westminster Press, 1972), 94.

10. Cf. Hamilton, "To each of the trespassers God speaks a word which involves both a life function and a relationship. Thus, the snake is cursed in his mode of locomotion, and his relationship with the woman and her seed is to be one of hostility. The woman shall experience pain at the point of childbearing and in relationship to her husband. The man will confront disappointments as a worker through his estrangement from the soil" (*Genesis Chapters 1—17,* 196).

This, in itself, would beget stress enough, but it is not all. Their interpersonal relationship would be affected directly. "Your desire will be for your husband, and he will rule over you" (3:16b). These words have been variously interpreted. The term translated "desire" (Hebrew *təshūqāh*) occurs only two other times in the Old Testament: Gen. 4:7 and Song of Sol. 7:10. In the latter, its meaning is romantic: "I belong to my lover, and his desire is for me." On this basis, the verse has been taken to mean that the woman's sexual desire for the man would lead, not to affection from him, but rather to domination by him and exploitation by him.[11]

Hamilton, however, points to the striking use of the same pair of terms: "desire" and "master" in Gen. 4:7, where the former denotes desire, not in a sexual sense, but in the sense of domination: "If you do not do what is right, sin is crouching at your door; it desires to have you, but you must master it." Hamilton suggests with probability that the same pair of terms occurring within a few verses of each other will carry the same meaning. "Applied to 3:16, the desire of the woman for her husband is akin to the desire of sin that lies poised ready to leap at Cain. It means a desire to break the relationship of equality and turn it into a relationship of servitude and domination."[12] But God predicts that the woman's attempt at domination will rebound against her, and instead of being the ruler, she will be the ruled.

The Fall has thus wreaked deadly havoc at the very apex of God's creation, that is, in the personal relationship between the pair in whom God reproduced His image and to whom jointly He entrusted the lordship of His creation (1:27-28). The joy of the man's discovery of one like himself, for whom he will forsake all others (2:23), is replaced by the expectation of contention and strife. To quote Hamilton again: "Far from being a reign of coequals over the remainder of God's creation, the relationship now becomes a fierce dispute, with each party trying to rule the other. The two who once reigned as one attempt to rule each other."[13]

---

11. So Wenham, *Genesis 1—15,* 81.

12. Hamilton, *Genesis Chapters 1—17,* 202.

13. Ibid. It may be noted that not all interpreters see the subjugation of the woman as the consequence of the Fall. Thus Wenham, arguing that the author "evidently does not regard female subordination to be a judgment on her sin" since woman, being made from man and named by him, was intended to be subordinate, takes the "rule" of the man predicted in 3:16 to refer to "harsh exploitive subjugation" (*Genesis 1—15,* 81). A fuller statement of this view may be found in Werner Neuer, *Man and*

We thus encounter the deadly element that constitutes the fount and origin of the abrupt descent from the creation ideal of marriage to that which we found to characterize biblical history to the time of Christ. In the haunting but eloquent words of Eichrodt:

> The masterly portrayal of the seduction and its consequences stresses *one* point as the central focus of all the rest, namely, that *the cause of all evil, the reason for distortion in the order of creation, was alienation from God*. . . . There is also a relentless description of *the consequences of this first conscious rejection of God in the disturbance of the very foundations of human existence, indeed of Man's own psychical constitution,* in that the abandonment of Man to the sufferings of life in all their manifold forms is explained by his expulsion from God's fellowship, and the inward destruction of the creature originally held in the will of God is displayed in his enslavement to the power of those sinful impulses which drive him on irresistibly through fratricide and the shedding of blood to the wickedness of a generation on whom the divine judgment of the Deluge falls.[14]

The somber reality with which marriage has to reckon after the Fall is the grievous wounding of the mutual concern and commitment that characterized the order of creation. The mutual concern and commitment do not die, but they are constantly threatened by the menace of distorted self-interest.

Divorce in the Teaching of the Old Testament

"The Old Testament presupposes the legitimacy of divorce," say Heth and Wenham.[15] They add that little is said about its operation, and that the one law that says anything is concerned with regulating divorce (Deut. 24:1-4). Nonetheless, their primary claim remains that in the Old Testament divorce is an accepted institution. This clearly poses a question. How can an institution that is inconsistent

---

Woman in Christian Perspective, ET Gordon J. Wenham (Wheaton, Ill.: Crossway Books, 1991), chap. 5, "Man and Woman in the Old Testament," and esp. Excursus 2, "The subordination of the woman in Genesis 3:16," 79-81. Coming after the picture of woman's creation in the previous chapter, not least of man's delight in finding a partner and his covenanting himself to her, it is difficult not to agree with Westermann that "the domination of the husband and the consequent subordination of the wife is seen as something which is not normal (hence as punishment)" (*Genesis 1—11,* 262). If it is intended in a positive sense, then it stands alone as such in the entire list of consequences of the Fall in 3:14-19.

14. Eichrodt, *Theology of the Old Testament,* 2:404.

15. Heth and Wenham, *Jesus and Divorce,* 106.

with the divine ideal not only remain uncondemned but be actively used by God? The propriety of the question must await clearer definition as we examine the Old Testament teaching about divorce. Meanwhile, it may be tentatively suggested that the perspective from which it is to be viewed in the Old Testament is from that of the redemption of a fallen society, which will be redeemed only as God involves himself in it incarnationally, entering into and taking hold of its institutions in all of their fallenness, not to approve them, but to grasp them in such a way as to transcend them.

We may proceed to put these issues to the proof by surveying the teaching regarding divorce in three main areas of the Old Testament where it is found.

1. Divorce in the Pentateuch

It is not difficult to find laws in the Pentateuch in which divorce as an existing institution is clearly presupposed. Two examples may be found in Deut. 22. The first refers to a husband who comes to dislike his wife (v. 13) and seeks to rid himself of her by claiming falsely that at the time of the marriage she was not a virgin (v. 14). The defense of the wife rests with her parents, who were responsible not only for vouching for her virginity at the time of marriage but also for preserving evidence of the same (vv. 15-17).[16] If the husband proved to be lying, he would be punished and fined (vv. 18-19a). The further significant part of the law reads, "She shall continue to be his wife; he must not divorce her as long as he lives" (v. 19b).

A parallel example in the same group of marriage laws concerns the rape of an unbetrothed virgin. The rapist is to pay the father of the girl the normal marriage payment and marry the girl (v. 29a-b).[17] Still more, "He can never divorce her as long as he lives" (v. 29c).

In both passages, divorce as an existing institution is taken for granted, and in the two instances cited, reasons are given as to why it may not be resorted to, both, apparently, for the protection of the wronged woman.

---

16. For discussion of the possible nature of this evidence, see J. A. Thompson, *Deuteronomy*, in *Tyndale Old Testament Commentaries* (Downers Grove, Ill.: InterVarsity Press, 1976), 235-36.

17. So Thompson, *Deuteronomy*, 237, and Gerhard von Rad, *Deuteronomy, a Commentary*, in OTL (Philadelphia: Westminster Press, 1966), 143. For the view that the "fifty shekels" represents damages, see Peter C. Craigie, *The Book of Deuteronomy*, in NICOT (Grand Rapids: Wm. B. Eerdmans Publishing Co., 1976), 295.

The most explicit law in the Old Testament concerning divorce is found in Deut. 24:1-4. Several points of major importance must be grasped if its meaning is not to be misunderstood. First, this law is not a law of divorce in the sense of legislating divorce into existence. No Old Testament law institutes divorce. It does accept (without approving) divorce as an existing institution and seek to curb its application in the specific case of the return of a woman to her first husband following divorce by or the death of her second husband. The heart of this law is to be found in verse 4: "Her first husband, who divorced her, is not allowed to marry her again after she has been defiled. That would be detestable in the eyes of the LORD. Do not bring sin upon the land the LORD your God is giving you as an inheritance" (v. 4).[18]

A second point of importance is the ground on which the husband divorces his wife: "He finds something indecent (Hebrew *'erwat dābār*) about her." The expression *'erwat dābār* means literally "the nakedness of a thing" and is frequently used metaphorically to denote sexual intercourse (Lev. 18:6-20). It is unlikely to carry that meaning in this context, however, since that would involve adultery, the penalty for which was death by stoning (Lev. 20:10; Deut. 22:22). The same expression is used in Deut. 23:14 to denote behavior that is improper or unbecoming, rather than immoral, and this is probably its meaning here.[19]

---

18. Much confusion has been created by misleading translation of this passage. Old Testament law falls broadly into two categories: command law (or apodictic law, to use the technical expression), introduced by some such phrase as "Thou shalt not," and case law (or casuistic law), which deals with a specific issue and is framed around the formula "If a man does (this) . . . then he cannot do (that)." Deut. 24:1-4 is a case law in which verses 1-3 describe the case in question and verse 4 defines the law for the particular case. This pattern is obliterated in KJV and other translations, giving the impression of legislating divorce into existence in verse 1 and adding further divorce laws in verses 3-4. That the only law laid down here is that in verse 4 is virtually the unanimous opinion of the commentators. Cf. S. R. Driver, *Deuteronomy,* in *The International Critical Commentary* (Edinburgh: T. and T. Clark, 1895), 265-66; von Rad, *Deuteronomy, a Commentary,* in OTL, ET, 150; P. C. Craigie, *The Book of Deuteronomy,* in NICOT (Grand Rapids: Wm. B. Eerdmans Publishing Co., 1983), 304-5. Read in this way, it becomes clear that divorce procedure had already become formalized, requiring: (i) a substantial reason: "something indecent about her" (1*a*); (ii) a written legal document: "he writes her a certificate of divorce" (1*b*); (iii) the formal serving of the same upon the wife: "[he] gives it to her" (1*c*); and (iv) the formal dismissal of the wife from his home: "[he] sends her from his house" (1*d*).

19. So Driver, *Deuteronomy,* 269; John Murray, *Divorce* (Philipsburg, N.J.: Presbyterian and Reformed, 1961), 12; Thompson, *Deuteronomy,* 243. Von Rad asserts that its meaning must have been clear in the time of Deuteronomy, otherwise it would have

The third point of substance in Deut. 24:4 is the reason given as to why her first husband may not marry her again: "She has been defiled," and such behavior would be "detestable" in the sight of the Lord and bring sin upon the land. The crux is the meaning of defilement. Murray contends that it is divorce per se that is defiling.[20] This is hardly persuasive, since, if it were so, it would stand as an objection to the first divorce and the second marriage. Craigie holds that the second marriage is adulterous, but both the form of the law as well as its content belie this.[21] Heth and Wenham argue that the assumption underlying the prohibition of restoration of the first marriage is that the first marriage created what is tantamount to a blood relationship, and therefore its restoration following a "divorce" and "second marriage" would be tantamount to incest.[22] If this is the primary concern, would one not rather expect the law to forbid divorce absolutely if "to seek a divorce is to try to break a relationship with one's wife that in reality cannot be broken"?[23] In fact, as we have seen, the law offers no criticism of the second marriage.

More likely the explanation can be found in the realm of cultic regulations. Many Old Testament passages witness to the aversion of having sexual relations with an unfaithful wife (Num. 5:11-31) or of male relatives having relations with the same woman (2 Sam. 16:21-22 and 20:3; Amos 2:7). Similar reasoning seems to lie behind the law that priests must not marry prostitutes or divorcés (Lev. 21:7),

---

been defined more precisely (*Deuteronomy, a Commentary,* 150). Craigie concludes that its meaning is now unknown (*Book of Deuteronomy,* 304). There is a clear discussion in Abel Isaksson, *Marriage and Ministry in the New Temple* (Lund, Sweden: C. W. K. Gleerup, 1965), 25-27, in which he concludes that indecent exposure on the part of the wife is what is in mind. The same conclusion is reached by Calvin M. Carmichael, *The Laws of Deuteronomy* (Ithaca, N.Y.: Cornell University Press, 1974), though by a different route (pp. 203-9). In his view, the reason she may not return to her first husband is the embarrassment caused him by her original offense. "The (male) concern with the public behavior of women in Mesopotamian society emerges clearly in the law codes" (209, n. 7).

20. "The remarriage on the part of the divorced woman is not expressly stated to be defilement irrespective of return to the first husband . . . (But) . . . whatever may be true of the second marriage, irrespective of return to the first husband, the moment return is envisaged, then with reference to the first husband, the woman has been defiled . . . It is the fact of divorce that bears the whole onus of ultimate responsibility for the defilement" (Murray, *Divorce,* 14-15).

21. Craigie, *Book of Deuteronomy,* 305-6.

22. Heth and Wenham, *Jesus and Divorce,* 109-10.

23. Ibid., 110. The best that Heth and Wenham can reply in answer to the question as to why the Old Testament does not ban divorce altogether is, "We are just not told" (ibid.).

and the high priest must marry only a virgin, marriage even with a widow being regarded as defiling (vv. 13-15). The sliding scale suggests strongly that we are in the realm of the cultic rather than the moral, a conclusion confirmed by the description of the relationship proscribed in Deut. 24:4 as "detestable" or an abomination to the Lord and bringing sin upon the land. Such language is used in Deut. 22 to describe the wearing of female clothing by men (and vice versa, v. 5) and the sowing of a field with two kinds of seed (v. 9).[24]

If we synthesize the evidence of the Pentateuch regarding divorce, we may say that divorce is accepted as a fact. This implies two things. First, it is not a divine institution nor part of the divine plan for marriage. Rather, it is part of the prevailing sinful situation, and insofar as God accepts it, He does so to bring out of it something better. It is significant, for instance, that the laws cited above referring to the husband who seeks to divorce a wife he has come to dislike by falsely accusing her of unchastity (Deut. 22:13-19) and to the unbetrothed virgin who is raped (vv. 28-29) not only punish the offending male but seek to protect the attacked woman by legislating that the husband may never divorce her. The law against remarriage to the first husband following the termination of a second marriage (24:1-4) likewise has as its effect the preservation of human sensitivities by enshrining within it a principle that prevents marriage and remarriage from becoming a cattle market.[25]

The second implication of the acceptance of divorce is, however, that divorce is recognized as accomplishing what it professes to accomplish. That is to say, it terminates an existing marriage and frees the divorced parties to remarry. Deut. 24:1-4 has no meaning if it does not mean this. This point does not depend upon the claim that the intent of the law was to discourage hasty divorce or similar arguments.[26] It depends upon the plain import of the passage that the first

---

24. Von Rad writes of Deut. 24:1-4, "The law refrains from giving a real reason for the negative decision. It contents itself with the very archaic comment that to remarry this woman would be 'an abomination before the Lord.' Thus the legal decision rests on very ancient cultic conceptions" (*Deuteronomy,* 150). To the same effect, see Thompson, *Deuteronomy,* 244. For a fuller discussion see Isaksson, *Marriage and Ministry,* 22-24.

25. Cf. George Adam Smith on Deut. 24:1-4, "It is not a law instituting divorce . . . No O.T. oracle or law institutes divorce. But the husband's right to divorce is accepted or permitted . . . and is put under regulations . . . in the interests of the wife" (*Deuteronomy,* in *Cambridge Bible for Schools and Colleges* [Cambridge, England: University Press, 1918], 276-77).

26. As Heth and Wenham appear to imply (*Jesus and Divorce,* 107-8).

marriage was terminated by due divorce, making possible the second marriage, and the second marriage was similarly terminated by divorce, freeing the woman to contract a further marriage. At this point the law intervenes, not to forbid a third marriage per se, but to forbid remarriage to her first husband. This is precisely what one would *not* expect if the contention were true that the one-flesh relationship of the first marriage remained unbroken and, indeed, unbreakable.[27]

2. Divorce in the Prophetic Literature

In dealing with the biblical picture of marriage, reference was made to the use of such imagery in the prophetic writings. It was pointed out that the use of marriage by the prophets to depict the relationship between God and His people was negative rather than positive; it described how things might have been but were not rather than how they were. It is to that negative side we now come, to the prophetic account of marriage failure and how God dealt with it in His relationship with Israel.

Two preliminary observations may be made that are important for understanding the background of the prophetic teaching. First, the use of marriage to describe God's relation to Israel is an extension of the idea of covenant.[28] In particular, it injects a strongly personal note into the relationship. Whereas a covenant might be no more than a political arrangement or a business transaction, marriage, as understood by a prophet such as Hosea, involved personal commitment and loyalty at the deepest level. As Pierre Grelot puts it, "There can be discerned the appearance of a new dimension of conjugal love itself, a personalization of the bond between the man and the woman which goes beyond the old view of fertility and the con-

---

27. Protagonists of the permanence of the "one-flesh" relationship reply, of course, that restoration of the first marriage is impossible because the one-flesh relationship is tantamount to blood relationship. Restoration of the marriage would therefore amount to incest. Cf. Heth and Wenham, *Jesus and Divorce,* 110. But on these terms, it is difficult to see how restoration of the marriage would have a different effect than the initial marriage, particularly since (as the theory in question maintains) the original relationship remained unbroken because unbreakable. Wenham himself concedes the oddness of the implication. "The result is paradoxical. A man may not remarry his former wife, because his first marriage to her made her into one of his closest relatives" (G. J. Wenham, "The Restoration of Marriage Reconsidered," *Journal of Jewish Studies* 30 [1979]: 40). The obstacle seems to be much more naturally explained in terms of cultic conceptions, as argued above.

28. The idea of covenant in the Old Testament is not static but shows variation and redefinition according to the needs of the given situation. For a history of this, see Eichrodt, *Theology of the Old Testament,* 1:45-69. A briefer account is R. E. Clements, *Old Testament Theology: A Fresh Approach* (Atlanta: John Knox Press, 1978), 96-103.

tinuance of the family."[29] This development, exhibited with tragic drama in the personal life of Hosea and applied by him and his successors, such as Jeremiah and Ezekiel, to the relationship between God and His people, constitutes the background against which we must examine the question, What happens when the marriage collapses?[30]

A second factor, which will be developed more fully later but should be kept in mind throughout, is the particular danger that attends the attempt to derive the law of divorce from the allegorical use of marriage. It must not be forgotten that the primary interest of the prophets is in Israel's religious fidelity to God and God's response to her religious infidelity. The marriage metaphor is used to illustrate this, but it should never be forgotten that it is marriage and divorce that are being used to illuminate the meaning of the religious covenant and not the religious covenant that is being used to explain marriage and divorce. There may be aspects of the religious covenant that have no counterpart in marriage and divorce, and to assume their presence where they do not exist can lead to a distortion of the prophetic teaching regarding marriage and divorce. On the other hand, there can be no question of a real analogy in some measure (as in the case of Hosea, the relation of God with His people is drawn directly from Hosea's personal marital experience).

The procedure from this point will be to set forth, as objectively as possible, the use made of marriage and divorce imagery by four prophets—Hosea, Jeremiah, Isaiah, and Malachi—and then to attempt to draw from this the implications for the biblical view of divorce.

The significance of Hos. 1—3 is twofold. Hosea is the first Old Testament writer to interpret God's covenant with Israel in terms of marriage, and his personal agony of betrayal by his wife becomes the means by which the meaning of God's covenant is conveyed to him. Thus one expects a very real analogy between what the law of marriage and divorce prescribes and how God treats His people who have been unfaithful to the terms of His religious covenant with them.

The story of the marriage and its collapse is told with less exactness than we might desire. As H. L. Ellison expresses it: "Unfortunately for us moderns, Scripture is more concerned with the message that arose from the marriage than with human interest in it. As

---

29. Grelot, "The Institution of Marriage," 46.
30. See Eichrodt, *Theology of the Old Testament,* 1:251-55; cf. 51-52.

a result there is hardly a feature in it that can be interpreted with certainty. What is more, *every* interpretation offered is in the last analysis subjective, so there is no point in counting heads and seeing which has the most and most impressive supports."[31] If this seems to doom to futility any attempt at interpretation, let it be said that the broad outline of the story is clear, and the large features carry the main message, even if more exact details are lacking.

Painting with a wide brush, one may say that the prophet's story has three main phases. The first is the marriage, in which Hosea obeys the command of the Lord: "Go, take to yourself an adulterous wife and children of unfaithfulness, because the land is guilty of the vilest adultery in departing from the LORD" (1:2). Whether this is to be understood literally as a divine directive to the prophet to marry a whore or whether the prophet writes from the vantage point of hindsight, describing his experience in the light of knowledge gained after the event, is a question into which we do not need to enter.[32] The material point is the reality of the marriage and the two sons and a daughter whom Gomer bore to Hosea (vv. 3, 6, 8-9).

The second phase is the collapse of the marriage. This is plainly implied in chapter 2, where although the prime focus of attention is the nation of Israel and its worship of pagan gods, yet the personal tragedy of Hosea is glimpsed fleetingly from time to time: most clearly in verse 2, where Hosea urges his children to rebuke their faithless mother, and in verse 23, where the names of the children are reversed (cf. 1:4, 6, 8-9).[33] The breakdown of Hosea's marriage is made clear beyond question in the second command he receives from the Lord: "Go, show your love to your wife again, though she is loved by another and is an adulteress" (3:1).

---

31. H. L. Ellison, *The Prophets of Israel, from Ahijah to Hosea* (Grand Rapids: Wm. B. Eerdmans Publishing Co., 1967), 97.

32. For a survey of the various suggestions that have been advanced see H. H. Rowley, "The Marriage of Hosea," in *Men of God* (London: Nelson, 1963), 66-97, esp. 94-97.

33. As might be expected, commentators differ as to the extent to which details of Hosea's personal story are to be found in chap. 2. Andersen and Freedman hold that 2:2-13 (Hebrew 2:4-15) make sense on a personal level; while in 2:14-23 (Hebrew 2:16-25) the focus is mainly on the nation. Even so, they admit that "some of the ideas apply mainly to Hosea and Gomer; some apply best to Yahweh and Israel; many make good sense in both sets. But the limitations restrain us from pushing analogies to explain difficult passages. . . . This double meaning continues all through 2:4-25, now one side, now the other, being uppermost" (Francis I. Andersen and David Noel Freedman, *Hosea,* in *The Anchor Bible* [Garden City, N.Y.: Doubleday and Company, 1980], 220; cf. 218).

A question of concern for us is, did Hosea divorce his wife? Interpreters are divided. Hans Walter Wolff expounds the entire sequence on the assumption that he did. "We can only infer that one day Gomer, having committed adultery, left Hosea and became the legal wife of another man."[34] On this view, chapter 2, though not depicted formally as a court scene, uses the speech forms of legal dispute.[35] "She is not my wife, and I am not her husband" (v. 2) is seen as a legal divorce formula.[36] By stripping her of her garments, the husband visibly repudiates his marriage obligation to clothe his wife (Exod. 21:10). When she becomes disillusioned with her new situation, she says, "I will go and return to my first husband" (Hos. 2:7, RSV).[37] The sequel to this comes in verses 19-20 where, in Wolff's view, the reconciliation of Gomer and Hosea is used to express the renewed covenant between God and Israel. The phrase "I will betroth you" is repeated three times (vv. 19-20). Wolff translates it "I will make you my own," attesting to the "binding, legal act of marriage" inasmuch as it "denotes the act of paying the bridal price."[38] To quote Wolff again, "The old marriage is not to be reconstituted, but a completely new one is to be created."[39]

If this interpretation is sound, then it has important implications for the Old Testament picture of divorce. For one thing, it is implied that not only did Hosea divorce Gomer for moral adultery, but God also "divorced" Israel for spiritual adultery. Indeed, Wolff affirms that the expression "for you are not my people, and I am not your God" (1:9) is the divine parallel to the judicial divorce formula, "for she is not my wife, and I am not her husband" (2:2), and meant the dissolution of the covenant between God and Israel.[40] Again, if the law of Deut. 24:1-4 was in force at that time, God was not only di-

---

34. Hans Walter Wolff, *Hosea,* in *Hermeneia,* ET (Philadelphia: Fortress Press, 1974), xxii.

35. Ibid., xxiii. See also 32.

36. Ibid., 33. Cf. Peter C. Craigie, *Twelve Prophets,* vol. 1 in *The Daily Study Bible* (Philadelphia: Westminster Press, 1984): "One must envisage Hosea and his children in the court; they address words to the judge in the presence of Gomer. Hosea's purpose in the lawsuit is to obtain a decree of divorce from his wife, and indeed his speech begins with the formal proclamation of divorce: 'She is not my wife and I am not her husband' (verse 2)" (19-20).

37. "My first husband" is a more exact rendering of the Hebrew text than "I will go back to my husband as at first" (NEB).

38. Wolff, *Hosea,* 52.

39. Ibid.

40. Ibid., 21-22, 27.

recting Hosea to act contrary to the law in remarrying a wife who had been married to another man but also doing so himself in entering into a new covenant with Israel (Hos. 2:18-23). In Wolff's words, "God does what is impossible according to the law."[41]

On the other hand, not all expositors are convinced that the text supports the conclusion that Hosea divorced his wife. Some contend that there is no evidence to show that Hosea's statement in 2:2 is a normal pronouncement of divorce.[42] Rather, it is to be understood as a declaration that they are no longer living as husband and wife. Gomer's offense is adultery (2:4; 3:1), and Hosea's intention is not to get rid of her but to win her back, an outcome that divorce would do little to bring about. Accordingly, the sequence of events recounts marriage breakdown rather than marriage dissolution. If there are points at which the language seems to go beyond this, for example, the return to her "first husband" (2:7) or the account of the new betrothal (v. 19), these are simply examples of how the marriage metaphor is influenced by the idea of God's covenant with Israel, which is Hosea's primary concern.[43]

It seems clear that given the uncertainties of the evidence and making due allowance for the metaphorical use of marriage to describe the covenant, it is claiming too much to say affirmatively that Hosea divorced his wife. This detracts little from the third phase of the event, which is the restoration of Gomer. The precise details of why Hosea had to buy her back, and from whom, remain obscure.[44] But what is not in doubt is the driving power behind God's command and Hosea's action—love. "The LORD said to me, 'Go, show your love to your wife again, though she is loved by another'" (3:1).

The order is remarkable inasmuch as it sweeps aside the legal prescription that the penalty for adultery was death (Lev. 20:10;

---

41. Ibid., 63.

42. Cf. James Luther Mays, "The specific complaint . . . is cited: 'she is not my wife, and I am not her husband.' This sentence has been identified as a declaration of divorce, but corroborating evidence for the identification from Old Testament times in Israel is lacking" (*Hosea,* in OTL [Philadelphia: Westminster Press, 1969], 37). See also Rowley, *Men of God,* 92, together with n. 2.

43. It is interesting to observe how Andersen and Freedman write with measurably varying degrees of certainty on this issue. "There is no evidence of a formal divorce" (128). "The woman is transformed by a 'second' marriage . . . The form of reinstatement implied by 2:4-25 is rather elusive. There is a hint of divorce, yet the husband continues to treat her as a wayward wife" (Andersen and Freedman, *Hosea,* 218).

44. A variety of theories is discussed by Rowley, *Men of God,* 90, n. 2. The details of 3:2 are discussed by Mays, *Hosea,* 57-58.

Deut. 22:22). Hosea was not to feel bound by the letter of the law in his treatment of Gomer any more than God was to feel bound by the letter of the law in His treatment of Israel. Yet there was a searching qualification. "And I said to her, 'You must remain as mine for many days; you shall not play the whore, you shall not have intercourse with a man, nor I with you'" (3:3, NRSV). As Mays comments pungently: "The woman must live in the prophet's house shut away from any opportunity to be a harlot, cut off from other men. Even he would not claim the conjugal rights of a husband, for what this stern imprisoning love seeks is not punishment, or mere possession, but the answer and response of the beloved. . . . He will not go in to her because more than anything he wants her to come to him. The pathos and power of God's love is embodied in these strange tactics—a love that imprisons to set free, destroys false love for the sake of true, punishes in order to redeem."[45]

We may turn next from Hosea to Jeremiah, whom Eichrodt describes as "the only man to have fully absorbed the preaching of Hosea."[46] The imagery of divorce comes into prominence particularly in chapter 3, a chapter that in thought and expression has much in common with the first three chapters of Hosea. Three points receive particular emphasis.

The first is that reconciliation between God and Israel is legally impossible. The reason for this is that the law of divorce forbids it. The chapter begins by summarizing the divorce law of Deut. 24:1-4, but as a rhetorical question: "If a man divorces his wife and she leaves him and marries another man, should he return to her again?" (3:1). It is true that in Jeremiah, unlike Hosea, no literal marriage is in view. Nevertheless, the marriage imagery is drawn upon metaphorically—in the specific form of the divorce law. This law makes clear that there is no possibility of God's returning to His earlier relationship with Judah. Her promiscuity with a multitude of other lovers had made her an adulteress (vv. 2, 3, 8b, 9, 10), and the law must take its course.[47]

Second, God is represented as making use of the divorce law. This is certainly implied in Jer. 3:1 and stated forthrightly in verse 8:

---

45. Mays, *Hosea,* 58.
46. Eichrodt, *Theology of the Old Testament,* 1:253.
47. W. L. Holladay suggests, with probability, that Jeremiah may be opposing the complacency that had arisen from Hos. 3:1-5. Cf. *Jeremiah 1,* in *Hermeneia* (Philadelphia: Fortress Press, 1986), 113. The repeated references to the fate of Israel in 3:6-13 lend credence to this view.

"I gave faithless Israel her certificate of divorce and sent her away because of all her adulteries." Thus, what is not stated explicitly or (as we saw) clearly implied in Hos. 3 is here expressed forthrightly. God himself divorced Israel.

Third, repentance alone could bring restoration. The mind-set of Judah was of superficial sentimentalism that failed to treat moral realities for what they were. "Have you not just called to me: 'My Father, my friend from my youth, will you always be angry? Will your wrath continue forever?' This is how you talk, but you do all the evil you can" (Jer. 3:4). "I gave faithless Israel her certificate of divorce and sent her away because of all her adulteries. Yet I saw that her unfaithful sister Judah had no fear; she also went out and committed adultery. . . . [She] did not return to me with all her heart, but only in pretense" (vv. 8, 10*b*).

It is important to be aware that the word translated "return" (Hebrew *shūb*) also means "repent." Jeremiah's emphasis on repentance, in contrast with Hosea where it is at most presupposed, is explicit and repeated. Its importance lies in this: while within the framework of the law the restoration of Israel as God's wife was impossible, yet God's creative grace could work beyond the limits of the law, bringing forgiveness and restoration. "Return, faithless people; I will cure you of backsliding" (v. 22*a*). Thus, what the chapter begins by declaring impossible becomes achievable through renewing mercy.

What is to be said of Jeremiah's characterization of divorce? It is important to remember that here, as with Hosea, divorce is being used metaphorically to describe religious infidelity. The latter is Jeremiah's prime concern, and when the illustration becomes too cramped for the religious reality, then it is the illustration that must yield. Thus, within the framework of the law a divorced wife could not be restored, but divine grace is bigger than the letter of the law. As William McKane points out, while God's divorce from Israel was legally attested by her final exile, yet "the intention of vv. 6-11 in connection with vv. 12-13 is to establish that the divorce is, nevertheless, not final."[48] The same point is implicit in the repeated urging of repentance upon Judah. The law of divorce makes no place for repentance; indeed, law by definition can make no place for repentance, since repentance is a religious rather than a legal category.

---

48. William McKane, *Jeremiah*, vol. 1 in ICC (Edinburgh: T. and T. Clark, 1986), 65.

However, the God who uses the law of divorce to convict and punish Israel is not inhibited by it from forgiving and restoring her where His mercy has brought her to repentance.

The third of the prophetic works in which the image of divorce is found is Isaiah, notably in chapters 40—66. Those chapters describe the return of the nation from exile. Throughout them Jerusalem is personified as a woman, an identification made in the well-known words of 40:2: "Speak tenderly to Jerusalem, and proclaim to her that her hard service has been completed, that her sin has been paid for, that she has received from the LORD's hand double for all her sins." In particular, Jerusalem is personified as a wife, and within this frame of reference three aspects of her condition are brought into focus.

First, Jerusalem protests plaintively that she is an abandoned wife. God has not merely forsaken her but forgotten her (49:14). She was a "a wife who married young, only to be rejected" (54:6) and, therefore, childless (v. 1). Indeed, she was "hated" (Hebrew śǝnū'āh, 60:15), "a technical term for a wife repudiated by her husband."[49]

Second, the charge that Jerusalem makes against God He returns against her by declaring that while indeed He abandoned her, it was not because of His unfaithfulness but rather because of hers. "Because of your sins you were sold; because of your transgressions your mother was sent away" (50:1b). Here the language used is that of divorce, to "send away" being the second act of the divorce procedure as is made clear in the first part of the verse.

Third, while it is true that she has been rejected, now she is to be miraculously restored. This is made plain in two ways. To begin with, she is to prepare to bear children. "'Sing, O barren woman, you who never bore a child; burst into song, shout for joy, you who were never in labor; because more are the children of the desolate woman than of her who has a husband,' says the LORD" (54:1). "For your Maker is your husband. . . . The LORD will call you back as if you were a wife deserted and distressed in spirit" (54:5a, 6a). Still more—and here the reality described breaks through the limits of the marriage metaphor—she already is the mother of a multitude of children, and they are streaming back to her from their Babylonian

---

49. So R. N. Whybray, *Isaiah 40—66,* in NCB (Grand Rapids: Wm. B. Eerdmans Publishing Co., 1981), 236. It is the term used of the "hated" wife in Deut. 21:15. John L. McKenzie comments finely, "The prophet toys with the idea of divorce" (*Second Isaiah,* in AB [Garden City, N.Y.: Doubleday, 1968], 139).

exile. "Lift up your eyes and look about you: All assemble and come to you; your sons come from afar, and your daughters are carried on the arm" (60:4).

Now two matters are of particular significance for the prophetic attitude to divorce. The first is that while Jerusalem evidently regarded her abandonment by God as divorce, He did not do so. Her complaint of desertion in Isa. 49:14, as well as receiving part of its reply in the remainder of that chapter, finds its precise riposte in the following chapter: "This is what the LORD says: 'Where is your mother's certificate of divorce with which I sent her away?'" (50:1). The question is rhetorical. Jerusalem can produce no certificate of divorce, because she was never given one. And where there is no certificate of divorce, there is no divorce. In God's intention, there never was a divorce. Separation—yes, because of her sins. But now that she has paid for her sins (40:1-2), the separation is over, and the broken marriage can be repaired. "'For a brief moment I abandoned you, but with deep compassion I will bring you back. In a surge of anger I hid my face from you for a moment, but with everlasting kindness I will have compassion on you,' says the LORD your Redeemer" (54:7-8). There is a difference at this point between Jeremiah and Isaiah. Whereas Jeremiah depicts Samaria's overthrow as God's divorce of Israel (Jer. 3:8), the parallel act for Judah is specifically repudiated in Isa. 50:1.

A second feature of importance in defining the prophetic attitude to divorce in Isa. 40—66 is the range of imagery used and the elasticity with which it is used. Thus, Jerusalem's abandonment is described not only in terms suggestive of divorce but also in terms suggestive of slavery (50:1), widowhood (54:4), and the deprivation of mother-love (49:15). By the same token, the reversal of her abandoned condition is depicted in terms of both the reconciliation of estranged marriage partners (54:5-8), as well as in terms of a completely new marriage (62:4-5). The latter passage reads: "No longer will they call you Deserted, or name your land Desolate. But you will be called Hephzibah, and your land Beulah; for the LORD will take delight in you, and your land will be married. As a young man marries a maiden, so will your sons marry you; as a bridegroom rejoices over his bride, so will your God rejoice over you." This freedom of application of the marriage metaphor, together with the supplementing of it by other metaphors, warns against the danger of attempting to deduce divorce law and the prophetic attitude to it from passages such as these. If they show anything in this regard, it is rather the sovereign grace of God to forgive and restore even where the law has been broken. The law is not disregarded, but it is not God's last word. It is this very fact that, in Isaiah, restrains God from using divorce as one of His instruments.

The last of the Old Testament prophetic writers to speak significantly of divorce is Malachi. Not all of the introductory issues regarding the prophecy of Malachi need be considered here. Some, however, are important for the interpretation of the passage concerning divorce (2:10-16). The first is that of historical setting. There is widespread agreement that Malachi addresses the same situation as Ezra-Nehemiah.[50] The same problems that preoccupied them preoccupied him.

While there is no reference in Malachi to the rebuilding of the Temple (the way in which worship had degenerated into a routine affair suggests that the reconstruction had taken place some time before), yet the religious battles facing Malachi were akin if not identical to those faced by Ezra and Nehemiah. The reluctance to support the Temple's financial upkeep (Mal. 3:8; Neh. 10:32-39; 13:10); the oppression of the poor and underprivileged (Mal. 3:5; Neh. 5:1-5); and, above all, intermarriage with those who did not share the Jewish faith (Mal. 2:10-11; Ezra 9:1-2; Neh. 13:1-3, 23-24)—all point to the same *general* period of the reestablishment of the Israelite faith in Jerusalem following the return from exile.[51]

A second issue in the interpreting of the divorce passage is the overall message of the book. There is a large measure of agreement that whatever other elements may be present—such as the concern for the proper practice of Temple worship, the preservation of the purity of the chosen people, and the advent of the divine messenger—the controlling theme that constitutes the baseline of all of these is the covenant. Joyce G. Baldwin sounds the right note when she says: "Fundamental to Malachi's teaching is the concept of covenant. It is implicit in the opening theme, the Lord's love for Israel

---

50. See, for example, the conclusions of representative commentators, such as S. R. Driver, *The Minor Prophets,* vol. 2 in *Century Bible* (Edinburgh: T. C. and E. C. Jack, 1906), 291, 293; Pieter A. Verhoef, *The Books of Haggai and Malachi,* in NICOT (Grand Rapids: Wm. B. Eerdmans Publishing Co., 1987), 159-62; Ralph L. Smith, *Micah—Malachi,* in WBC (Waco, Tex.: Word Books, 1984), 298.

51. The *precise* chronological relationship between Malachi and Ezra—Nehemiah, whether prior to, contemporary with, or subsequent to the latter, is a matter of much more debate. See the commentaries referred to in the previous note. This question of *relative* relationship does not concern us here.

(1:2-5), and the book ends with a call to fulfill the obligations of the covenant as expressed in the law (4:4)."[52] Steven L. McKenzie and Howard N. Wallace have demonstrated the frequency with which covenant is mentioned in Malachi, arguing that this constitutes the background to the violations of the covenant alleged throughout the book.[53]

A third preliminary issue is whether the divorce in mind is metaphorical or literal. We need not treat every point of the argument. Suffice it to say that there are some phrases in Mal. 2:10-16 that could bear the meaning of religious infidelity: "marrying the daughter of a foreign god" (v. 11) has been taken to mean engaging in the worship of a false goddess; and flooding "the LORD's altar with tears" (v. 13) has been understood as a ritual in which the aforementioned goddess, in the persons of her worshipers, weeps for her male counterpart. The whole passage is thus taken as an attack on syncretistic worship, an attack, it is claimed, that is in keeping with the message of the rest of the book.[54]

Amid many difficulties[55] some things seem reasonably clear, and they tend to weigh in favor of a literal interpretation.[56] First, the end of verse 15, "and do not break faith with the wife of your youth," is most naturally understood to refer to marriage in a literal sense.[57] If this is so, then, as Baldwin affirms, it constitutes a guide

52. Joyce G. Baldwin, *Haggai, Zechariah, Malachi,* in *Tyndale Old Testament Commentaries* (Downers Grove, Ill.: InterVarsity Press, 1972), 216.

53. Steven L. McKenzie and Howard N. Wallace, "Covenant Themes in Malachi," CBQ 45 (1983): 549-63, esp. 559-60. Their main point is secure, whatever be thought of their theory regarding 3:13-24.

54. For a full statement of this view see Abel Isaksson, *Marriage and Ministry,* 27-34. Isaksson concludes: "The prophet's attention is concentrated all the time on the true religion. Malachi is a priestly reformer, not a prophetic renovator of the ethics of marriage" (32).

55. Chap. 2, verse 15 has been described as "one of the most difficult verses in the Old Testament" (R. C. Dentan, quoted in Ralph L. Smith, *Micah—Malachi,* 324); while Smith himself describes the whole passage as "one of the most important yet most difficult . . . in the book of Malachi" (325). Joyce Baldwin adds: "It is impossible to make sense of the Hebrew as it stands, and therefore each translation, including the early versions, contains an element of interpretation" (*Haggai, Zechariah, Malachi,* 240).

56. For a point-by-point refutation of Isaksson's view, see Ralph L. Smith, *Micah—Malachi,* 323-24.

57. On the metaphorical view: that attachment to a false god is in mind, the logic of the argument requires that "the wife of your youth" is a reference to the God of Israel. This is unusual, since God is usually referred to as Israel's *husband.* Isaksson admits that this is untypical but defends it nonetheless (*Marriage and Ministry,* 33).

to the interpretation of this verse and, in turn, of the passage as a whole.[58] Second, on this basis, the first half of the verse presumably refers likewise to marriage and in particular seems to echo Gen. 2:24: "Has not the LORD made them one? In flesh and spirit they are his. And why one? Because he was seeking godly offspring."[59] Third, there is no justification for saying that the idea of divorce does not fit the overall message of the book. It is quite correct to claim, as Isaksson does, that the prophet is concerned about religion.[60] But far from meaning that mixed marriages with non-Jews were an "ethical" as opposed to a "religious" matter, Malachi's message is quite the reverse; that is, such marriages were having a directly religious effect by mingling pagan rites with the pure worship of God.

What, then, is Malachi's argument in this passage?[61] His point of departure is the unity of creation. Since all were the creation of one God, they ought to be one. One Father makes one family. But far from acting as one family, they were breaking faith with one another in breach of God's covenant with their forefathers (2:10). This breaking of faith took two forms. First, it took the form of religiously mixed marriages, marriage to worshipers of foreign goddesses, all the while bringing offerings to the Lord (vv. 11-12). Second, it took the form of divorce from "the wife of your youth" (vv. 14-15).

It is possible, as Verhoef suggests, that the two offenses were connected, that the divorces took place in order to make possible the marriages with pagan wives.[62] The language implies also that an influential reason was the desire to replace an older woman, less attractive from the scars of age, with a more youthful and vivacious partner.[63] The offensiveness of such an action lay not only in the shabby injustice of using a woman until she was past her prime and then casting her on the scrap heap, but primarily in the breaking of the lifelong covenant made to her on marriage in the presence of God. "The LORD is acting as the witness between you and the wife of your youth, because you have broken faith with her, though she is

---

58. Baldwin, *Haggai, Zechariah, Malachi*, 240.
59. For alternative understandings of the meaning of "one," see Ralph L. Smith, *Micah—Malachi*, 323.
60. See n. 54 above.
61. For a structural analysis of the passage that underlies and sustains the argument, see Verhoef, *Books of Haggai and Malachi*, 175-76, 264-65.
62. Ibid., 275.
63. The expression "the wife of your youth" in the Old Testament commonly denotes the physical powers of attractiveness, reproduction, etc., at their pristine best. Cf. Isa. 54:6 and especially the very frank, figurative descriptions of Ezek. 23:8, 19-21, 23.

your partner, the wife of your marriage covenant" (v. 14). It is this behavior that evokes the exclamation "I hate divorce" from the covenant God of Israel (v. 16).[64]

The net effect of both offenses is the same: the disparagement and even endangering of the worship of the true God of Israel. The religiously mixed marriages entail the defilement of the nation's worship at the same time as they threaten its future existence. For the reason God "made them one" (i.e., male and female in marriage) was "because he was seeking godly offspring" (v. 15).[65] But godly offspring are the last thing likely to be produced in a home into which religious division has been injected for such frivolous reasons. Nor will intense and even frenzied religious observance serve to put things right. Not bringing offerings to the Lord (v. 12); not weeping and wailing to gain God's attention (v. 13); not offering a sacrifice so vigorously that one is spattered with the victim's blood (v. 16)—nothing will avail save keeping the covenant. "So guard yourself in your spirit, and do not break faith" (v. 16b).[66]

It is worth pausing to summarize the teaching of this remarkable passage on marriage and divorce. The first thing that is striking is that here, as in Gen. 2:24, marriage is understood as a covenant (2:14). Scholars who favor the cultic interpretation of the passage do so because, among other reasons, the understanding of marriage as a covenant rather than as a contract is inconsistent with common practice throughout the history of Israel, as we ourselves discovered earlier.[67] However, the idea of marriage as a covenant was never wholly lost, as is made clear in Hos. 1—2, as well as in other contexts, such as Ezek. 16:8, 59-62 and Prov. 2:17. Moreover, there is

---

64. Against the claim that "I hate divorce" is an unlikely rendering, see Ralph L. Smith, *Micah—Malachi,* 323, 324; and Verhoef, *Books of Haggai and Malachi,* 278-79.

65. For reasons for interpreting the Hebrew text this way, see Ralph L. Smith, *Micah—Malachi,* 321, 324.

66. Verhoef argues plausibly for understanding the text thus (*Books of Haggai and Malachi,* 279-80).

67. Isaksson says flatly that "a really quite decisive argument against interpreting these verses as dealing with marriage and divorce is that the O. T. concept 'covenant' is quite incompatible with what marriage meant at this period. Marriage was not a contract entered into by man and wife with Yahweh as witness but a matter of commercial negotiation between two men. The prospective husband paid the bride's father a sum of money and in this way the bride, who, in legal terms, was quite incapacitated, passed into the possession of her husband" (*Marriage and Ministry,* 31). McKenzie and Wallace make essentially the same observation in different terms. "If Mal. 2:13-16 concerns divorce, it is in striking contrast to the law of divorce in Deut. 24:1-4" ("Covenant Themes in Malachi," 552-53, n. 14).

every reason why Malachi, for whom covenant is a fundamental theme, would readily make the connection that the reason why God's covenant with Israel was being nullified was because the infidelity of husbands to wives was opening the door to pagan infiltration via mixed marriages. The breach of God's covenant with the nation was being accentuated by the breach of the marriage covenant. The language of Mal. 2:10, 15 is strongly reminiscent of Gen. 1—2 and may well represent a recovery of the marriage ideal of creation.

A second distinctive feature of the teaching of this passage following directly from the first is that divorce is represented as a clear departure from the will of God, who declares, "I hate divorce" (2:16). If it has been correctly maintained that Malachi refers to the covenant marriage of Gen. 2:24, it is hardly plausible to contend that the divorce God is said to hate is the kind discussed in this passage (i.e., the kind whose design was to discard an aging wife and marry a younger woman who was a pagan), but that Malachi fully accepted divorce as conventionally practiced on the basis of Deut. 24:1-4.[68] It is much more probable that Malachi's view is an application to a particular situation of a general rejection of divorce that he believed to be God's will. If this is correct, then Joyce Baldwin is right in concluding that "Malachi's plea prepares the way for the teaching of Jesus (Matt. 5:31-32; 19:4-9)."[69]

The third notable feature of Malachi's teaching is his insistence that no amount of religious observance can make the practitioners of divorce acceptable to God. "You weep and wail because he no longer pays attention to your offerings or accepts them with pleasure from your hands" (2:13). We may now ask, Where did Malachi go from there? Did he advocate the dissolution of mixed marriages? Did he affirm the impossibility of forgiveness for those who refused to do this? The answer is, we do not know. All we know for certain is that he endeavored to prevent divorce. The logic of his position

---

68. This view is maintained by Stephan Schreiner. For references, see Ralph L. Smith, *Micah—Malachi*, 324.

69. Baldwin, *Haggai, Zechariah, Malachi*, 241. Isaksson agrees that this is the import of Malachi's teaching if marriage is being spoken of literally in the passage in question. "He goes far beyond Dt. 24:1-4, and indeed seems to set himself in downright opposition to what is written there about divorce. He has an almost N. T. conception of marriage. He comes very close to what is said about marriage in the Synoptic pericope on divorce (Mt. 19:3-12; Mk. 10:2-12). He even explains the indissolubility of marriage in the same way as Jesus in this pericope, viz. from the idea of God as creator (v. 10)" (*Marriage and Ministry*, 30).

would seem to permit only one possibility, namely, that religiously mixed marriages be dissolved, but there is no specific statement to that effect. For that conclusion we have to look to his contemporaries Ezra and Nehemiah.

When we attempt to put together the various views of and attitudes toward divorce expressed by the prophets, whether in regard to the literal dissolution of marriages or the figurative use of the image to express religious realities, what kind of picture emerges? To begin with, it seems clear that divorce as an institution is accepted as a fact and used accordingly, without being either approved or disapproved. This conclusion seems to be required by the metaphorical use of the image, according to which God himself is said to have divorced Israel (Jer. 3:8). At the same time, there is no clear evidence at the literal level that Hosea divorced Gomer, while Malachi represents God as hating divorce.

Yet another feature of the prophetic picture is the underlining of the covenant aspect of marriage. The effect of this is to underscore the dimension of personal commitment over that of contractual relationship. It comes to its most vivid expression in Hosea's refusal to abandon his unfaithful wife, while in Malachi the prophet excoriates those who would send away their wives to whom they had covenanted themselves in their youth. This aspect is not absent from the metaphorical application; if Jeremiah can depict God as having divorced Samaria, then the insinuation in Isa. 50:1 that God has divorced Judah is groundless. His covenant loyalty made it impossible (Isa. 54:7-8).

This leads naturally to a third feature that recurs in the prophets: God is not the prisoner of the law—even His own law. The law may prescribe the death penalty for adultery (Deut. 22:22), but this is not God's purpose for either Gomer or Israel. In Peter Craigie's words: "The divine call impels him to action, but the divine law appears to prohibit the action to which he is called. . . . How can God ask Hosea to do what is prohibited in divine law? The question is phrased wrongly! Love always precedes law. If law took preeminence, there would be no gospel in either Old or New Testament. . . . But divine love is a force that knows no bounds; law may follow love to give some structure to the forms of love, but it can never have preeminence."[70]

---

70. Craigie, *Twelve Prophets,* 28.

As was seen earlier, substantially the same point is made by Jeremiah, though in somewhat different form.[71] Within the framework of the story of Hosea, the stress falls chiefly upon the determination of divine love to pursue the faithless partner. In Jeremiah, the accent falls on the possibility of restoration if only there is repentance. "'Return, faithless Israel,' declares the LORD, 'I will frown on you no longer, for I am merciful,' declares the LORD, 'I will not be angry forever. Only acknowledge your guilt'" (Jer. 3:12-13a). To quote Craigie again, commenting on Jer. 3:1-5: "To the reader who has not even pondered the possibility of repentance, the opening statement in this section on repentance suggests that it might not be possible! That is the legal perspective presupposed by the opening analogy, but before the chapter is complete, the requirements of law will have been overwhelmed by the compassion of grace."[72]

What all of this amounts to has been well stated by G. W. Bromiley. While pointing out that the marriage metaphor is only one of many used by the prophets to denote Israel's relationship to God, and that the metaphor of God as husband has distinct limitations (for example, in failing to suggest the truth that not only wives commit infidelity), he concludes that the point of overriding importance is that "God acts as he does toward Israel with a view to redemption and restoration."[73] The prophetic insight that God's distinguishing work is redemptive in character and purpose is one we should not allow to slip beyond our field of vision.

3. Divorce in Ezra-Nehemiah

The final contribution to the picture of divorce presented in the Old Testament comes from Ezra-Nehemiah.[74] However the precise historical relationship of the two men is to be understood, the problem they confronted and the circumstances that gave rise to it are not in doubt.[75] At a point approximately 80 years after the return of

---

71. Chap. 2, 59-61 (above).

72. Peter C. Craigie, *Jeremiah 1—25,* in WBC (1991), 51-52.

73. Bromiley, *God and Marriage,* 34. Cf. 32-33.

74. The two books constituted a single entity according to Jewish tradition. Not until the third century of the Christian era is there evidence of their separate existence. For a summary of the evidence, see H. G. M. Williamson, *Ezra, Nehemiah,* in WBC (1985), xxi-xxii.

75. The various permutations suggested, together with the arguments for and against, need not be gone into here, since the position adopted does not affect the issue under consideration. Suffice it to say that a recent treatment, such as that of Williamson, *Ezra, Nehemiah,* xxxix-xliv, argues cogently for the traditional order.

the first group of exiles from their captivity in Babylon, a second group returned under the leadership of Ezra, who is described as "a teacher well versed in the Law of Moses" (Ezra 7:6) and a "priest and teacher, a man learned in matters concerning the commands and decrees of the LORD for Israel" (v. 11). The years since the first return had witnessed the rebuilding of the Temple with the blessing of Cyrus, king of Persia, while Ezra returned with the approval and assistance of King Artaxerxes (vv. 11-28).[76]

Not long after Ezra's return, the leaders brought to his attention the fact that "the people of Israel, including the priests and the Levites, have not kept themselves separate from the neighboring peoples with their detestable practices. . . . They have taken some of their daughters as wives for themselves and their sons, and have mingled the holy race with the peoples around them. And the leaders and officials have led the way in this unfaithfulness" (Ezra 9:1-2). The solution eventually proposed and implemented by the people with the approval of Ezra was: "Now let us make a covenant before our God to send away all these women and their children, in accordance with the counsel of my lord and of those who fear the commands of our God. Let it be done according to the Law" (10:3, cf. vv. 10-11, 16-17, 44).

On the face of it what was counseled and effected here was the divorce of those who had intermarried with non-Jewish people of the land, even when children had been born to such marriages (10:3, 10, 44).[77] This was done "according to the Law" (v. 3). The law appealed to was evidently that of Deut. 7:1-5, which forbade intermarriage with the inhabitants of Canaan, "for they . . . will turn your sons away from following me to serve other gods" (v. 4a). That is to say, although the language used in Ezra 9:2 is racial ("they . . . have mingled the holy race with the peoples around them"), the underlying motive was religious: "You are a holy people to the LORD your God" (Deut. 7:6a).[78] Marriage with foreigners as such is not forbidden in the Old Testament, but when it posed a threat to the purity of

---

76. For an overview of the historical background from Cyrus to the return of Ezra, see Ezra 1—8.

77. For a note on the translation problem of Ezra 10:44, see Williamson, *Ezra, Nehemiah,* 144-45.

78. So D. J. A. Clines, *Ezra, Nehemiah, Esther,* in *New Century Bible Commentary* (Grand Rapids: Wm. B. Eerdmans Publishing Co., 1984), 117-18. For a contrary view, see Williamson, *Ezra, Nehemiah,* 131-32.

Israel's faith as it did when it became a widespread practice, then it was outlawed.

However, another law appears to have played a part in the decision. The law of Deut. 7:1-5 banned intermarriage with the people of the land, but it said nothing of what was to become of such marriages once contracted. Ezra 10:3, on the other hand, implies that the wives and even children of such unions are to be sent away "in accordance with the counsel of my lord [sc. Ezra] and of those who fear the commands of our God. Let it be done according to the Law." H. G. M. Williamson suggests that Ezra may have persuaded them that such marriages were inherently "unseemly" or "shameful" within the terms of Deut. 24:1, and that accordingly the law of divorce would apply to them.[79] It is worth noting that the word translated "leaves" in Deut. 24:2 is from the same root *(yātsā')* as that rendered "send away" in Ezra 10:3, so that there is a verbal link between the two passages.[80]

---

79. Williamson, *Ezra, Nehemiah,* 151. Likewise Clines, *Ezra, Nehemiah, Esther,* 126-27. Williamson points out that a high degree of "interpretative contextualization," probably traceable to the teaching of Ezra, takes place in Ezra 9 (Williamson, *Ezra, Nehemiah,* 130-31). Ezra 9:11-12 in particular draws upon Deut. 23:6, which forbids treaties of friendship with the people of the land. Again, commenting on Ezra 9:1, Williamson writes: "In the present verse we see how, once conditions had changed beyond the point where the law could be applied literally, its principle was nevertheless upheld" (130).

80. It is frequently pointed out that the terminology used in Ezra 9 and 10, and Neh. 13:25-27 to refer to marriage to and divorce from foreign women is not that normally used in the Old Testament but is unique to Ezra-Nehemiah. Thus, the term used for "marry" denotes "to cause to dwell or live with" (Hebrew *yāshab*). Again, the normal term for "divorce" (Hebrew *shālah*) is displaced by the term "separate" (Hebrew *bādal*). On this basis, some have concluded that divorce in the sense of termination of marriage is not in mind. J. Carl Laney holds that legal separation alone is in view (House, *Divorce and Remarriage,* 26, together with n. 19, where he retracts his earlier opinion that divorce is intended). William Heth argues that, since the marriages were a defiance of God's law *ab initio,* they were not marriages at all, therefore the question of divorce does not arise (in House, *Divorce and Remarriage,* 88-90). However, the employment of unusual—and somewhat contemptuous—terminology for marriage and divorce would seem to have a different purpose: namely, to express the depth of the revulsion of Ezra and the remorse of those who had contracted such marriages. In Williamson's words, it probably reflects a "pejorative attitude to these unions." However, to say that such marriages were forbidden is not to say they were not marriages at all. It is not difficult to find examples of foreign marriages with disastrous religious consequences where the regular marriage terminology is used (e.g., Samson's marriage to the Timnathite girl [Judg. 14:2-3, 8 where the conventional term for marry—Hebrew *laqah*—is used] and the account of Solomon's foreign marriages in 1 Kings 11:1-6 where the same word is used in the quotation from the law itself that forbade such marriages [Exod. 34:16]).

The problem apparently was not solved permanently by Ezra's action, because it arose again later in the time of Nehemiah (Neh. 13:23-29). The course of action followed by Nehemiah is not wholly clear (aside from such vivid details as beating some of the men and pulling out their hair [v. 25]). There is no mention of the breaking up of such families as in Ezra's time. All that is required of them is an oath to avoid such marriages, the example of Solomon being quoted as a solemn warning (vv. 25-26). Some interpreters hold that this was all that was demanded,[81] Williamson speculating that either the number involved was small or Nehemiah lacked the authority to enforce Ezra's more radical solution.[82] Clines, on the other hand, while admitting that the evidence is unclear, suggests that the oath itself carried with it the commitment to terminate such marriages. This would especially be so in the case of Joiada (Neh. 13:28), one of the sons of the high priest (who might therefore himself become high priest), since the law states specifically, "He must . . . marry . . . only a virgin from his own people" (Lev. 21:14).[83] It would certainly be odd if Nehemiah drew back from Ezra's position, and the probability is that he did not. At the same time it must be admitted that the evidence is not specific.

It is not relevant to our concern to pass judgment on the validity of the action of Ezra (and probably of Nehemiah also). Williamson describes it as "among the least attractive parts of Ezra-Nehemiah, if not of the whole Old Testament";[84] and it is difficult to disagree with Clines's conclusion that "the breaking up of families was a horrible thing."[85] At the same time, it must be seen against its own background, which was the stage of salvation history that required the corporate commitment of a nation to God's unfolding purpose of salvation. That marriages to pagans undermined this cannot be denied. At the same time, it must be stated firmly that what may have been appropriate in Ezra's day is not to be taken as a matter of abiding and universal validity. On the contrary, while Paul affirms that Christians should marry only fellow Christians (1 Cor. 7:39), he states equally clearly that believers married to non-Christians should take no initiative to break such marriages (vv. 12-16).

81. See F. Charles Fensham, *The Books of Ezra and Nehemiah,* in NICOT (Grand Rapids: Wm. B. Eerdmans Publishing Co., 1982), 267; Williamson, *Ezra, Nehemiah,* 399.

82. Williamson, *Ezra, Nehemiah,* 398-99.

83. Clines, *Ezra, Nehemiah, Esther,* 246-48.

84. Williamson, *Ezra, Nehemiah,* 159.

85. Clines, *Ezra, Nehemiah, Esther,* 118.

The point of relevance for us is that in the time of Ezra and Nehemiah we see the practice of divorce being resorted to, not as part of God's declared will, but as an act less evil than the threat that would be posed to His saving plan by the perpetuation of mixed marriages with pagans.[86]

Before leaving the Old Testament it may be useful to attempt to summarize the attitude to divorce depicted there. Indeed, it may well be asked if there is a single, unified attitude to divorce rather than a series of incompatible estimates of it varying all the way from divine hatred of it proclaimed by Malachi to the enforcement of it in God's name by Ezra. The following observations may serve to bring into due relationship the contending perspectives.

First, it may be affirmed with confidence that divorce is nowhere presented as a divine institution. Never is it advanced as part of God's plan or approved as part of His design. On the contrary, as we saw in chapter 1, God's design for marriage is lifelong commitment expressed in covenantal promise made in the presence of God. That it came to mean anything less than that is traceable to the destructive power of sin.

Second, while divorce is no part of God's design, it is a fact of human experience. As such, it has to be reckoned with as part of the context within which God pursues His redemptive purposes. God is represented as engaging with it in at least three ways. Sometimes He is represented as restricting it so that its evil effects are curbed. This is the meaning of the law recorded in Deut. 24:1-4. Again, at other times He is depicted as using divorce as an existing reality to further His purposes: either the imagery to express His rejection of Israel (as in Jer. 3:8) or the institution itself to safeguard the continuance of His saving work in history (as in Ezra-Nehemiah).[87] Yet

---

86. Williamson gives a sensitive overview both of how Ezra's "solution" might have been evaluated in his own day, as well as how it might be evaluated from a New Testament perspective (Williamson, *Ezra, Nehemiah,* 159-62). Cf. also Clines, *Ezra, Nehemiah, Esther,* 133-34.

87. Clines quotes R. North as saying in this connection, "The dangerous and casual claim that 'God's rights outweigh all human considerations' can only be called fanaticism" (Clines, *Ezra, Nehemiah, Esther,* 118). In the context of salvation history, it is surely more to the point to say, with James Orr, that "at whatever point revelation begins, *it must take man up at the stage at which it finds him";* and "revelation can be held responsible only *for the new element which it introduces*—not for the basis on which it works, or for everything in the state of mind, or limited outlook, of the recipient, with which it happens to be associated" (*The Problem of the Old Testament* [London: Nisbet, 1906], 472-73). The entire section on the Progressiveness of Revelation (465-77) is worth consulting.

again, amid the decay of love and loyalty, the covenant aspect of marriage is retrieved and elevated as the original and perpetual purpose of God (as by Malachi).

Third, grace takes precedence over law. Covenants should not be broken, but they can be and are broken. The covenant of marriage is no exception. But even here grace, not law, has the last word. The law says that an adulteress should be stoned, but Hosea is enjoined by God to defy the law and receive his wife back (Hos. 3:1). Jeremiah sees God as showing grace to Judah, even though He has divorced her (Jer. 3:8) and the law declares there shall be no reconciliation (v. 1).

What this amounts to is a deepening of the idea of covenant beyond that of a legal agreement, legally enforceable, to that of a relationship in which the parties to the covenant are viewed, not as legal entities, but as human persons. This is precisely what takes place in the Book of Jeremiah in which the old covenant is displaced by the new covenant whose essence is an inward relationship with God effected by an inward transformation of the people's hearts (31:31-34). In Eichrodt's words: "In Jeremiah all the emphasis is on God's fresh creative activity and the position of greatest prominence is reserved for the relationship of the individual heart to God; in place of an unchanging statutory order he stresses God's redemptive work. This emphasis on the personal element in man's communion with God . . . gave a somewhat different stamp to the conception of the covenant."[88] Tracing this development through Ezekiel and beyond, Eichrodt concludes that the legal and the personal aspects are both necessary to do justice to the picture of God.[89] "If the idea of the establishing of the covenant especially illuminates God's truth and faithfulness, yet the imagery of the Father, the Husband, the Re-

---

88. Eichrodt, *Theology of the Old Testament*, 1:59. The same point is made in somewhat more technical terms by R. E. Clements. Criticizing Mendenhall's sharp distinction between vassal-treaty covenants and promissory covenants, Clements contends that, after Judah's overthrow, covenant theology "came to look beyond the uncertainties of a conditional covenant agreement with God to the greater certainties of the divine grace and love . . . God will not only set the conditions of the covenant in his Torah, but he will himself, by his action within the human heart, give the power and strength to fulfil them (cf. Ezek. 36:26-27) . . . It becomes synonymous in effect, though not in name, with a covenant of promise" (*Old Testament Theology*, 102-3). For a fascinating statement of personal relationship as the inner core of covenant, see E. W. Nicholson, *God and His People, Covenant and Theology in the Old Testament* (Oxford: Clarendon Press, 1986), 210-17.

89. Eichrodt, *Theology of the Old Testament*, 1:59-63.

deemer, the Shepherd enable us to understand a little better his goodness, long-suffering and love."[90]

It is this same covenanting God who has provided for His creatures the gift of marriage that is both covenant and relationship. Since they are His creatures and marriage is His gift, He is a party to the covenant as witness. May we not expect to find in His administering of the covenant of marriage that same combination of fidelity and compassion evidenced in the administering of His covenant with Israel, especially because, in the Old Testament, the two are so frequently compared?

90. Ibid., 69.

3 Divorce in the New Testament

THE STARTING POINT for any treatment of divorce in the New Testament must be the teaching of Jesus. This takes us directly to the Gospels. It is true that the Gospels were not the earliest books of the New Testament to be written, just as it is true that they are not the earliest documents containing information about Jesus' teaching on divorce. That honor belongs to Paul's first letter to the Corinthians. However, the Gospels seem more intent on recording Jesus' teaching on the subject with the application of it being secondary. With Paul it is the other way around. True, the line cannot be drawn sharply in either case but seems a fair generalization.

Of equal significance is that Paul plainly regards the teaching of Jesus on divorce as the benchmark of his own teaching on the subject. In 1 Cor. 7 he makes a clear distinction between the teaching of Jesus, "I give this command (not I, but the Lord)" (v. 10), and his own teaching, which has no precedent in the teaching of Jesus, "I, not the Lord" (v. 12). Clearly then, the earliest New Testament writer to write about marriage and divorce was in possession of a tradition of Jesus' instruction on that subject that he regarded as the point of departure of his own. In taking the teaching of Jesus as our starting point, we are following the practice of the earliest Christian writer known to us.

Divorce According to Jesus

Our concern now is to seek to uncover and interpret the teaching of Jesus on divorce as this is presented to us in the Gospels.[1] It is worth remembering that Matthew, Mark, and Luke, for all their overlapping, are more than just attempts to give a verbal report of what a tape recorder would have picked up had it been invented when Je-

---

1. In effect this means the first three Gospels (the "Synoptics"), since John's Gospel makes no reference to the subject of divorce.

sus was teaching. Each is written to a different situation with different needs. Consequently, the selection of material and its arrangement is determined by what each individual author perceived to be most applicable to the situation he was addressing.[2]

With this understanding, we shall now look at the accounts of Jesus' teaching on divorce given in the Gospels.

1. According to Luke

Luke's account of Jesus' teaching on divorce is brief and is a convenient place to start. The passage reads, "Anyone who divorces his wife and marries another woman commits adultery, and the man who marries a divorced woman commits adultery" (16:18). This is a very early form of Jesus' teaching about divorce even if Luke was not the earliest Gospel to be written. The chief reason for so regarding it is that, unlike Paul's account of Jesus' teaching in 1 Cor. 7:10-11, it refers to divorce as an action open only to males. This was the case only among Jews, which suggests an original background for this saying in Palestine during the ministry of Jesus.[3]

What then is the import of the saying? The context, both local and remote, gives notoriously little help. As to the latter, the so-called central section of Luke's Gospel (9:51—19:10) has occasioned endless debate and little agreement as to its controlling theme.[4] As for the immediate context, chapter 16 is concerned primarily with warnings about wealth and as Marshall observes, "The restatement of the law on divorce appears oddly in a section devoted primarily to teaching about wealth."[5]

---

2. Cf. Graham N. Stanton, "The evangelists do intend to tell us about the 'story' of Jesus, but they are also addressing the needs and circumstances of their own Christian congregations" (*The Gospels and Jesus* [Oxford: Oxford University Press, 1991], 6). This twofold task of the Gospel writers Stanton characterizes as "the dual perspective of the evangelists" (5).

3. Joseph A. Fitzmyer comments, "The Lucan saying is thus cast completely from the OT or Jewish point of view . . . Underlying it are the Palestinian and OT ideas of the wife as the chattel of the husband" (*The Gospel According to Luke X—XXIV,* in AB [Garden City, N.Y.: Doubleday and Company, 1985], 1120). A similar view is expressed by Heinrich Baltensweiler, *Die Ehe im Neuen Testament* (Zurich: Zwingli Verlag, 1967), 60-62.

4. For a brief overview see I. Howard Marshall, *The Gospel of Luke,* in *The New International Greek Testament Commentary* (Grand Rapids: Wm. B. Eerdmans Publishing Co., 1978), 400-402. Marshall concludes that "the real importance of the section lies in the teaching given by Jesus" (401), though he immediately qualifies that statement (401-2).

5. Ibid., 614.

However, verses 14-18 have a certain coherence around the theme of the law, particularly its relation to the kingdom of God. In this connection, a double emphasis is found. First, a sharp contrast is made between outward conformity to the law and conformity at the level of the heart (vv. 14-15). Second, the coming of the kingdom of God with the ministry of John the Baptist is seen as a decisive turning point in that regard (v. 16). The meaning of this event is not that the law is overturned, quite the reverse (v. 17). The saying about divorce is now introduced as an illustration of this changed state of affairs.

The first part of the saying affirms that the man who divorces his wife and marries another commits adultery (v. 18a). The statement carries two implications revolutionary for Jesus' hearers. The first is that marriage is permanent and consequently any "additional" marriage is adulterous. Such a declaration would have been startling to the Jews of His day, among whom divorce was an accepted custom and practiced widely.

More startling than the redefinition of marriage would have been the redefinition of adultery, because within Judaism (taking its lead from the Old Testament) only husbands could be victims of adultery. A married man who consorted with the wife of another was deemed to have committed adultery against the husband whose wife he had taken, not against his own wife whose position simply was not taken into account. The formulation of verse 18a makes no mention of the marital status of the "other" woman or even whether she was married at all. The implication is that the victim of the husband's adultery was his original wife. G. J. Wenham comments aptly, "By this pronouncement Jesus binds husbands to their wives with the same exclusiveness as wives were bound to their husbands under the old covenant. A real reciprocity between spouses is thereby implied by Jesus' teaching."[6]

The second part of the saying declares that "the man who marries a divorced woman commits adultery" (v. 18b). This simply applies to the divorced wife the principle applied in the first part of the verse to the divorcing husband. The marriage that is permanent for one partner is permanent for both; hence any man who marries a divorcé becomes guilty of adultery inasmuch as he is marrying another man's wife.

---

6. G. J. Wenham, "Gospel Definitions of Adultery and Women's Rights," *Expository Times* 95 (1984): 331.

The overall thrust of Jesus' saying then is that with the coming of the kingdom of God, a new dimension of depth has been added to the meaning of life under the rule of God. The yardstick for godly living is no longer the surface meaning of the law, but the divine design in all its absoluteness—in the case of marriage, permanence—is brought to bear and sweeps aside any lesser standard as being inconsonant with God's will.

2. According to Mark

In contrast with Luke's account of the teaching of Jesus about divorce, which is brief and largely lacking in context, Mark's account is fuller (10:2-12) and much more lively. As to its wider context, it stands at the beginning of Jesus' final return to Judea,[7] which means His death, as He has stated repeatedly (8:31; 9:31; 10:32). It takes the form of an argument between Jesus and the Pharisees[8] when the latter ask Jesus a test question about divorce (10:2-9). The discussion is completed privately between Jesus and His disciples when Jesus sums up His teaching for them (vv. 10-12).

The controversy with the Pharisees was launched by their question as to whether it was lawful for a man to divorce his wife, "testing Him" (v. 2, NASB). The last two words indicate that the Pharisees were less interested in learning Jesus' view than in setting a trap for Him. It is possible that Jesus had already gained notoriety for expressing rigid views on divorce. If He replied to the question negatively, He could at once be charged with contradicting the Law of Moses (not to mention the laws of the Roman Empire, which permitted divorce) and, in general, of adopting an extreme position on the issue.[9] On the

---

7. This conclusion is not affected by the uncertainties of the text at this point. For a discussion of the various options, see C. E. B. Cranfield, *The Gospel According to St. Mark*, in *Cambridge Greek Testament Commentary* (Cambridge: Cambridge University Press, 1977), 317-18. Bruce M. Metzger et al. reach the same conclusion in *A Textual Commentary on the Greek New Testament* (New York: United Bible Societies Corrected Edition, 1974), 103.

8. On the textual problem of the mention of the Pharisees, see Metzger, TCGNT, 103-4.

9. It is sometimes suggested that a negative answer would have been impossible, since divorce was accepted universally at least in some cases. From this it is inferred that the question is unreal and the entire incident fabricated. However, there is evidence to suggest that, in some sects of Judaism, a more stringent attitude was adopted toward divorce at this time. The sect of the Dead Sea Scrolls at Qumran appears to have been such a group, as is implied in the Temple Scroll, column 57 lines 17-19. For a discussion, see J. A. Fitzmyer, "The Matthaean Divorce Texts and Some New Palestinian Evidence," *Theological Studies* 37 (1976): 197-226, esp. 213-21. Rejection of divorce by Jesus could have caused Him to be branded as part of the lunatic fringe of Judaism.

other hand, if He replied to the question affirmatively, He could then be drawn into the debate between the Jewish schools of Shammai and Hillel as to the grounds on which divorce was permissible.[10]

Jesus, however, turned the tables by focusing attention on the Mosaic Law and specifically on its permanent intention rather than its situational permissiveness. The law to which the Pharisees appealed was Deut. 24:1-4 whose design, far from being to approve let alone institute divorce, was to limit and restrict it. The particular restriction they quoted was that a divorced wife must be given a certificate of divorce and not simply be turned out of the house on her husband's say-so.[11] Jesus set that aside as a temporary concession to human stubbornness: a law designed to restrain evil rather than promote good. God's real pattern for marriage is seen in the creative act at the beginning when He made one male for one female. That design finds fulfillment when a man leaves his father and mother and is united to his wife so that the two become one flesh (Gen. 2:24). The real answer to the question of whether divorce is lawful is therefore not the Mosaic concession but the divine intention. "Therefore what God has joined together, let man not separate" (Mark 10:9).

Jesus' engagement with the Pharisees is followed by a period of private discussion with His disciples. A summary of this is set forth in verses 11 and 12. Verse 11 states the implication of Jesus' understanding of the creation design from the side of the divorcing husband. "Anyone who divorces his wife and marries another woman commits adultery against her."

This statement is remarkable on several counts. First, it stands in formal tension with verse 9, "Therefore, what God has joined together, let man not separate." If man does, in fact, separate what God has joined, it is a breach of the divine plan for marriage. Verse 9 is not formulated in legal terms; if it were, it would read, "What God has

---

10. This aspect is explicit in Matthew's Gospel (19:3-9). It is possible that the Marcan version is an account of the same story adapted for Gentiles, to whom the debate between Jewish parties would be meaningless. See Morna D. Hooker, *The Gospel According to St. Mark,* in *Black's New Testament Commentary* (Peabody, Mass.: Hendrickson Publishers, 1991), 235.

11. David Daube argues plausibly that the reason for legislating this was that the woman would have proof of divorce. He writes, "The main reason for introducing the bill had no doubt been to enable a woman to prove that she was divorced." He adds in a footnote, "Prior to the bill there might be dire consequences if she or her family wrongly believed that divorce had taken place" ("Repudium in Deuteronomy," in *Neotestamentica et Semitica,* ed. E. E. Ellis and M. Wilcox [Edinburgh: T. and T. Clark, 1969], 238).

joined together, man *cannot* separate." It is rather an assertion of the divine design for marriage over every human deviation from it. The divine plan always stands in judgment over the human reality.

A second notable feature about verse 11 is that it recognizes the worth of the divorced wife as a person in her own right. In Judaism, only the husband had the right of divorce; a wife not only lacked this right but was not regarded as an injured party in the event of infidelity. An adulterous husband was regarded as having committed adultery only against the husband of the woman with whom he had misconducted himself. An adulterous wife, on the other hand, was regarded as having committed adultery against her husband. A married woman was capable of doing wrong but not of being wronged. This subpersonal understanding is overturned here by the declaration that an unfaithful husband commits adultery against his own wife.

In verse 12 the implication of the divine design of marriage is stated from the viewpoint of a divorcing wife. Everything that is said of a divorcing husband in verse 11 is repeated of a divorcing wife in verse 12. This implies the same departure from Jewish law as was noted in verse 11. If a married woman may be the victim of divorce, she may also be the culpable instigator of divorce. The recognition of her personal moral worth brings with it not only the possibility of being a wronged victim but also the moral responsibility for using her moral status in a moral way.

It is worth pausing to draw attention to some of the implications of the Marcan account. First, the main point stressed in the dialogue between Jesus and the Pharisees is that there is a vast difference between what God permits in a situation where the power of sin is already effecting its deadly work and what He enjoins as His pure and absolute will. The Jews of Jesus' day, as those of earlier days, assumed that since the law contained a commandment regarding divorce (Deut. 24:1-4), it must be "commanded" by God in accordance with His will. Actually no Old Testament law institutes divorce and, as pointed out, Deut. 24:1-4, far from approving it, is an attempt to rein in some of its more brutal effects upon women.[12] As Cranfield

---

12. See S. R. Driver, *Deuteronomy,* in ICC on Deut. 24:1-4, "The law is thus not, properly speaking, a law of divorce: the right of divorce is assumed as established by custom." Cf. G. A. Smith on the same passage, "It is not a law instituting divorce . . . No Old Testament oracle or law institutes divorce. But the husband's right of divorce is accepted or permitted . . . and is put under regulations . . . in the interests of the wife . . . or [to] ensure deliberation on the husband's part before he completes the act" (*Deuteronomy,* in *Cambridge Bible,* 276-77).

points out, Jesus is not setting the command of God against that of Moses; rather He is bringing out the real meaning of Deut. 24:1. "A distinction has to be made between that which sets forth the absolute will of God and those provisions which take account of men's actual sinfulness and are designed to limit and control its consequences."[13] If one wants to know God's absolute will regarding marriage, it is found in Gen. 2:24, "The two will become one flesh" (Mark 10:7). Jesus expresses the meaning of this in the following words, "So they are no longer two, but one. Therefore what God has joined together, let man not separate" (vv. 8-9).

Second, the overriding import of the entire passage is to insist that God's standard is for marriage to be permanent and lifelong. This is not only the point of Jesus' reference to the creation ideal but also the irresistible conclusion from His statement to the disciples in verses 11 and 12. It is significant that no exception is mentioned, and it cannot be argued convincingly that any is implied.

Third, it is implied in verses 2-12 that the absolute will of God regarding marriage, as expressed in the creation ordinance, is capable of fulfillment. The concession made by Moses on account of the hardness of human hearts is set aside in favor of the original command to lifelong fidelity. This is made explicitly clear in verses 11-12 where divorce and remarriage is flatly said to entail adultery. On this two questions are in order. To begin with, we may inquire what it is that makes possible now the observance of a law whose repeated breaching prompted the concession made by Moses. The answer is even more explicit in Matthew than in Mark, but even here it is not in doubt. It is simply that with Jesus has come the reign of God and the power of God, making possible Kingdom behavior.[14] As David Catchpole has expressed it, "The one scheme which can set Moses aside and argue from creation is eschatology: Jesus presupposes that the end time has already come. The declaration regarding divorce belongs to the central concerns of the mission of Jesus. Participation in the present age alone is the hallmark of exclusion from the kingdom."[15]

---

13. Cranfield, *Gospel According to Mark,* 319.

14. This entire section of Mark's Gospel is concerned to show the necessity of Christ's death for the coming of the Kingdom. For references to the Kingdom in the surrounding context, see Mark 9:47; 10:14, 23, etc.

15. Catchpole, "Synoptic Divorce Material," 125.

Other questions that present themselves are these: Is not hardness of heart to be found even after the coming of Jesus—indeed, even among His followers? If so, is there still room for the Mosaic concession? The answers may well be yes. If so, then it must be regarded as it is in Deuteronomy, namely, as a concession to human sinfulness and not as part of the divinely ordained order. To quote Cranfield again: "Human conduct which falls short of the absolute command of God is sin and stands under the divine judgment. The provisions which God's mercy has designed for the limitation of the consequences of man's sin must not be interpreted as divine approval for sinning. When our sinfulness traps us in a position in which all the choices open to us are still evil, we are to choose that which is least evil, asking for God's forgiveness and comforted by it, but not pretending that the evil is good."[16]

Fourth, it has been noted that Jesus is depicted here speaking of divorce as a legal resource open to both wife and husband (vv. 11-12). The accuracy of this has been questioned on the grounds that in Judaism only the husband had the right of divorce, and in the Matthaean parallel (Matt. 19:9), this is the only possibility that is envisaged. However, Jesus may have spoken of divorce as an expedient open to wives. The case of Herodias, who had made use of Roman law to divorce her husband, Herod Philip (who was also her uncle), was a cause célèbre during the ministry of Jesus; indeed, John the Baptist's denunciation of it had cost him his head (Mark 6:17-29). Jesus may well have had this in mind,[17] not to mention the prevailing practice in the Gentile world.[18]

But there is an aspect of this saying of Jesus involving an extension of Jewish divorce practice that is even more important. As has been noted, in rabbinic law only males were regarded as parties injured by adultery. Jesus sweeps this restricted view aside, redressing the imbalance of the law of divorce that, until then, had operated to the disadvantage of women. This in itself carries yet another implication—that while in this saying Jesus is intent on ruling out divorce and remarriage, the effect of His extension of prevailing law is to affirm the innocence of an injured party. This raises at least the ques-

---

16. Cranfield, *Gospel According to Mark,* 320.

17. F. F. Bruce, *The Hard Sayings of Jesus* (Downers Grove, Ill.: InterVarsity Press, 1983), 59-60.

18. Cranfield, *Gospel According to Mark,* 321.

tion if not the possibility of remarriage after divorce in a context whose overt purpose was to exclude that very thing.

3. According to Matthew

Matthew records two pronouncements of Jesus concerning marriage and divorce. The first occurs at 5:32, the second at 19:3-12. Our procedure will be to consider each in its individual setting, to draw attention to the features each has in common with the teaching of Jesus in Luke and Mark, and finally to concentrate on the feature that is unique to the two passages in Matthew.

The first saying constitutes one of the so-called antitheses or contrasting statements in the early part of the Sermon on the Mount, statements constructed around the pattern "You have heard that it was said . . . but I tell you" (5:21, 27, 33, 38, 43). The Sermon on the Mount has sometimes been described as the Law of the Kingdom of Heaven, and Jesus has been depicted as the new Moses declaring the new law from the Mount of Beatitudes as Moses handed down the old law from Mount Sinai.[19] Undeniably the Sermon on the Mount is concerned with law in some sense. "Do not think that I have come to abolish the Law or the Prophets; I have not come to abolish them but to fulfill them. . . . For I tell you that unless your righteousness surpasses that of the Pharisees and the teachers of the law, you will certainly not enter the kingdom of heaven" (vv. 17, 20). The question is, In what sense is the Sermon on the Mount to be taken as law?

The Sermon on the Mount clearly cannot be viewed as a legal code, compliance with which can be policed, measured, and penalized as with a civil code of law. No external yardstick can measure the presence of lust or anger or hatred in the heart, and it is these that are the concern of the "laws" of Matt. 5:31-48. It is nearer the mark to say that the concern of the Sermon on the Mount is with what may be called—borrowing the language of Matt. 5:17—"fulfilled law," that is to say, law that finds observance not merely at the level of performance but at the level of inward assent and compliance. No law is truly kept when outward conformity to it is accompanied by inward rejection of it and resistance against it. It is this harmony between spirit and performance that is the hallmark of life in the kingdom of God. The assumption on which the Sermon on

---

19. A brief, critical examination of this view may be found in W. D. Davies, *The Sermon on the Mount* (Nashville: Abingdon Press, 1966), chap. 1.

the Mount is written is that such inner compliance is possible. The law of the kingdom of God clearly presupposes the presence of the kingdom of God, and on that the Sermon on the Mount is based.[20] The presence of the kingdom of God implies the presence of the power of God, making possible the realization of God's design and demands.

Against this background we may now turn to the saying on divorce in Matt. 5:31-32. Verse 31 reads, "It has been said, 'Anyone who divorces his wife must give her a certificate of divorce.'" There is an evident allusion here to Deut. 24:1 where it is accepted that a man might not order his wife to depart from his house simply by word of mouth. In such a case she would have no proof that she had really been divorced and had not just absconded, and she must be given legal evidence. It would appear that what Jesus has in mind here is not the specific ruling contained in Deut. 24:1-4 that deals with the case of a woman who has been twice-married and twice-divorced. The rule is concerned to legislate that when her second husband has divorced her, she may not return to the first. Jesus' primary concern appears rather to be with the mentality that had come to prevail in the Jewish religion of His day that said, "Divorce is perfectly acceptable provided you observe the proper procedures."

In thundering repudiation of this outlook, Jesus replies, "But I tell you that anyone who divorces his wife, except for marital unfaithfulness, causes her to become an adulteress, and anyone who marries the divorced woman commits adultery" (Matt. 5:32). Several features of this saying deserve comment. First, Jesus speaks as one who has the authority to give the law its definitive interpretation. Hence the emphatic (and repeated) phrase, "But I tell you" (vv. 22, 28, 32, 34, 39, 44). We have already seen that the law of the Kingdom implies the presence of the Kingdom. That Jesus prescribes the law for the Kingdom implies further that the presence of the Kingdom implies the presence of Jesus (vv. 17, 20).

Second, the consequences of divorce are stated in terms of their effect on the wife rather than the husband. This stands in contrast

---

20. The placing of the Sermon on the Mount in Matthew's Gospel strongly favors this conclusion. Note especially Jesus' announcement of the Kingdom in 4:17, His ministry described in 4:23-25 in which He is shown exercising the power of the Kingdom, and the echoes of Isa. 61:1ff. in the Beatitudes. The point is made briefly in Joachim Jeremias, *The Sermon on the Mount* (Philadelphia: Fortress Press, 1963), 24-35, and more fully in Robert A. Guelich, *The Sermon on the Mount: A Foundation for Understanding* (Waco, Tex.: Word Books, 1982), chap. 3.

with both Mark and Luke where it is said that a husband who divorces his wife and marries another commits adultery (Mark 10:11[21]; Luke 16:18*a*). In Matt. 5:32 the effect of divorce is to "[cause] her to become an adulteress" (v. 32*c*). The perspective assumed is that of the Judaism of Jesus' day in which only a husband could initiate divorce proceedings and, further, in which adultery could be committed only against another man. Since a married woman was viewed as the property of her husband, any breach of marital vows was an offence only against her husband. Jesus speaks of divorce as an offence against the divorced wife here. The reasoning appears to be that in a society where a woman's place was the home, a divorcé would have to marry again, if only to survive,[22] and such marriage would amount to adultery: "Anyone who marries the divorced woman commits adultery" (v. 32*d*).

This expression of the consequences of divorce would surely have a stunning effect on the contemporary Jewish mind. To begin with, it would have involved an earthquake in their evaluation of women. In legal terms women did not count. Jesus' declaration that remarriage following divorce was tantamount to adultery would have been even more stunning. As has already been seen in our review of Mark's account, divorce was an accepted institution in Judaism. The only disagreement was in regard to the grounds on which it was permissible. This appears to have been precisely the point of Jesus' critique. The real matter for debate was not on what grounds divorce should be permissible but whether divorce was permissible at all.

There are few ways in which Jesus could have challenged prevailing standards more breathtakingly than this. Without doubt, in seeking to take the measure of Jesus' words we must read them in their setting alongside the other sayings in the Sermon on the

---

21. It is, of course, stated in Mark 10:11*c* that the adultery committed by the husband is "against her," viz. his wife. While this presupposes rejection of the prevailing view in Judaism that, in matters of divorce the wife did not count as an involved legal party, it remains the case that the Marcan saying focuses on the husband: he commits adultery. In the Matthaean saying, the effect of divorce on the husband is ignored, attention being placed on its effect on the divorced wife and anyone who may marry her.

22. H. Benedict Green comments, "A woman sent away by her husband would normally (unless it was still possible for her to return to her father's house) be forced to cohabit with another man or starve. Jesus puts the responsibility for this situation squarely on the husband" (*The Gospel According to Matthew,* in *New Clarendon Bible* [Oxford: Oxford University Press, 1980], 84).

Mount. In the verses immediately preceding these, Jesus speaks of plucking out the eye that causes one to look lustfully upon a woman and so being able to observe the seventh commandment (Matt. 5:28-29). In subsequent verses He enjoins, "Give to the one who asks you, and do not turn away from the one who wants to borrow from you" (v. 42) as the Christian alternative to the law of revenge (v. 38). Similar examples from later parts of the Sermon on the Mount are sayings against storing treasures on earth (6:19) and about not worrying about what one will eat or drink or wear (6:25). In the divorce saying, He is not branding Judaism as being guilty of mass adultery. There is no indication that He would have countenanced a campaign to unravel "adulterous" marriages or sort out legitimate children from illegitimate. As D. A. Hagner has put it, "The point of speaking of remarriage as involving 'adultery' is simply to emphasize the wrongness of divorce."[23] The point of the Sermon on the Mount in its entirety is to proclaim the divine standard, not in legal terms, but in moral terms and to affirm that God has provided the grace to live in accordance with it.

A third notable feature of the divorce saying in Matt. 5:32 is that it contains an exception. This is striking. The parallel sayings in Mark 10:11-12 and Luke 16:18 give no hint of any exception. Both appear to teach in an unqualified way that any divorce is a breach of the divine standard. Matt. 5:32 (together with 19:9) affirms a single exception, "except for marital unfaithfulness." Why this exception? What is this exception? Why is it recorded only by Matthew? These questions are evidently critical. It will be best not to address them until account has been taken of the additional instance of this phrase in its related context in Matt. 19:3-12. We shall then be able to evaluate the issue in the light of all of the evidence in the Gospels.

---

23. Donald A. Hagner, *Matthew 1—13*, in WBC (Dallas: Word Books, 1993), 33a: 125. The same point is being made, albeit in more technical terms, by W. D. Davies and D. C. Allison when they write of verse 32 as a whole: "Jesus' saying about divorce was, when first delivered, probably intended to be more haggadic than halakhic; that is, its purpose was not to lay down the law but to reassert an ideal and make divorce a sin, thereby disturbing then current complacency . . . Jesus was not, to judge by the synoptic evidence, a legislator. His concern was not with legal definitions but with moral exhortation (cf. 5:27-30)" (*The Gospel According to St. Matthew,* in ICC [Edinburgh: T. and T. Clark, 1988], 1:532). To similar effect, see Raymond F. Collins who argues that the legal form is here being used prophetically, as in 5:22a-b, which is hardly to be made the basis of legal enactment (*Divorce in the New Testament* [Collegeville, Minn.: Liturgical Press, 1992], 169). Cf. 209-10.

The teaching in Matt. 5:32, which takes the form of a saying, in 19:3-12 takes the form of a story, specifically, a story of conflict between Jesus and certain Pharisees on this issue. In some respects there is a measure of resemblance between this account and that in Mark 10:2-12. Both fall into two parts, the first part detailing the debate between Jesus and the Pharisees (Mark 10:2-9; Matt. 19:3-9), the second describing private discussion between Jesus and His disciples (Mark 10:10-12; Matt. 19:10-12). However, there are significant differences between the two.

First, there is a distinctively Jewish flavor in Matthew's account that is absent from Mark's. In Mark, the point of debate is a straightforward either-or question, "Is it lawful for a man to divorce his wife?" (10:2b). Is divorce permissible or isn't it? A yes or no answer is expected. In Matthew the question is more finely nuanced, "Is it lawful for a man to divorce his wife for any and every reason?" (19:3b). This carefully stated question points to the particular Jewish setting, because Pharisees were divided as to the grounds on which divorce was permissible.

The difference arose from divergent interpretations of the expression denoting the cause of divorce in Deut. 24:1. The Hebrew expression *('erwat dābār)* means literally "the nakedness of a thing" and probably denotes any kind of improper or indecent behavior.[24] The range of English translations—"some uncleanness" (KJV), "some indecency" (RSV), "something objectionable" (NRSV), "something indecent" (NIV), "something offensive" (REB)—gives some idea of the scope for interpretation. Jewish interpreters had divided themselves into two main groups on this issue. The conservative school of Shammai, dating from the first century B.C., took it to mean "unchastity" and would permit divorce for no other reason. The more liberal school of Hillel, stressing the phrase "if she becomes displeasing to him" together with the word "thing," took it to refer to almost anything—"even if she spoiled a dish for him . . . or he found another fairer than she" (Gitt. 9-10). Jesus was thus being lured into taking sides in a piece of Jewish party warfare.

---

24. So Driver, *Deuteronomy*, in ICC, 270. Driver notes that in Deut. 23:14 "the same expression is used, not of what is immoral, but only of what is unbecoming. It is most natural to understand it of *immodest* or *indecent behaviour*" (271). The word *'erwāh* is frequently used in the Old Testament of indecent exposure as in Gen. 9:22-23 and (figuratively) Ezek. 16:37.

Jesus' response was in the same vein as in Matt. 5:32. The paramount issue was not that divorce should be done in the right way or for the right reason. The paramount question was whether it should be done at all. He makes this point by quoting from two parts of the creation narratives in Genesis. "At the beginning the 'Creator made them male and female,' and said, 'For this reason a man will leave his father and mother and be united to his wife, and the two will become one flesh'" (Matt. 19:4-5). The first part of the quotation comes from Gen. 1:27, the second from Gen. 2:24. The former is interpreted by Jesus as meaning that God made one man for one woman; the second is illustrated in the act of marriage by the husband's leaving his parental home and becoming one flesh with his wife. From this follows the conclusion: "So they are no longer two, but one. Therefore what God has joined together, let man not separate" (Matt. 19:6).

What this amounts to is that marriage is part of God's creation design. By it a new and unique unity is created, sealed by the solemn covenant of the two parties, expressed in oneness of family and flesh, and effected by God himself. Divorce was therefore never part of God's plan or intention.

This bold and conclusive claim by Jesus that divorce was not part of God's design was clearly open to what looked like a devastating objection the Pharisees were not slow to raise. If divorce was contrary to God's will, why was it in the Bible—in the Law of Moses, no less? Jesus' reply is made in two ways. To begin with He makes a distinction between what the law *commanded* and what it *permitted.* "'Why then,' they asked, 'did Moses command that a man give his wife a certificate of divorce and send her away?' Jesus replied, 'Moses permitted you to divorce your wives because your hearts were hard. But it was not this way from the beginning'" (vv. 7-8). Because the procedure for divorce was embodied in Deut. 24:1-4, it was concluded by Jews in Jesus' day that divorce was part of the divine plan and perfectly acceptable to God. Jesus shattered that illusion by pointing out that divorce was never commanded by God.[25] As we saw in our study of Mark 10:2-12, it was *permitted* by God but always represented a departure and a decline from God's will at creation.[26]

---

25. This implication would be particularly stunning to Jesus' hearers since in Judaism in His day a husband was *required* to divorce an adulterous wife. The Mishnah declares, "If a man was suspected of intercourse with a married woman and (the court) dissolved her marriage with her husband, even though he married her they must take her from him" (Yeb. 2.8). Again, in a section dealing with the suspected adulteress, it

The reference to God's creative will, already treated at length in Matt. 19:4-6 and repeated in verse 8*b,* becomes the springboard for the second step in Jesus' reply: the permitting of divorce was occasioned by human sin and stubbornness, not by God's creative design. Jesus not only demolishes the notion that divorce was part of God's plan but also implies that the drift of the Mosaic concession was to restrain divorce as commonly practiced and so point toward the recovery of the creation ideal.[27]

This leads then to Jesus' concluding formulation: "I tell you that anyone who divorces his wife, except for marital unfaithfulness, and marries another woman commits adultery" (v. 9).

In comparing the formulation of Matt. 19:9 with that of 5:32, it is evident that the former is framed in terms of its effect on the divorcing husband—if he divorces and remarries, he commits adultery. In this respect, it is thoroughly in keeping with the Judaism of Jesus' day. Matt. 19:3-9 thereby concludes echoing the Jewish background with which they begin.

Two other points may be observed regarding 19:9. The first is that it shares with 5:32 an exception not found in any other of the Gospels—"except for marital unfaithfulness." The precise meaning of these words is of great importance and will require extended examination. For this reason it will be best to postpone treatment of them until the remainder of the passage has been considered. A second point worth noting arises from the observation made earlier that the episode in 19:3-9 takes the form of a conflict story. Just as 5:31-32 is a prophetic saying rather than a regulation, so a conflict story—which

---

reads, "As she is forbidden to the husband so is she forbidden to the paramour, for it is written, 'And she is become unclean,' and again, 'And she is become unclean'" (Sot. 5:1). It has been noted earlier that the law of the Roman Empire at that time also required the divorcing of an adulterous wife.

26. It is notable that in Mark 10:3-4 the verb "command" is used by Jesus and "permit" by the Pharisees—both in reference Deut. 24:1. R. H. Gundry comments, "Either Jesus wants the Pharisees to answer with Genesis instead of Deuteronomy, according to Mark; or, more likely, he means that Moses gave the commandment in Deuteronomy to cover the matter of divorce. Matthew reverses the verbs to avoid the wrong impression that Moses commanded divorce as such" (*Matthew: A Commentary on His Literary and Theological Art* [Grand Rapids: Wm. B. Eerdmans Publishing Co., 1982], 380).

27. Cf. Gundry, "Moses' law runs in the opposite direction from divorce with remarriage . . . In all of this (Jesus) does not pit God's original intent against the Mosaic provision so much as he harmonizes the Mosaic provision with God's original intent" (ibid.).

frequently concludes with a summarizing saying—is intent on expressing opposite views rather than conveying codified regulations. As R. F. Collins expresses it: "The nature of the genre is such that it presents contrasting positions. Matthew would have respected the laws of the genre only if a sharp contrast is drawn between the position espoused by Jesus and that proposed by his opponents. . . . In any case, the climax of an argumentative setting is not the place for the introduction of the fine distinctions of casuistic law."[28]

Just as in the Marcan account the exchange with the Pharisees is followed by a private inquiry by Jesus' disciples, so the debate in Matthew is followed by an account of the disciples' response to the teaching Jesus has just given. However, the account in Matthew is significantly different from that in Mark in several respects, and this constitutes the second major unique feature of Matthew's version in comparison with Mark's. Mark simply indicates that when the public altercation with the Pharisees was over, the disciples inquired privately about what Jesus had just said (Mark 10:10), and Jesus responds with the summarizing saying in verses 11-12. In Matthew the picture is much more vivid. There the disciples give a specific response to what Jesus has just taught: "If this is the situation between a husband and wife, it is better not to marry" (Matt. 19:10). Clearly, what Jesus said was significantly different from what the disciples had believed so far and was not received by them with great enthusiasm. Their reaction was that if marriage was as binding as Jesus had just declared it to be, it was better not to marry at all. For Jews to whom marriage was virtually a duty, this was an extreme conclusion indeed and demonstrates the dominance of the Jewish perspective at the end of Matthew's account as at the beginning.

To this Jesus replies, "Not everyone can accept this word, but only those to whom it has been given" (v. 11). There is some uncertainty as to what "this word" refers to.[29] If it refers to the immediately preceding statement of the disciples, then Jesus is agreeing that not all have the power to lead a celibate life and only those who

---

28. Collins, *Divorce in the New Testament,* 210.

29. The manuscript evidence is divided at this point, the majority text reading "this word" and Codex Vaticanus and its allies reading "the word," which could be taken to mean "the Word" (i.e., Jesus' message as a whole, and His teaching on marriage and divorce as a particular part of it). Metzger indicates that the UBS editors found the evidence indeterminate and therefore compromised (TCGNT, 48-49). The decision must be made on the basis of content rather than textual evidence.

have that power should follow that path. In this case Jesus' words will be a warning against an extreme and impetuous reaction to His teaching. On the other hand, "this word" may refer to Jesus' teaching in verses 3-9, in which case Jesus was saying that His teaching about the binding character of marriage is indeed demanding and none should imagine that they can keep it in their own strength.

However, as Jesus goes on to say, one is not left to one's own strength. The point is made by development of the disciples' reference to celibacy. Originally made by them as a reductio ad absurdum of Jesus' teaching—"If what you say is true, we may as well be celibates!"—it is taken up by Jesus to press the demands of the Kingdom to the last degree. Just as some are born to a life of celibacy by physical defect and others choose celibacy by resorting to surgical procedure, so some accept the life of celibacy because of fidelity to Jesus' teaching regarding the permanence of marriage. Those who receive the kingdom of heaven find that the power of the Kingdom is equal to the demands of Kingdom living. The question is that of faith in the power of God. "He who has ears to hear, let him hear" (Matt. 11:15, NASB). "The one who can accept this saying should accept it."

It seems clear that the former interpretation is to be rejected. Jesus' extolling of marriage as a divine ordinance in verses 3-6 would be ineptly followed by advice that only those should marry who could not help it. Jesus is pointing out the danger of marital failure and warning those who would be His followers to count the cost. The warning is not to be read as being addressed to a special class of followers who are called to a life of celibacy; it is addressed to all who would be Christ's disciples. It is punctuated with a similar formula Jesus used in His public preaching. "Let anyone with ears listen!" (Matt. 13:9, NRSV). "Let anyone accept this who can" (Matt. 19:12, NRSV; cf. 13:11; 19:11, NRSV).

We may turn now to the third notable difference between the accounts of Matthew and Mark. While Jesus' teaching according to Mark is absolute, according to Matthew Jesus allowed divorce and remarriage in one instance—marital unfaithfulness. With this we come to Matthew's exceptive clauses present in both 5:32 and 19:9. It is not too much to say that the interpretation of these three-word clauses has not only given rise to widespread debate but also exercised a large effect in the formulation of widely divergent views of what Jesus taught regarding divorce and remarriage. A survey of some representative English translations gives some indication (albeit limited) of the variation in interpretation as well as of the doctrinal differences that could result. Thus, the exceptive clause in Matt. 5:32 is rendered variously as "saving for the cause of fornication" (KJV), "except on the ground of unchastity" or similar phrasing with the word "unchastity" (RSV, NASB, NRSV, REB), and "except for marital unfaithfulness" (NIV). A similar picture emerges in 19:9, where KJV reads "except it be for fornication"; RSV, NRSV, and REB use the word "unchastity"; NASB renders "except for immorality"; and NIV retains "except for marital unfaithfulness."

Clearly, much turns on the translation and interpretation of the word lying behind "fornication," "unchastity," "immorality," "marital unfaithfulness." The Greek word is *porneia,* whence English words such as "pornography." The various understandings of the exceptive clauses derive from divergent understandings of this term. It might be thought that the problem could be readily resolved by looking up the word in a Greek dictionary. Unfortunately, it is not quite so easy. Words are slippery and can change their meaning, and their precise shade of meaning in a given setting depends on the ability to detect the appropriate nuance. To further complicate things, the Greek of the New Testament is now a dead language, so developing an "ear" for differing shades of meaning is correspondingly harder.

Before turning to the evaluation of the various suggestions that have been advanced, it may be useful to list some of the factors that condition the meaning of a New Testament word such as *porneia.* The root meaning is the starting point, but no more than that. Its use in the language of the times is a significant factor in gauging its field of meaning, but of prime significance for a New Testament word are the biblical contexts. These are, starting from the circumference and moving to the center, the context of the Bible as a whole, the context of the entire New Testament, and particularly the context of related types of literature within the New Testament—in this case the first three Gospels. Moving toward the center there is the context of the book in which the words—in this case, the exceptive clauses—stand: the purpose for which it was written, the social and religious situation that it addressed, the literary character of the material in which the exceptive clauses are used. Finally, there is the understanding placed upon this material by the Church in the age after the apostles. Such evidence cannot be given definitive status. The Early Church was as capable of misunderstanding and misinterpreting the texts as the Church in any other age. On the other hand, the Early Church was nearer to the writing of the Gospels than we are;

they had access to traditions largely lost to us, and they spoke the same language as the Gospel writers.

These factors and techniques cannot be applied here in any thoroughgoing way without extending the length of this book intolerably. It will serve to have them in mind as checks and balances or as touchstones to which the contending interpretations have to answer.

With these considerations in mind we may now turn directly to the main interpretations that have claimed the allegiance of biblical scholars. This in itself could quickly become a morass because the number of interpretations is not small. Abel Isaksson lists 7,[30] R. F. Collins counts 12,[31] while a recent symposium counts at least 4 as being Christian![32] Happily, Collins feels able to consign 9 of the views he lists to "the exegetical curiosity cabinet" (a phrase he borrows from Joachim Gnilka).[33] Isaksson likewise dismisses cursorily 3 of the 7 views he treats.[34] It is clear that not all of the interpretations advanced in the history of exegesis are of equal weight. We may confine our attention to those best able to meet the criteria set out above and that have attracted a measurable degree of academic and ecclesiastical support in the history of the Christian Church.

Separation Without Divorce or Remarriage

This view, in which the word "separation" denotes discontinuance of married life by legal sanction, maintains that divorce, in the sense of the dissolving of a marriage bond, is powerless to do what it purports to do. In a word, there is no such thing as divorce. The bond cemented by marriage is unbreakable and subsists, whatever the parties to a marriage or ecclesiastical authorities or lawyers may claim to the contrary. Marriage is indissoluble because it is indelible. Since divorce is impossible, remarriage is likewise impossible, simply piling one empty pretense upon another. The most that Scripture allows in cases of marriage failure is separation. This is what is conveyed in the exceptive clauses.

As might be expected, this view is expounded with variations from one exponent to another, and important differences will be noted as we proceed. Broadly speaking, however, the various formu-

---

30. Isaksson, *Marriage and Ministry*, 128-42.
31. Collins, *Divorce in the New Testament*, 109-205.
32. House, *Divorce and Remarriage*, 1990.
33. Collins, *Divorce in the New Testament*, 199. Cf. 203, 205-7.
34. Isaksson, *Marriage and Ministry*, 128-29, 131.

lations follow much the same lines. Fundamentally, the position rests on what is taken to be the biblical teaching regarding marriage. This is derived principally from the creation narratives in Gen. 2:24: "For this reason a man will leave his father and mother and be united to his wife, and they will become one flesh."[35]

The claim that marriage is here taught to be indissoluble is based on three features.[36] First, the language "leave his father and mother" implies a public act, bespeaking the intention to establish a new family unit. Second, the expression "be united to his wife" is covenant language. Other renderings of the phrase are "cleave unto his wife" (KJV), "clings to his wife" (NRSV), denoting not only physical closeness but loyalty, indeed, loyalty through thick and thin (Ruth 1:14; 2 Sam. 20:2). Moreover, as the One who, by His creative act, created the woman out of the man, God is the Witness and Creator of this covenant. Third, the result of this covenant-union is that the pair becomes "one flesh."

Here, upholders of the view that marriage is indissoluble, while interpreting the *effect* of marriage similarly, understand the *means* by which this is achieved rather differently. All are agreed that "one flesh" denotes the physical act of marriage and, beyond that, what J. Carl Laney calls "a mystical spiritual unity."[37] On this basis he concludes, "The concept of one flesh seems to imply that the marriage bond is indissoluble."[38] For Heth this is insufficiently conclusive.[39] It is not enough to demonstrate that the marriage bond *should* not be broken; what needs to be shown is that it *cannot* be broken. This he endeavors to do by appealing to the Levitical laws of relationship according to which marriage creates relationships of the same binding character as blood.[40] Inasmuch as blood relationships cannot be un-

---

35. For a discussion of this verse, see above, 112-13, 124-25.

36. For an exposition of the verse in question along these lines, see J. Carl Laney in House, *Divorce and Remarriage,* 16-21. William A. Heth writes approvingly of Laney's essay in House, *Divorce and Remarriage,* 55-60. Heth's own essay in the same volume expounds the Genesis passage on similar lines (74-78).

37. Ibid., 19.

38. Ibid., 20.

39. Heth's comment, "I am still not sure, however, if Laney understands the kinship aspect of marriage in the specific way that I tend to think of it" (House, *Divorce and Remarriage,* 57), seems to be directed to Laney's ambivalence on this point.

40. Commenting on Lev. 18:7-8, 16, parts of a series of forbidden sexual relationships that extends to verse 18, Heth points out that the forbidding of sexual relations between a man and his stepmother (v. 8) or a man and his brother's wife (v. 16) implies that marriage creates as close a bond as blood, so that marriage within that bond is in-

done, it follows that the marriage relationship cannot be undone either.[41] This is held to be the meaning implied in the man's exclamation in Gen. 2:23: "This is now bone of my bones and flesh of my flesh." At the same time not every proponent of the "separation only" position finds it necessary to appeal to anything more objective in establishing this case than God's will and human nature. The distinguished exegete Jacques Dupont writes: "The principle of indissolubility stems from the will of the Creator, written into the complementary character of the man and the woman. Marriage is not just a simple contract between persons. The will of the spouses is not the only thing to give their union its stability. The union of the spouses finds its principle in the design of God who created them male and female. Divorce ignores a fundamental law of nature, itself an expression of the will of the Creator."[42]

It was this teaching that Jesus reaffirmed in Luke 16:18 and Mark 10:11-12, where no exception is mentioned. This teaching is reaffirmed in Matt. 5:32 and 19:3-12. There (as is indeed also the case in Mark 10:2-12) Jesus is ostensibly going back behind current teaching and behind even Moses' teaching to God's design at creation. All of these factors create a strong presumption against Jesus' permitting any exceptions; on the contrary, it is exceptions that He is engaged in sweeping aside. On what grounds, then, is it maintained that clauses that self-evidently have the form of exceptions do not have that force?

Several factors are appealed to. First, some defenders of the view under consideration appeal to the language. Dupont, for example, maintains that the word translated "divorces" in the exceptive

---

cestuous. For marriage partners, this implies that marital intercourse has the effect of relating them as closely as parents and children (ibid., 80). Heth concludes, "The Mosaic legislation in Leviticus 18—of moral relevance today—makes it clear that legal divorce does not dissolve 'one flesh' nor the extended relationships that arise through a consummated marriage covenant" (ibid., 82). For an exegesis of Lev. 18 along these lines, see Wenham, *Book of Leviticus,* in NICOT, 253-58.

41. Heth writes, "The biblical kinship view of marriage . . . suggests that just as parents cannot 'cut off' their children from being their own flesh and blood, no matter how disreputable or immoral they may be so a man cannot 'divorce' or sever the kinship relationship with his wife, who is his own flesh and blood through the covenant and consummation of marriage" (House, *Divorce and Remarriage,* 87).

42. Dom Jacques Dupont, *Mariage et Divorce Dans L'Évangile* (Bruges: Desclée de Brouwer, 1959), 34 (my translation).

clause (Greek *apoluein*) and which is rendered "puts away" in the King James Version denotes separation rather than divorce as such.[43]

Second, it is held that the grammar of Matt. 19:9 speaks against the conclusion that divorce with right of remarriage is what is in mind. It is significant that the verse does not read "Whoever divorces his wife and marries another, except for fornication, commits adultery," implying that remarriage is permissible following divorce on the single ground of fornication. The verse rather reads "Whoever divorces his wife, except for fornication, and marries another commits adultery." That is to say, what is really being defined here is divorce; the concern of the statement is not to legislate for remarriage but to prescribe an exception regarding divorce. This is certainly the case in the earlier exceptive saying in 5:32,[44] which implies three things. First, remarriage by the wife following divorce is adulterous (v. 32b). Second, divorce by the husband is adulterous inasmuch as it leads to the wife's remarriage (v. 32a). Third, divorce by the husband is adulterous except in cases of the wife's unchastity (v. 32a).[45] There is no mention of the husband's freedom to remarry, not even in this third circumstance. The purpose of the saying is to indicate in what circumstances divorce by a husband does not involve him in adultery. Essentially these same things are repeated in 19:9, albeit in somewhat compressed form. The exceptive clause, it is argued, expresses an exception, not to the principle that whoever puts away

---

43. Dupont bases his conclusion as much on the entire clause as on the single word "divorce." Arguing that Jesus is using a kind of oriental paradox, he holds that, whereas Jesus' hearers would have expected Him to say, "Whoever divorces his wife is free to remarry," Jesus, in fact, says, "Whoever divorces his wife and marries again commits adultery" (ibid., 146). Jesus has thereby given the verb "divorce" a new meaning (145).

44. Adherents of this view hold that verses 31-32 of Matt. 5 are part of the context that begins at verse 27, pointing to the linking preposition and the abbreviated introductory formula with which verse 31 begins. This means that verses 31-32 are a further example of Jesus' interpretation of the seventh commandment, "Do not commit adultery." J. J. Kilgallen writes, "It is important to take notice of the distinction emphasized in verses 27-32. If Jesus, on the one hand, extends the law against adultery to include looking lustfully at a woman, He may have objections of a type to deal with; if, on the other hand, He extends the law against adultery to include divorce, He has another kind of objection to deal with, namely, that the Law allows for divorce. It is because of this 'permission' for divorce that Jesus specifically and explicitly includes divorce in His 'definition' of adultery" ("To What Are the Matthaean Exception-Texts [5:32 and 19:9] an Exception?" *Biblica* 61 [1980]: 103).

45. G. J. Wenham comments, "Matthew 5:32a is thus adding a new idea: that divorce by itself is also adultery, unless it be for unchastity" ("Matthew and Divorce: An Old Crux Revisited," *Journal for the Study of the New Testament* 22 [1984]: 104).

his wife and marries another commits adultery, but rather to the principle that a man may not put away his wife.[46] It is maintained that this is not only a possible meaning of the Greek text but the natural meaning of it.[47]

A third reason advanced in favor of understanding the exceptive clauses to refer to separation rather than divorce is the context in which they stand. This is particularly the case in 19:9, where the context is very full. The question posed by the Pharisees is sharply defining: "Is it lawful for a man to divorce his wife for any and every reason?" (v. 3); and the thrust of Jesus' reply is similar: "Therefore what God has joined together, let man not separate" (v. 6). The attempt to deflect this response by appealing to the Mosaic "permission" of divorce is neutralized by Jesus' pronouncement in verse 9. The general drift of the debate, therefore, far from leading one to expect concessions, encourages the opposite expectations.[48] That this was what was given appears to be confirmed by the response of the disciples: "If this is the situation between a husband and wife, it is better not to marry" (v. 10). If Jesus was simply opting for either of the views then prevailing in Judaism at that time—the Shammaite or Hillelite options described above or some variation on them—then the response of the disciples is very difficult to understand. In essence, they would have been declaring their inability to do what the followers of Shammai (to refer to the sterner option) did, namely, resort to divorce only in cases of a wife's unchastity. If, on the other hand, Jesus has just taught that marriage is indissoluble and separation was permissible only in some cases, and then with no right to remarriage, the disciples' misgiving is fully intelligible.

---

46. Heth and Wenham write, "The construction of Matthew 19:9 basically indicates that we are dealing with two conditional statements, one that is qualified and one that is unqualified or absolute: (1) A man may not put away his wife *unless* she is guilty of adultery. (2) Whoever marries another after putting away his wife commits adultery. Or, to paraphrase the idea in another way: 'Putting away for reasons other than unchastity is forbidden; and remarriage after every divorce is adulterous'" (Heth and Wenham, *Jesus and Divorce*, 117).

47. The point is technical. The account above has sought to avoid technical language. The technical, syntactical details may be found in Dupont, *Mariage et Divorce*, 102-3, 147-50, and in G. J. Wenham, "The Syntax of Matthew 19:9," JSNT 28 (1986): 17-23. A brief but lucid summary is given in Heth and Wenham, *Jesus and Divorce*, 51-52.

48. Cf. Alfred Plummer, "We can hardly believe that our Lord, after setting aside the Mosaic enactment as an accommodation to low morality, should himself have sanctioned what it allowed" (*An Exegetical Commentary on the Gospel According to Matthew* [Grand Rapids: Baker Book House, 1909, reprint 1982], 82).

A fourth reason alleged in support of the separation understanding is the setting of Matthew's Gospel as a whole. No interpretation will have much credibility if it cannot show why the exceptive clauses are found in Matthew's Gospel only. This is just another way of saying that one must show positively what the meaning of the exceptive clauses is and, further, demonstrate that it fits the situation to which Matthew's Gospel was addressed, insofar as we can reconstruct it. It is probable that we have insufficient evidence to define the precise setting of the Gospel,[49] but certain broad concerns seem to be indisputable. Prominent among these was the relation of Christianity to the Law of Moses, which, in turn, raised practical problems for Jewish converts. Not least among these was how the Jewish requirement of the divorce of an adulterous wife was to be reconciled with Jesus' absolute prohibition of divorce. As David Hill has expressed it pungently, "A man was not just allowed, but was *compelled,* by Jewish law (in New Testament times) to divorce his wife when fornication before marriage was discovered (cf. Matt. 1:19; Deut. 22:13ff.) or adultery detected."[50] This problem is addressed by the exceptive clauses that declare that, in such circumstances, the husband may divorce his wife without incurring the condemnation that would otherwise be his under Jesus' teaching. However, such divorce would bring no right to remarry.[51]

The fifth reason given in support of the separation view is that this was the view held in the Early Church. Indeed, William Heth places this argument at the head of his list. "The first reason I do not believe that Matthew 19:9 should be interpreted as permitting remarriage after divorce in the event of marital unfaithfulness is that this idea was foreign to the early church."[52] Again, "The early Christian writers understood the 'divorce' which Jesus seems to permit

---

49. For example, scholars disagree regarding the stage of the controversy reflected in the Gospel: whether the Jewish Christians were still synagogue worshipers or whether the church had already broken with the synagogue but was still under social and moral pressure from that source. For recent evaluations of the evidence, see R. T. France, *Matthew, Evangelist and Teacher* (Grand Rapids: Zondervan, 1989), 81-122, and Graham N. Stanton, *A Gospel for a New People: Studies in Matthew* (Louisville, Ky.: Westminster/John Knox Press, 1993), 113-68.

50. Hill, *Gospel of Matthew,* 125.

51. Collins quotes Alexander Sand as characterizing this position as a recourse offered to Jews *(privilegium Judaicum).* Collins himself would see that privilege as probably applying also to those wishing to comply with the civil law. "It served as a conscience clause for those who lived in a society ruled by law" *(Divorce in the New Testament,* 212).

52. House, *Divorce and Remarriage,* 95.

for unchastity as mere separation from bed and board, and not the 'dissolution' of the marriage. These early interpreters of the Greek New Testament had a built-in cultural, social, and linguistic grid that served them in their reading and interpretation of the Gospels—and Matthew's was the most popular in the Early Church. As far as I am aware, the early Greek-speaking fathers never discuss or debate the question of what the exception clause qualifies."[53]

The cumulative force of this case is considerable, even if not every point is equally cogent. For example, the claim that the verb "puts away" denotes something less than divorce is difficult to sustain, not least since it is used twice in the same context (vv. 3 and 8) to mean "divorce" in the sense of dissolution of marriage with right to remarry. Again, the argument that the clause structure in verse 9 indicates that the exception refers to the right to divorce only and not to the right to remarry makes Matthew's writing not merely compressed but clumsy inasmuch as he gives the impression that he is speaking throughout of one and the same person, when in reality (on this view) he is speaking of two different cases. As to the situation addressed, the proposal described above (of Jews wrestling with the Jewish *requirement* of divorce of an unfaithful wife) would seem to fit it insofar as we know it, though it is not the only possibility, as we shall see.

It would appear that the data do not readily support the *precise* position under examination, namely, separation without actual divorce and therefore without the possibility of remarriage. What may be said with confidence is that the *general* thrust of this interpretation toward a narrow rather than a broad attitude toward divorce is well-supported. The overall force of the entire passage (19:3-12) points indisputably in this direction. Also of weight in its support is the claim that the Early Church held this view, an argument that, as we have seen, Heth places first in his list.[54] Even if the rigidity of the Early Church's attitude to divorce can be overstated,[55] and showed a

---

53. Ibid., 104.

54. See the quotations above at notes 52 and 53.

55. The exposition of the Early Church view in Heth and Wenham, *Jesus and Divorce*, chap. 1, contains nuances that the summary statements quoted above lack. Thus it is noted that Hermas, a Roman Christian writing not later than 150, insists that an adulterous spouse *must* be put away, and that while remarriage is forbidden so as not to preclude reconciliation, a repentant adulterer should be received back no more than once. On both points Hermas has gone beyond Scripture (Heth and Wenham, *Jesus and Divorce*, 23-26).

certain margin of variation,[56] its overall position leans clearly toward a restrictive view according to which divorce was unacceptable for any reason or, if accepted for serious reasons such as adultery, did not bring with it the right to remarry.

Divorce for Adultery Only, with Right of Remarriage

An alternative interpretation of the data of the first three Gospels is that divorce is permitted on the grounds of adultery, and that with divorce, understood as the dissolution of an existing marriage, comes the right to remarry. This has been the prevailing view within Protestantism since the time of the Reformation.[57] Indeed, it has sometimes been labeled the Erasmian view inasmuch as it was first propounded in 1519 by Erasmus of Rotterdam from whom it was derived by Luther and other of the Reformers.[58]

While there have been variations among those who have held this view, just as there are among those who adhere to it today, the foundations upon which it rests are common to all. In an important measure the "divorce for adultery with right to remarry" position is less distant from the "separation only without the right to remarry" view than might appear at first sight. Stated otherwise, it might be described as the "no divorce or remarriage save with a single exception" view. One may expect to find significant areas of common ground. The question at issue between the two positions is whether the admission of any exception is not only possible without exploding the biblical idea of marriage but also in fact capable of being found in the biblical texts. Inasmuch as the sayings on divorce in Mark 10:2-12 and Luke 16:18 make no mention of the possibility of divorce at all, it follows that the chief evidence on which this position depends is the exceptive clauses in Matt. 5:32 and 19:9. Broadly speaking, the argument is developed in the following stages.

First, it is claimed that the natural meaning of the words used and the natural force of the grammatical forms or structures employed point plainly to a real exception or exceptions to the other-

---

56. See Appendix, "Marriage and Divorce in the Early Church to the Time of Augustine."

57. For a survey of the first 150 years, see V. Norskov Olsen, *The New Testament Logia on Divorce: A Study of Their Interpretation from Erasmus to Milton* (Tübingen, Germany: J. C. B. Mohr, 1971).

58. This, notwithstanding the fact that it is found 1,100 years earlier in the writings of Ambrosiaster. See Appendix.

wise firm rule against divorce and that the exception specified as justifying divorce is adultery. It will be worthwhile to look at each category of evidence in turn.

As to the terms employed, two are significant. The first is the verb variously translated "set free," "release," "send away," "dismiss," "divorce" (Greek *apoluein*). The claim is that in the contexts of the exceptive clauses, this term denotes divorce in the legal sense implying the termination of a marriage and with it the right to remarry. In Matt. 5:31 this is very clearly its meaning. The verse is, indeed, drawn from Deut. 24:1, 3, where divorce procedure is being defined and the reference to the "certificate of divorce" (Greek *apostasion*) places the matter beyond doubt. Precisely the same term is used (albeit in two different grammatical forms) in Matt. 5:32, which is translated, "But I tell you that anyone who divorces *[apoluein]* his wife, except for marital unfaithfulness, causes her to become an adulteress, and anyone who marries the divorced woman *[apoluein]* commits adultery." It would be surprising if the word should change its meaning between verses unless there is something in the context to require this. Whether there is remains to be discussed. What seems indisputable is that the import of the verse is that whoever divorces his wife save for the reason given makes her an adulteress, as does any man who marries her, since, apart from the reason given, divorce does not really take place; the original marriage remains.

The same line of argument applies in Matt. 19:3-9. The question posed in verse 3, "Is it lawful for a man to divorce *[apoluein]* his wife for any and every reason?" plainly presupposes the dispute between the parties of Shammai and Hillel as to the reasons for which divorce was permissible. The reply of Jesus' questioners to His response that divorce was not part of God's plan on any terms (v. 6) evokes this counterquestion (v. 7): "Why then . . . did Moses command that a man give his wife a certificate of divorce and send her away *[apoluein]*?" To this Jesus retorted, "Moses permitted you to divorce *[apoluein]* your wives because your hearts were hard. But it was not this way from the beginning. I tell you that anyone who divorces *[apoluein]* his wife, except for marital unfaithfulness, and marries another woman commits adultery" (vv. 8-9). The reasoning here is parallel with that in 5:32.

Proponents of the "divorce for adultery with right to remarry" interpretation are therefore correct in claiming that the verb used, whether translated "send away" or "divorce," constitutes no obstacle against their view. The term in itself can mean "separate" or "divorce."[59] Its meaning in the verses under consideration is determined by the context and in no small measure by the second important word, "adultery" (Greek *porneia*).

It is decisive to the view under consideration that the Greek word *porneia,* translated "adultery," should in fact bear that meaning in the exceptive clauses. The term occurs 26 times in the New Testament and is used "of every kind of unlawful sexual intercourse."[60] In some instances it is distinguished from adultery (Matt. 15:19; 1 Cor. 6:19); in others, adultery is apparently included in a more comprehensive use of the term (Rom. 1:29; 2 Cor. 12:21).[61] As to its meaning in Matt. 5:32, exponents of the view under consideration maintain that this is its natural meaning in that context. Thus John Murray, pointing out that the case envisaged is of an offended husband and duly noting that *porneia* may be used broadly, concludes that the form *porneia* would naturally take within a marriage relationship is adultery. "What Jesus sets in the forefront is the sin of illicit sexual intercourse. It is, of course, implied that such on the part of a married woman is not only fornication but also adultery in the specific sense, for the simple reason that it constitutes sexual infidelity to her spouse. And this is the only case in which, according to Christ's unambiguous assertion, a man may dismiss his wife without being involved in the sin which Jesus proceeds to characterize as making his wife to be an adulteress."[62]

Matt. 19:9 is described by Murray as "the most pivotal passage

---

59. Dupont who, as was seen, upholds the "separation without divorce or remarriage" view, concedes as much. Indeed, he sees the giving of a new sense to an old word as part of Jesus' debating strategy. "Jesus could have declared quite simply that he did not admit that divorce had the power to dissolve marriage. The precise logic of professors would have been satisfied, but Jesus was speaking to Orientals whose wits are less hidebound. He says to them: divorcees who remarry commit adultery. An absurd statement if one starts out with the idea that divorce dissolves marriage, and if one adopts the principle that Jesus was obliged to use the words in the sense his questioners gave them. Jesus does not seem to be troubled by such constraints. To change the usual sense of words is exactly his way of making people understand that he does not accept the ideas of his background" (Dupont, *Mariage et Divorce,* 146).

60. W. Bauer, W. F. Arndt, F. W. Gingrich, F. W. Danker, *A Greek-English Lexicon of the New Testament and Other Early Christian Literature,* 2nd ed., rev. and aug. from Bauer's 5th German ed. of 1958 (Chicago: University of Chicago Press, 1979). Hereafter BAGD, s.v.

61. In Hermas, *Mandates* 4.1.5 *porneia* is used explicitly with the sense of adultery.

62. Murray, *Divorce,* 20-21. Cf. France, "The more natural meaning here is adultery by the wife" (*The Gospel According to Matthew,* in *Tyndale New Testament Commentary* [Leicester: InterVarsity Press, 1987], 123).

in the New Testament" respecting divorce because here alone are brought together in a single context the exceptive clause ("except for fornication") and the remarriage clause ("and marries another").[63] The question of remarriage following divorce is raised explicitly here. The immediate point, however, is the force of the term *porneia*. The context of 19:9 is even fuller than that of 5:32. The narrative begins with the Pharisees' question to Jesus as to whether a man may divorce his wife for any cause (v. 3). Jesus' reply falls into two parts. First, He quotes two passages from the creation narrative—the statement that from the beginning God made them male and female (v. 4), and next the saying from Gen. 2:24 that the married pair become one flesh (v. 5). The second part of Jesus' reply is His comment on these sayings. This consists of an emphasis of their import by stating the conclusion that "they are no longer two, but one [flesh]" (v. 6*a*) and by the imperious command that what God has joined together human beings are not to tear apart (v. 6*b*). Verses 7-8 describe the scribal objection that Moses had permitted divorce, which Jesus meets by pointing back to the creation design. Then follows the central saying: "I tell you that anyone who divorces his wife, except for *[porneia]*, and marries another woman commits adultery" (v. 9).

Unlike 5:32, which is concerned with the effect of divorce on the wife, 19:9 focuses on the consequence of divorce for the husband. This is that if he remarries following divorce for any reason other than illicit sex, he becomes an adulterer. Since the relationship under discussion is that between husband and wife, it is concluded by upholders of this view that the form of illicit sex in mind is most naturally understood to be adultery.[64]

---

63. Murray, *Divorce*, 33.

64. Cf. T. R. Edgar, "The meaning in this context, therefore, is decisive for determining the nature of the exception. Matthew 19:9 is a discussion concerning the valid basis of divorce and states that some type of illicit sex on the part of the wife is the only proper basis for divorce. Therefore, the most natural way to interpret *porneia* is with the meaning 'adultery.' A less likely, but plausible, opinion is that *porneia* does not have a specific reference here but refers to any type of illicit sex, including incest, homosexuality and sodomy. However, in a context concerning husbands and wives, particularly when using the term *porneia* for the wife's conduct and *moichao* for the husband's, it is certain that the primary reference is to the sin of adultery" (in House, *Divorce and Remarriage*, 162). It is significant that William Heth, who subscribes to the "divorce but no remarriage" position, says of this, "I tend to agree with Edgar that a wife's adultery is probably the most natural way to understand the reference to *porneia* in the context of the exception clauses" (ibid., 203). Other scholars who share this view (though with varying degrees of conviction) include Ulrich Luz, *Matthew 1—7* (Minneapolis: Augsburg, 1989), 304-5; W. D. Davies and Dale C. Allison, *Gospel According to St. Matthew,*

It is claimed, then, by adherents of the "divorce for adultery with right to remarry" position that not only is it possible to understand the language of Matt. 5:32 and 19:9 in a way consistent with this view, but also this is the most natural understanding of it in the contexts in which these verses stand.

A further consideration enters into the case for this view in 19:9, namely, the grammatical form or syntax employed. As noted above, 19:9 is the only verse that brings together both an exceptive clause and a clause regarding remarriage. It is the positioning of the former in relation to the latter that gives to the verse the pivotal significance seen in it by Murray, as noted earlier. The details of the issue have already been spelled out[65] from the perspective of the "separation without divorce or remarriage" view and need not be recited here. Suffice it to say that if the exceptive clause is placed after the phrase "anyone who divorces his wife," it is held that only divorce is being approved; whereas, if it stands after the expression "anyone who divorces his wife and marries another," then not only divorce but also remarriage is being approved. Since in the Greek text the former is the case, the passage is claimed to support the "separation but no divorce" viewpoint by proponents of that stance.[66]

This claim has been contested by those who find in the exceptive clauses permission for divorce and remarriage on the ground of adultery.[67] As with the contrary claim, this also may be expressed in technical terms. But put simply, Murray raises three objections against it.

First, when an exception is being stated in Greek, everything to which it is an exception is expressed first, followed by the exception. However, in the Greek text of Matt. 19:9 the exceptive clause stands

---

1:529-31; D. J. Harrington, *The Gospel of Matthew,* in *Sacra Pagina* Series (Collegeville, Minn.: Liturgical Press, 1991), 1:87-88; D. A. Hagner, *Matthew 1—13,* 124-25. For a contrary view that, however, takes little account of the connection of thought of the exceptive clauses, see Isaksson, *Marriage and Ministry,* 133-35.

65. See above, 98-99.

66. See above, 98-99, and n. 46.

67. The case is fully stated by Murray, *Divorce,* 35-43. It should be noted that not all supporters of this view make as much of this argument as others do. For example, D. A. Carson, while affirming that Matt. 19:9 must mean, "Anyone who divorces his wife and marries another commits adultery—though this principle does not hold where *porneia* is present," nevertheless observes that attachment of the exceptive clause to the divorce rather than the remarriage clause is not decisive "since every other place breeds ambiguities" (*Expositor's Bible Commentary* [Grand Rapids: Zondervan, 1984], 8:414).

in the middle of the general statement: *"put away his wife* except for fornication *and marries another."* On the "separation but no remarriage" interpretation the verse is thus taken to mean, "But I say to you that whoever puts away his wife and marries another commits adultery—only a man may put away (but not divorce) his wife for the cause of fornication." The thought is intelligible enough; the question is whether this is a clear and natural way of expressing it.

Second, the ruling idea of the verse has to do with committing adultery as the main verb indicates. The exceptive clause must relate to this in one way or another, and the only way in which it can do so is via the verb that activates the principal verb, that is, via the expression "and marries again." What this amounts to is that the impact of the exceptive clause cannot be sealed off from the verb "and marries again" as the "separation without remarriage" view contends.

Third, Murray maintains that the exceptive clause is in exactly the right position to refer *both* to the combination of factors resulting in adultery, divorce and remarriage, *and* to the one exception where that consequence does not follow, namely, in cases of adultery.[68]

The net result of the argument thus far is that both the terms employed and the grammatical structure of Matt. 5:32 and 19:9 show that the natural meaning of these verses is that the putting away of one's wife followed by remarriage entails adultery with one single exception, namely, when the wife has already committed adultery. In that case, and in that case alone, a husband is free to relieve himself of his wife and likewise free to enter into another marriage.

A further point of great importance that distinguishes the "divorce for adultery" view from the "separation only" view emerges sharply at this point. This is not simply that the former view admits the possibility of divorce (at least in one case) whereas the latter denies it absolutely, but that behind the former view lies the assumption *that the marriage bond can be broken.* As noted earlier, the "separation only" position maintains that the reason why divorce is impossible is because the marriage bond is indelible. In the act of two becoming one flesh, a union is created that neither divorce nor any other device has the power to undo.

Murray argues strenuously against such a position on three counts. He points out, to begin with, that Mark 10:4, Matt. 5:31, and

---

68. For Murray's complete and technical exposition of these points, see *Divorce,* 39-41.

19:7—all refer to the Mosaic permission of divorce (Deut. 24:1-4) that accepted that divorce terminated a marriage, thereby making possible the contracting of another. Assuming, as he does, that the exceptive clause refers to adultery, Murray infers that the core of Jesus' dissent from the Mosaic provision was not to deny the reality of divorce but rather to restrict the grounds on which it was permissible. Again, Murray argues that there is something distinctly anomalous in a situation in which the marriage bond is said to remain intact and yet the partners live as though it no longer existed. "To provide for and sanction permanent separation while the marriage tie remains inviolate is something that is alien to the whole tenor of Scripture teaching in regard to the obligations that inhere and are inseparable from the marital bond."[69] Finally, he argues that an indissoluble marriage bond would have made impossible the observance of the injunction to purity in 1 Cor. 6:15-17, where a wife had abandoned herself to prostitution.

Not all of Murray's arguments against marital indissolubility are equally weighty. One factor particularly notable is that even while affirming the possibility of divorce for adultery, he insists strongly on the unique quality of the first marriage. Referring to Deut. 24:1-4, where, as was seen above, a woman divorced by her first husband was permitted a second marriage but, if that failed, was denied the right to return to her first husband, Murray comments: "The second marriage effects an unobliterable separation from the first husband. This implies a unique relation to the first husband."[70] The position of D. A. Carson is equally notable in that while affirming the possibility of dissolution in cases of adultery, he nonetheless asserts that mar-

---

69. Ibid., 43.

70. Murray's explanation of the character of this uniqueness is not particularly lucid. He writes, "Although divorce may be given and a certain freedom granted to the divorced persons, yet there is an unobliterable relationship that appears, paradoxically enough, in the form of an unobliterable separation in the event that a second marriage has been consummated on the part of the divorced wife . . . While not stigmatized as adultery in terms of the Mosaic economy, nevertheless, it is not at all certain that the remarriage is not regarded as involving defilement. It may very well be that the evil attaching to divorce and the abnormal situation in which the woman is placed as the divorcee of her first husband are regarded as casting their shadow over the second marriage even though the second marriage is not placed in the category of adultery and civil or ecclesiastical penalty is not appended" (ibid., 14-15). The cogency of this explanation—hesitating as it is—is open to question. Either a marriage is dissolved or it is not. Murray is clear in concluding that dissolution is possible.

riage is grounded in the order of creation and cannot be merely a covenantal relationship.[71]

By way of evaluation it may be said that the position under review possesses formidable strengths. There can be no doubt that from a linguistic and syntactical perspective it rests on a possible interpretation of the two passages in Matthew's Gospel containing the exceptive clauses. Beyond that narrow, though indispensable, base, however, it encounters difficulties. For example, it has difficulty explaining why in the Marcan and Lucan parallels no exceptions are mentioned—particularly in the case of Mark where the question regarding the permissibility of divorce makes explicit reference to the exception allowed by Moses (10:4).[72] Not only so, but to understand the exception as adultery creates great problems of interpretation within the contexts in which the exceptive clauses stand.

For one thing, what is implied is that, having rejected the Mosaic permission of divorce in favor of a return to the creation picture of marriage as permanent, Jesus should in the next breath approve divorce in certain cases. This is true in Matt. 5:32 but is especially clear in 19:3-9, where Christ goes out of His way to condemn the Mosaic regulation as a concession to hardness of heart. Is it likely that, having condemned the concession, He should proceed forthwith to legislate for its continuance? "We can hardly believe," says Plummer, "that our Lord, after setting aside the Mosaic enactment as an accommodation to low morality, should himself have sanctioned what it allowed."[73] Again, the view in question has difficulty in explaining the reaction of the disciples in Matt. 19:10-12 to Jesus' teaching if all He has done is rule that divorce for adultery is the only alternative to lifelong marriage.[74] Such was the teaching of the

---

71. EBC, 8:412.

72. Murray's reply that the exception is taken for granted in Mark and Luke is essentially an argument from silence. His prior suggestion that the question posed in Mark is confined to the justifiability of the grounds for divorce mentioned in Deut. 24:1-4 would make the question purely antiquarian, which manifestly it was not (Murray, *Divorce*, 51-52).

73. Plummer, *Exegetical Commentary*, 82.

74. Matt. 19:10-12 has been interpreted in at least two ways: (*a*) The expression "this word" (v. 11) has been taken to refer to the disciples' comment in verse 10, "It is better not to marry." On this view, verses 10-12 are concerned with the respective merits of celibacy and marriage, Jesus teaching that celibacy is a gift received only by some, not all. Furthermore, the gift is exercised "on account of the Kingdom of heaven" understood as for the sake of the service of God. For exposition, see D. J. Harrington, *Gospel of Matthew*, 273-77; W. D. Davies, *The Setting of the Sermon on the Mount* (Cam-

school of Shammai; indeed, prevailing Jewish law *required* the divorce of an adulterous wife. Thus, while verbally possible, the "divorce for adultery" view has difficulty reconciling itself with the teaching of the Gospels as a whole, as well as with the cultural background of Jesus' ministry. Any view that cannot meet these touchstones will not have a strong claim to credibility.

Divorce to Meet Circumstances Unique to First-Century Jewish Christians

A third understanding of Jesus' teaching accepts that, as recorded in Mark and Luke, He forbade divorce absolutely. The question then arises, What is the import of the exceptive clauses found in Matt. 5:32 and 19:9? While more than one response is given to this question, all have this in common, that the explanation is sought in the background of Matthew's Gospel in general and in a Jewish element in its readership in particular.

On this view it is seen as no accident that the exceptive clauses are found only in Matthew's Gospel. On the contrary, this is precisely what would be expected in a Gospel addressing what seem to be Matthew's aims. Matthew's Gospel is characterized by what appear at first sight to be mutually exclusive interests. On the one hand there are features that reflect or address a Jewish mind-set. These include the emphasis on Jesus' ministry as the fulfillment of Old Testament prophecy, His attitude to the Old Testament law and scribal interpretation of it, and His controversies with the representatives of the Jewish religion. Only Matthew records that Jesus saw himself as

---

bridge, England: Cambridge University Press, 1966), 393-95; F. J. Moloney, "Matthew 19, 3-12 and Celibacy," JSNT 2 (1979): 42-60. *(b)* The expression "this word" is taken to refer to Jesus' teaching as a whole in verses 3-9; specifically to forbidding of remarriage following divorce in verse 9. In this case, the disciples' reply is that, in face of so stringent a position, it is better to avoid marriage altogether than, having indulged the sexual appetite, to risk being deprived of its indulgence. Jesus concedes that His teaching is not easy but points out that God's grace makes possible what is impossible otherwise (v. 11) and illustrates His point by citing three occasions of sexual abstinence: natural defect, emasculation, and choice in the interests of a greater good. It is clearly the third that is the focus of His argument. He is not teaching that celibacy is preferable to marriage, which would contradict His declaration in verses 4-6 that marriage is a gift of God given at creation. Rather He is saying that *sometimes* celibacy is preferable to marriage—and in particular to remarriage following divorce. For exposition, see Pierre Bonnard, *L'Évangile Selon Saint Matthieu* (Neuchâtel: Delachaux & Nestlé, 1963), 284; D. Patte, *The Gospel According to Matthew* (Valley Forge, Pa.: Trinity Press International, 1996), 266-68; W. Heth in House, *Divorce and Remarriage,* 105-7.

sent only to "the lost sheep of Israel" (10:5-6; 15:24), and many of the issues discussed, such as how to present offerings at the Temple (5:23-24), or the payment of the Temple tax (17:24-27), would have meaning (let alone interest) only for Jews. On the other hand, this same Gospel evinces a vision that encompasses all nations. Jesus' birth is welcomed by foreign visitors (2:1-12); He begins His ministry in "Galilee of the Gentiles" (4:12-17), and its scope is the world (13:38; 28:18-20).

At the same time, there is distinct evidence of tension between these two emphases—not merely as ideas but as attitudes within the community to which Matthew was written. The faith of the centurion in Jesus' power to heal is praised as greater than any seen in Israel and is viewed as a symbol of the displacement of the sons of the Kingdom by outsiders (8:5-13); a similar conclusion is drawn from the parable of the vineyard (21:43); while the example of the scribes and Pharisees is trenchantly criticized in chapter 23.

How these contending emphases are to be resolved, whether on the assumption of a group of Christian Jews and God-fearers withdrawing from the synagogue or a mixed Jewish Christian and Gentile church in process of splitting or having already split, is a point of much debate.[75] There is no need for it to be resolved here. What is important is the recognition of such an element in the background to which Matthew's Gospel was written. That it affected the discussion regarding divorce seems clear from the fact that in 5:31-32 and 19:3-10 (in contrast with Mark 10:11-12) divorce is assumed to be the right of the husband alone—a state of affairs that existed in Judaism but not in the Gentile world.

Against a general background of this sort, the precise force of the exceptive clauses, and specifically of the word *porneia,* has been variously defined. At least three options merit consideration.

---

75. For two recent, full discussions of the various options proposed, see France, "The Setting of the Gospel," *Matthew, Evangelist and Teacher,* chap. 3, and Stanton, "The Parting of the Ways," *Gospel for a New People,* Part II, esp. chaps. 5-6 and Conclusions to Part II. Stanton proposes the following reconstruction of events, "At first Jews who had become Christians within the communities with which the evangelist was associated maintained their Jewish loyalties and most aspects of their Jewish identity. However, gradual acceptance of some Gentiles led to intolerable tensions between Christian and non-christian Jews. Matthew wrote his Gospel partly in order to strengthen his readers' resolve to continue to accept Gentiles" (281).

1. The Ground of the Exception as Premarital Unchastity

As was noted earlier, the word *porneia* has a wide field of meaning, hence the fact that it has been translated as "unchastity," "fornication," "adultery" in the exceptive clauses themselves in Matt. 5:32 and 19:9 (to mention no other passages where the word is used). Nor are these the only possible shades of meaning. There is evidence of narrower uses in the Greek Bible, one of which denotes unchastity on the part of a woman prior to marriage. The law of Deut. 22:13-21 says that a girl who, after marriage, is found not to have been a virgin at the time of marriage is to be stoned to death because she has been promiscuous (Greek *ekporeusai,* Deut. 22:21, LXX). Part of the reasoning behind this is that a betrothed woman was regarded as committed to her husband-to-be and, indeed, was spoken of as his wife (Deut. 22:23-24). Since the terms of the marriage were flawed, the marriage was invalid, but even so it had to be terminated by a formal divorce.

There is an example of this very thing in Matt. 1:18-25 in which Joseph, on discovering the condition of Mary, his betrothed, plans to divorce her, although they had not yet been married (vv. 18-19). The claim is that this is what is referred to in the exceptive clauses.[76] In that case, the exceptive clauses were directed to Jewish Christians who, on learning of Christ's teaching of the indissolubility of marriage, would have raised the question about unchastity before or during betrothal. The exceptive clauses will indicate that in such cases divorce would be permissible, though it should be noted that in mind here is not dissolution of marriage, since a true marriage never existed. The divorce, then, would not be a divorce so much as a declaration of annulment.

This interpretation has been objected to chiefly on the grounds that the meaning suggested, while not textually impossible, is not obvious from the context,[77] and that in the case of Matt. 5:32, it presents no antithesis to verse 31.[78] The latter objection would hold only if *porneia* were given a generic sense, but as defined in the view expounded above, it is hard to see that this claim holds. As to the

---

76. Cf. Isaksson, "Linguistically speaking, the most probable meaning of *porneia,* when used in a statement of a legal nature about a married woman's crime, is undoubtedly premarital unchastity" (*Marriage and Ministry,* 140). The full exposition (135-42) should be consulted.

77. So Atkinson, *To Have and to Hold,* 117.

78. So Hagner, *Matthew 1—13,* 124.

former, it is true that nothing in the local contexts suggests this particular shade of meaning. All that can be maintained is that it is consistent with the background of the Gospel and an example of precisely this import stands in the first chapter, as has been noted.

2. The Ground of the Exception as Marriage Within Prohibited Degrees of Relationship

Another interpretation proposed for the term *porneia* in the exceptive clauses is marriage within degrees of affinity or blood relationship prohibited by the Levitical code in Lev. 18:6-18. Such relationships were considered defiling among Jews. There is evidence of this use of the term in parts of the New Testament. One instance is in the so-called Decree of the Council of Jerusalem in Acts 15:28-29: "It seemed good to the Holy Spirit and to us not to burden you with anything beyond the following requirements: You are to abstain from food sacrificed to idols, from blood, from the meat of strangled animals and from sexual immorality *[porneia]*."

The context makes clear that the problem confronting the council was whether or not Gentile converts to Christianity must be required to observe the Mosaic Law (v. 1). This was primarily a question of the ceremonial law, which to Gentiles meant little or nothing, but to the Jews meant a great deal, since it involved matters of religious purity that their ancestors had observed for generations. Indeed, Gal. 2:11-14 makes plain that the possibility of table-fellowship (and therefore the Lord's Supper) between Jews and Gentiles turned on this very thing.

The first three items listed in Acts 15:29 belong clearly to this category: the eating of food sacrificed to idols, of blood, and of the flesh of animals slaughtered in a way that did not conform to *kosher* requirements. The eating of any of these rendered a person ceremonially unclean in Jewish eyes. It is a safe presumption that the fourth item in the list, *porneia,* belongs to the same class.[79] Gentile Christians did not need a council decree to tell them that adultery was to be avoided; the seventh commandment told them that. But they might need to be told that Jewish scruples regarding the relation-

---

79. For an examination of the textual problem and its exegetical implications, see Metzger, TCGNT, 429-34. Two discussions of the contending interpretations are Kirsopp Lake and Henry J. Cadbury, *The Beginnings of Christianity* (London: Macmillan, 1933), 5:204-9, and F. F. Bruce, *The Book of the Acts,* in *New International New Testament Commentary,* rev. ed. (Grand Rapids: Wm. B. Eerdmans Publishing Co., 1989), 295-96.

ships within which marriage was permissible were narrower than those of pagan society and that disregard of these might pose a threat to the unity of the Church.

The meaning of the term *porneia* in 1 Cor. 5:1 appears to be of the same character. The "sexual immorality" spoken of in the text is defined as "a man [having] his father's wife." Gordon Fee explains, "The problem is incest, a man taking a wife of his father other than his own mother and living with her sexually in an ongoing relationship. . . . What cannot be known is what had happened to the father, whether there had been divorce or death. In either case what is forbidden by all ancients, both Jewish and pagan, is the cohabiting of father and son with the same woman."[80] Here again, then, *porneia* is being used in an abbreviated sense.

That such a view was intelligible in Jesus' day seems to be supported by evidence from the Dead Sea Scrolls where marriage to a niece is roundly denounced.[81] Still more important, it makes sense of the situation to which Matthew's Gospel appears to be addressed. Like the decree of the Jerusalem Council, its destination seems to have been Syria, if not Antioch specifically,[82] precisely the location where the dispute regarding the observance of the Mosaic Law by Gentile Christians broke out (Gal. 2:11-14; Acts 14:26—15:1).

Again, it has reference to a problem of long standing in Judaism, namely, the terms on which Gentile converts to Judaism could be admitted as proselytes. Judaism tended to tolerate in proselytes marriage relationships that were unacceptable to Jews because they fell outside the limits prescribed in Lev. 18. The exact form of the problem in Matthew has been variously defined, according to whether the directive is thought to have been written for the benefit of Jewish Christians or Gentile Christians. Ultimately this makes little difference, since its aim was to facilitate relations between the two groups. Thus Bonnard and Baltensweiler[83] see it as specifying the

---

80. Fee, *First Epistle to the Corinthians,* 200 (see the whole passage).

81. Cf. *Covenant of Damascus* V 7b-11a, with J. A. Fitzmyer, "Matthaean Divorce," in TS 37:220-21.

82. Acts 15:22, 23, 30. For a recent discussion of the destination of Matthew, see France, *Matthew, Evangelist and Teacher,* 91-95. France writes, "The majority of scholars today tend to opt cautiously for the origin of the gospel being somewhere in Syria" (92).

83. Bonnard reads the prohibition against the background of Jewish casuistry that permitted proselytes to maintain some unions forbidden in Lev. 18. The exceptive clauses would thus represent a tightening of current practice among Jewish Christians, restricting divorces to those specified in the Levitical code. In short, pagan converts to

terms on which proselytes might be admitted into the (Jewish) Christian community. Crossan likewise sees the initiative—or pressure—coming from "pagans wishing to fraternize with Jewish Christians."[84] Or it may have a concession to conservative Jewish Christians to maintain their traditional standards in this regard (though this is perhaps less likely). Either way, the meaning and outcome are the same. *Porneia* refers to purity barriers between Jewish and Gentile Christians that must be removed if the two groups are to form a single community.

This interpretation has much to be said for it. It fits what is known of the social background of Matthew's Gospel, and it uses the key term in a sense it can clearly bear. Yet it is not without its critics.[85] The weightiest criticisms of it reduce to the claim that it does not really fit the contexts in which it is used. This is alleged in two respects. First, it is claimed that there is no clear indication that the exceptive clauses apply only to Gentile converts, a claim held to be verified by the fact that no single church father ever took the saying in the sense proposed.[86] Second, it is alleged that whether *porneia* bears the sense of "prohibited marriage" elsewhere, that is not its natural meaning here. The exceptive clauses clearly refer back to Deut. 24:1, where the matter under discussion is valid marriages sundered by divorce.[87]

Proponents of this view do not find these objections unanswerable, and the interpretation has distinguished supporters. Following a listing of the main interpretations F. F. Bruce writes: "Most probable is the view that the exceptive clause is designed to adapt the ruling to the circumstances of the Gentile mission. If this is so, the term "unchastity" has a technical sense, referring to sexual unions that, while they might be sanctioned by use and wont in some parts of

---

Christianity in Jewish Christian churches are in mind (Bonnard, *L'Évangile Selon Saint Matthieu,* 69, 283). Identical with Bonnard's view is that of Heinrich Baltensweiler, *Die Ehe im Neuen Testament,* 87-101.

84. Dominic Crossan, "Divorce and Remarriage in the New Testament," in *The Bond of Marriage: An Ecumenical and Interdisciplinary Study,* ed. William W. Bassett (Notre Dame, Ind.: University of Notre Dame Press, 1968), 21-26, esp. 25-26.

85. For serious critiques, see Dupont, *Mariage et Divorce,* 110-14; Isaksson, *Marriage and Ministry,* 129-31; E. Lövestam, "Divorce and Remarriage in the New Testament," JLA 4 (1981): 54-58; Luz, *Matthew 1—7,* 304-6.

86. Luz, *Matthew 1—7,* 305; Lövestam, "Divorce and Remarriage in the New Testament," 56.

87. Luz, *Matthew 1—7,* 305; Dupont, *Mariage et Divorce,* 111-12.

the Gentile world, were forbidden by the marriage law of Israel. It is a matter of history that the Church's traditional marriage law, with its list of relationships within which marriage might not take place, was based on that of Israel. What was to be done if two people, married within such forbidden degrees, were converted from paganism to Christianity? In this situation the marriage might be dissolved."[88]

3. The Exception as a Concession to First-Century Jewish Christian Conscience

Another type of interpretation understands the exception in Matt. 5:32; 19:9 as a clarification of, and even concession to, constraints belonging peculiarly to the situation of Jewish Christians in the first century. Again, there are variant forms of this view, not all of which need to be noted here. Two may be considered.

R. F. Collins finds the backdrop of the exceptive clauses in the divorce law then prevailing in Judaism and the Roman Empire. This law did not merely permit but *required* the divorce of an unfaithful wife. Collins suggests that Jews who either had conformed to this law and later wished to become Christian or who, already Christian, felt bound in conscience by their traditional law or the law of the empire might find themselves torn by Jesus' unequivocal ban on divorce. It is to these that the exceptive clauses are directed, indicating that such divorce is not a breach of Jesus' ban, since it falls within the boundaries of His ban. "The adulterous wife could, and probably should, be dismissed. Forbidden to her husband, she was also forbidden to any other man. The one who dared to marry her was guilty of adultery."[89]

An alternative form of this view is advanced by E. Lövestam. The Jewish setting of the Matthaean sayings is shown in that the right of divorce is assumed to be restricted to the man and the emphasis of the sayings is on the responsibility of the man if he divorces his wife. "This is where the exceptive phrase comes in. According to Jewish marital laws the wife could cause the breakup of a marriage by being unfaithful and the man had no say in the matter. If the wife was unfaithful, it was thus she, and not the man, who was responsible for the divorce. When the teachings in question are intended for people

---

88. Bruce, *Hard Sayings of Jesus,* 61.

89. Collins, *Divorce in the New Testament,* 213. The entire section beginning on page 207 should be consulted. This view assumes that *porneia* denotes adultery, and thus the position comes close to the "separation but no remarriage" view expounded above. Cf. Heth in House, *Divorce and Remarriage,* 93.

with this background, they relieve the man in this case of the responsibility for the divorce and its consequences. The wife bears it. That is what the exceptive clause means."[90] Lövestam is careful to point out that what is being sanctioned in these sayings is not the marital regulations prevailing among Matthew's readers. "No more than in the version in Mark do the logia on divorce in Matthew then imply a sanction of the marriage laws which applied for the addressees . . . the marito-legal regulations which applied for the addressees are presupposed in Matthew and within this framework people are taught the radical will of God on marriage and divorce."[91]

Both of these proposals have merit. They do not strain the meaning of the key terms; they fit plausibly into the social setting of Matthew's Gospel as well as into the overriding concerns of the Gospel. But while they are compatible with the verses in question, they are not required by them. Indeed, it may be argued that since the one fits as credibly as the other, there is nothing compelling about either. That would be to overlook the elements common to both, as well as their greater cogency than some of the interpretations considered earlier.

Following this lengthy examination of the ways the exceptive clauses have been understood, we may ask how the competing interpretations may be evaluated. The two fullest accounts of Jesus' teaching about divorce, Mark 10:2-12 and Matt. 19:3-12, presuppose a significant divergence between His view and that commonly held by the Pharisees—a view they traced to Moses' teaching in Deut. 24:1-4. This divergence is confirmed both by the disciples' reaction to it (especially in Matt. 19:10-12) and Jesus' overriding of Moses by affirming God's original design for marriage at creation (Mark 10:6-9; Matt. 19:4-6, 8*b*). We are thus led to expect a different understanding than what is prevailing in current Jewish teaching. This in fact is what we find.

In Mark 10:6-9 the permanence of marriage as God's plan at creation is affirmed, and in the private teaching to the disciples in verses 10-12 it is restated in such a way as to exclude any exception. Similar teaching is found in Luke 16:18, even though the context offers little or no help in explaining it. Matthew's account makes sub-

---

90. Lövestam, "Divorce and Remarriage in the New Testament," 61.

91. Ibid. Cf. 62. As Lövestam implies earlier, the purpose of the exceptive clauses is not to say something about the right to divorce but to address a different problem (58-59).

stantially the same points as Mark, including the Pharisees' appeal to Moses and Jesus' appeal to God's creation design. The only substantive difference in the Matthaean narrative is the presence of the exceptive clause in 19:9, also found earlier in 5:32, which otherwise agrees with Luke 16:18. For Jesus to inject an exception permitting divorce when His words have just precluded it does not simply create a clash with Mark and Luke, it creates a tension within the Matthaean sayings themselves.

For this reason, as well as for those listed above in the critique of it, the "divorce for adultery" view must be set aside. Quite apart from its absence from Christian interpretation until its relatively modern appearance at the time of Erasmus, it does not offer a convincing account of all the features of the texts.

The "separation only" theory gives a much more adequate account of the facts as was suggested in the evaluation of it earlier. However, not only does it strain the meaning of some key words as well as the grammatical structure of the verses (as was noted), but it also, like the "divorce for adultery" view, stands in tension with Mark and Luke as well as within itself by injecting an exception where the context leads one to expect no such thing.

This directs us toward the group of interpretations that see the exceptive clause as bearing upon circumstances or situations unique to Jewish Christians in the first century. It is not easy to decide among the options considered; indeed, it may not be possible to demonstrate definitively that one and only one is the meaning intended. We may not have enough information about the situation addressed to define this with precision, but neither may it be necessary. All that is required is the demonstration that an interpretation is available that gives words and grammatical structures a meaning natural to themselves and consistent with the overall context of the passages, as well as with the situation to which the Gospel appears to be directed.

Of the three alternatives proposed, the first, premarital unchastity, appears to be least likely. It is true that the Gospel begins with an example of this very thing in 1:18-25, but no evident link seems to be made with the later divorce sayings.[92] Besides the problems for this view spelled out above, there is the question as to

---

92. It has, indeed, been argued that Mary's situation in relation to Joseph prior to the birth of Jesus constituted a case of adultery in Jewish law, and this, in turn, has been used to fix the meaning of *porneia* in Matt. 5:32; 19:9 as being the same. See D. C. Alli-

whether it is likely that in the church to which Matthew is writing, premarital unchastity and only that would have been the problem agitating Jewish Christians. It cannot be ruled out, but its plausibility is not great.

The same cannot be said of the second form considered, namely, marriage within the prohibited degrees of relationship. For this, a formidable case has been mounted,[93] as was seen earlier. In addition to enabling the text to be read naturally, it addresses what is known from many sources to have been a source of heart-searching and friction in the New Testament Church, namely, the terms on which Jewish Christians and Gentile converts might associate.[94] The problem of marriage relationships deemed to be improper might well have been common in a Jewish Christian church in Palestine that was already including Gentiles in its mission. In that setting, especially if the Jewish roots of the church were in danger of being lost, such an emphasis might have seemed proper.

But perhaps open to fewest objections are those explanations that see the exceptive clauses as an attempt to put at ease Jewish Christian consciences troubled by Jesus' absolute prohibition of divorce. This would be particularly true of Lövestam's version of this view.[95] According to this, the exceptive clause does not deal at all with grounds on which one may seek divorce but only with the implications of a divorce imposed upon a Christian that is not of his or her seeking. As Lövestam points out, this is precisely the problem to which Paul refers in 1 Cor. 7:15, where a believer is deserted by an unbelieving spouse, and the answer is the same in both places. "Their situation is in principle in line with what is assumed in the exceptive clause in Matthew."[96]

---

son, "Divorce, Celibacy and Joseph (Mt. 1:18-25 and 19:1-12)," JSNT 49 (March 1993): 3-10. But it is questionable if this argument can be sustained. In Deut. 22, adultery is treated separately (v. 22) from premarital unchastity (vv. 13-21), and while the penalty for both is death by stoning, yet in the latter case execution takes place outside the home of the woman's father (v. 21) (i.e., the primary offense lies against her father who was deceived into believing that he was betrothing a virgin daughter [and expecting the appropriate bride-price] rather than against the husband).

93. The weightiest statement of that case is Baltensweiler, *Die Ehe im Neuen Testament*.

94. A more recent account of this view giving special attention to the social setting of the gospel is Moloney, "Matthew 19, 3-12 and Celibacy," JSNT 2 (1979): 42-60.

95. R. F. Collins's statement of this position falls under some of the objections to the "separation without remarriage" theory. See n. 51.

96. Lövestam, "Divorce and Remarriage in the New Testament," 65.

If the foregoing argument regarding the exceptive clauses is sound, then several conclusions follow with regard to them. The first is that inasmuch as they were addressed to a highly individual situation in the Early Church, namely, the problem of Jewish-Gentile relationships, they are unlikely to have any direct relevance today. This would certainly be the case with the "premarital unchastity" and "prohibited degrees" interpretations (though the latter might apply in rare circumstances or distant societies). As for the "desertion" view (the third interpretation), we have direct teaching on that in a setting complicated by Jewish-Gentile differences in Paul's teaching in 1 Cor. 7.

A second inference that may be drawn is that the line of argument followed would help to explain the absence of reference to such a Jewish-conditioned interpretation in the literature of the Early Church outside the New Testament. A striking feature of that literature is the almost total absence of specific treatment of the exceptive clauses,[97] on the one hand, and the uniform assumption that the New Testament passages affirm the permanence of marriage, on the other. Baltensweiler, who champions the "restricted relationships" view, points to the "paradoxical result" that ensued when Matthew's Gospel moved from its original Jewish Christian setting into the world of Hellenistic Christianity; the exceptive clauses were understood in a moral sense.[98]

The third inference is that the exceptive clauses, far from spelling out grounds on which divorce is permissible, in fact, do no such thing. They actually deal with complications arising for Jewish Christians from Jesus' total prohibition of divorce. These problems—whichever precise interpretation of the exceptive clauses be preferred—arise within a strictly Jewish Christian context in the first century and have little, if any, application outside of that context.

At this point it may be well to attempt a brief summary of this

---

97. See Appendix.

98. Baltensweiler, *Die Ehe im Neuen Testament,* 102. The same development is observable in the textual history of the decrees of the Council of Jerusalem in Acts 15:20. F. F. Bruce, having interpreted the decrees in a ceremonial sense to facilitate fellowship between Jewish and Gentile Christians, continues, "At a later time, when the issue dealt with by the apostolic council was no longer a live one, the provisions moved by James and adopted by the other leaders were modified so as to become purely ethical injunctions; thus the Western text makes James propose that Gentile converts 'abstain from idolatry, from fornication and from bloodshed, and from doing to others what they would not like done to themselves'" (*Book of the Acts,* 296).

lengthy examination of Jesus' teaching on divorce, even if a full statement must await consideration of the evidence of the rest of the New Testament, especially Paul. The first thing that stands out clearly is that in a setting riven by debate about grounds upon which divorce was right, Jesus affirmed that divorce was no part of God's will at all. It never had been, not even in the Mosaic Law that permitted it because of human hard-heartedness (Deut. 24:1-4). Never had it been part of God's plan. On the contrary, the divine design in creation had been for lifelong marital faithfulness (Gen. 2:24). Moreover, with the arrival of God's reign in himself, the original design had been reinstated. Such a message can only have fallen like a bombshell into the middle of the religious world of Jesus' ministry in which divorce and remarriage were taken for granted.

Second, if we ask how Jesus intended this to be applied in practice, there is less evidence to go on. The form of the divorce sayings in the Synoptic Gospels shows some application of them to different situations. In addition, the fact that some of them, such as that in Matt. 5:32, are not constructed like legal statements, suggests they were not intended to be either interpreted or enforced with legal rigor. For guidance in this matter we need evidence of how they were understood and applied by Jesus' followers. We may look to the apostle Paul for this.

Divorce According to Paul

Our second main source for reconstructing New Testament teaching on divorce is the letters of Paul, particularly 1 Cor. 7 where the subject of marriage and divorce is treated most fully. As noted at the beginning of this chapter, the teaching of Paul is pivotal in two respects. First, he clearly regards the teaching of Jesus as the foundation of his own teaching and so is an important witness to what Jesus' teaching meant. Second, much more than Jesus, Paul is under pressure to apply Jesus' teaching to real-life situations, including some that could not even have arisen during the ministry of Jesus, such as the breakdown of marriages between pagan and Christian partners. Paul thus becomes an important guide not only in regard to the content of Jesus' teaching but in regard to how it should be applied at the level of actual life and experience.

In attempting to gain an accurate picture of Paul's teaching on divorce we shall first look briefly at the attitudes to it that would have been found in Corinth, as well as at any other factors in Paul's relations with the Corinthians that will enable us to read what he wrote with more understanding. Next, we shall look at the general lines of Paul's teaching in 1 Cor. 7 that will condition his teaching on divorce. Finally, we shall turn to what he says specifically about divorce.

The Background of the Situation at Corinth

We need to take the measure of several factors likely to have a conditioning effect on our understanding of Paul. The first is the attitude to divorce held in the Jewish and Roman worlds. As constituting the background Paul was addressing, it might very well influence how he expressed himself on the subject and thereby shed light on his meaning.

The Jewish element in the Corinthian church was shown not only by its origination as a split from the synagogue (Acts 18:1-8) but also by 1 Cor. 7:18, where it speaks of some in the church who were circumcised. Reference was made in chapter 2 to the teaching of the Old Testament. While in no way did it regard divorce as of divine origin, it tolerated it as a necessary evil.[99] It was also pointed out in chapter 2 that divorce was a subject of debate and disagreement within Judaism at this time, the school of Shammai holding that divorce was permissible only on the grounds of the wife's immorality and the school of Hillel contending that anything that displeased her husband was a sufficient reason.[100] It has been claimed that the practice of the followers of Shammai differed little from that of the followers of Hillel, and that even if pious Jews maintained a high view of marriage, they regarded divorce (with the right to remarry) as preferable to a life of misery.[101] What this amounts to is that those of Jewish background in the Corinthian church would not, on the basis of their Jewish upbringing, have looked askance at divorce and would, on the same basis, have assumed that where divorce was granted, the right to remarry came with it.[102]

The Corinthian church, however, evidently contained a significant element of pagan origin, as the problem of attendance at idol worship—to mention no more—clearly shows (e.g., 1 Cor. 8:1-6). The point of importance here is that after its destruction in 146 B.C.,

---

99. See chap. 2, 53-54.

100. See chap. 2, 45-46, together with notes 3, 4, and 5.

101. See Atkinson, *To Have and to Hold,* 106-8.

102. The Mishnah states, "The essential formula in the bill of divorce is, 'Lo, thou art free to marry any man'" (Gitt. 9.3). It may be added that the Mishnah *required* divorce in cases of adultery (Sot. 5.1).

Corinth was refounded in 44 B.C. by Julius Caesar as a Roman colony. As such, not only would the Roman element be dominant, but Roman culture and Roman law would prevail.[103] Roman law had required no formalities for either the making or breaking of a marriage; marriage and divorce were strictly a private affair. However, by the time of Augustus concern for the declining birthrate led to encouragement of marriage (including penalties against the unmarried) as well as the institution of a legal process of divorce, including the requiring of divorce in cases of adultery.[104] Hence those of pagan background would have been accustomed to the practice of divorce, including the freedom to remarry that came with it.

A second background factor for which allowance must be made in understanding the teaching of 1 Cor. 7 is the state of Paul's relations with the Corinthians. It was argued above that this was one of considerable strain,[105] not least because of the Corinthian preoccupation that what it meant to be truly "spiritual"[106] allied with their suspicion that Paul was less than he might be in that regard. Consequently, he must cajole rather than confront them, quote their words while at the same time qualifying them. It is important therefore to read the chapter sensitively, aware that Paul was alert to the susceptibilities of his readers and concerned to avoid saying either too much or too little.

A third influencing factor (that underlies the second) appears to have been a distinct tendency toward asceticism on the part of the Corinthians or at least some of them. The drift of Paul's argument that sexual abstinence between married persons should not be permanent and is not obligatory (1 Cor. 7:1-6), that those married are not to seek to dissolve their marriages (v. 27), and that marriage is not a sin (v. 28) can only be directed to a mind-set that was main-

---

103. Cf. Gerd Theissen, "The 'new' Corinthians lived in a center of a country the culture of which had by that time become a 'myth.' They did not really *live* within this culture. If in many aspects of life they stood in continuity with Greek traditions, the use of Latin in their inscriptions and the construction of an amphitheater show how very un-Greek, in other ways, was their style of life" (*The Social Setting of Pauline Christianity* [Philadelphia: Fortress Press, 1988], 100).

104. For details, see Hugh Last, "The Social Policy of Augustus," in *The Cambridge Ancient History*, ed. S. A. Cook, F. E. Adcock, and M. P. Charlesworth (Cambridge, England: Cambridge University Press, 1979), 10: sections 5—7.

105. Chap. 1, 31-33.

106. For a brilliant overview of the entire Epistle from this perspective, see Fee, *First Epistle to the Corinthians*, 6-13.

taining the contrary. Jeremy Moiser has argued cogently (whatever might be said of some of the details of his position) that the two questions Paul seems to have been asked by the Corinthians were, "Although the end is near, surely there is not, as some scrupulous Christians maintain, an obligation on the married to renounce sexual pleasures and prepare themselves by prayer?"[107] And second, "Although the end is near, surely there is no obligation on the unmarried to stay as they are?"[108] These questions Paul deals with respectively in verses 1-24 and 25-40 of 1 Cor. 7.

The delicacy of Paul's problem was that he himself believed that it was better for all to be unmarried as he was (v. 7), and that in view of the "present crisis" it was better for the unmarried to remain so (vv. 26, 29-31). Indeed, it is entirely probable that it was the misunderstanding of Paul's example, if not of his teaching, that gave encouragement to the Corinthian ascetics, just as his teaching about the Second Coming had been misunderstood—with unfortunate results—in Thessalonica (2 Thess. 3:6-15). The decisive difference between Paul and the ascetics in Corinth was that whereas he believed the unmarried state was preferable on account of the existing situation, they believed it was wrong as a matter of principle and inconsistency with true spirituality.[109] Hence the need for him to say repeatedly that those who decline to take his advice, and proceed to marry, have committed no sin (vv. 28, 36).

A fourth factor conditioning Paul's teaching regarding both marriage and divorce in 1 Cor. 7 was his view of the sociopolitical situation then prevailing, which he characterized as "the present crisis" (v. 26) or "the shortness of the time" (v. 29). The former expression indicates a situation already existing, which Paul further describes by the word "tribulation" in verse 28, while the latter places it within the context of the suffering the Church must endure while it awaits the coming consummation (Rom. 8:18). In such a situation, which would be especially testing for those with family responsibilities, Paul's advice is that Christians should remain in the station in which they were at conversion (1 Cor. 7:17-24). He applies this to circumci-

---

107. Jeremy Moiser, "A Reassessment of Paul's View of Marriage with Reference to 1 Cor. 7," JSNT 18 (1983): 110.

108. Ibid., 112.

109. Cf. Fee, "His problem therefore is how to affirm celibacy without at the same time affirming their asceticism" (First Epistle to the Corinthians, 323; see his further remarks to the same effect on 330, 333, 341).

sion and slavery as well as to marriage;[110] indeed he affirms that this is his rule "in all the churches" (v. 17*b*).

There are only two exceptions to this rule Paul will countenance within the sphere of marriage. One is in a mixed marriage that the pagan partner refuses to continue (v. 15), so that the Christian partner has no option. The other is in the case of "virgins" (vv. 25-28, 36-38). Precisely what is denoted by this expression is greatly debated.[111] It appears to refer to betrothed couples, for whom Paul's rule to "remain as they are" would condemn them to a state of permanent betrothal. This, indeed, is what Paul recommends but with two important qualifications.

First, Paul's counsel is his own, not the Lord's, and is to be treated as the advice of a trustworthy spiritual guide (vv. 25, 40). At the same time Paul does not enforce it as a command. On the contrary, the touchstone is not Paul's opinion but whether or not the men of such couples feel that the refusal to marry would be unfair to the women who were betrothed to them (v. 36) or, again, whether the men in question have the self-control to forgo marriage (v. 37).

Second, if couples in this situation marry, they have committed no sin (vv. 28, 36, 38). Paul did not regard marriage as sinful per se; he simply thought it was undesirable in certain circumstances.

These four considerations entered importantly into the background of the agitation in the church in Corinth about marriage. They should be kept in mind as we turn next to Paul's specific teaching about divorce.

Paul's Direct Teaching About Divorce in 1 Cor. 7

There are at least two sections of the chapter in which Paul addresses directly the question of divorce, the first being verses 10-11. The structure of the chapter is important in giving guidance as to the category of individuals he has in mind at each successive stage. First Corinthians 7 is the first passage in the Epistle where Paul evidently takes up a question the Corinthians had addressed to him, "Now for the matters you wrote about" (7:1). The telltale formula indicating that this is so is the expression "Now for," or words to that effect. It

---

110. "Nevertheless" (Greek *ei me*) certainly refers to the negative verb in verse 15, "is not bound" (so Fee, *First Epistle to the Corinthians*, 309, n. 12). However, that in turn is linked in thought to verses 12-14, of which it is the opposite.

111. For a survey of the possibilities, see Fee, *First Epistle to the Corinthians*, 325-27.

occurs again in verse 25, suggesting that Paul is moving on to another question. This implies that in chapter 7 he deals with two questions relating in some way to marriage.

As was argued earlier, the first question appears to be concerned with sexual relations and marriage. Accordingly in verses 1-7 Paul addresses those who, following the principle that "it is good for a man not to have sexual relations" with a woman (v. 1b, mar.), either practiced abstinence within marriage or avoided marriage altogether.[112] His reply is that such a course is acceptable for those who, like himself, have received the gift of continence (v. 7); for others it would be a high road to immorality (v. 2) and should not become the norm within marriage (v. 5).

Next, he turns to "the unmarried and the widows" (v. 8), who are probably to be understood as the "demarried"; that is, those who had been married but had become unmarried through bereavement.[113] His counsel to them is identical with his counsel to the first group. While the single state is good—it was Paul's own state[114]—it is not the only acceptable option, and if they are not controlling themselves,[115] it is not merely *good,* "it is *better* to marry than to burn with passion" (v. 9, emphasis added).[116] If the pursuit of abstinence merely results in incontinence, then the goal has become self-defeating.

---

112. That Paul has these two categories in mind, and not just the married, seems clear from verse 2 in which he affirms that each man should have his own wife and each woman her own husband. Accordingly the preferred translation of verse 1b should be that quoted in the text (which represents the NIV margin) and not that of the NIV text, "It is good for a man not to marry," implying that Paul is addressing the unmarried, which is plainly not so as verses 3-5 make clear.

113. "The unmarried and the widows" is an odd combination, not least because Paul has just addressed the unmarried in verses 1-2. It is probable that the Greek word literally rendered "unmarried" should be translated "widowers," a sense that it could carry in Hellenistic Greek. For details, see Fee, *First Epistle to the Corinthians,* 287-88.

114. While verse 7 leaves Paul's marital state undefined beyond implying that he was single, verse 8 implies that he was a widower. Many interpreters lean to this conclusion on the ground that, as a rabbi, Paul must have been married (for references, see Fee, *First Epistle to the Corinthians,* 288, n. 7). F. F. Bruce advances the further possibility that he may have been deserted by an unbelieving wife, as described in verse 15 (*1 and 2 Corinthians,* 68, 70).

115. There is no equivalent in the Greek text for the word "cannot" in "if they cannot control themselves" (v. 9a, NIV). The verb is a simple indicative, "if they are not controlling themselves," implying immoral conduct.

116. Following from the interpretation suggested in note 114, the meaning of verse 9b will be that marriage is better than being devoured by sinful passion. Cf. Fee, "Paul is not so much offering marriage as the remedy for the sexual desire of 'inflamed youth' . . . but as the proper alternative for those who are already consumed by that desire and are sinning" (*First Epistle to the Corinthians,* 289).

This brings Paul to a third group who are of direct interest to our concern, those who are "demarried" by divorce (vv. 10-11). Since the immediately following verses are addressed to "the rest" (v. 12), and their contents show the reference is to mixed marriages in which one partner was Christian and the other pagan, it is a fair inference that those referred to in verses 10-11 are both Christians. Indeed, this has been the assumption throughout verses 1-9. Therefore, taking verses 10-11 in the flow of the chapter as a whole—indeed of the entire Epistle—in which the overriding concern is how to be truly "spiritual," it would seem that some married Christians in Corinth had concluded that since "it is good for a man not to have sexual relations" with a woman (v. 1*b,* mar.), the most spiritual thing a married Christian could do was to bring the marriage to an end—by divorce. The reasoning that the Christian answer to sexual immorality was no sex at all was thus being pushed to its final limit. That is to say, far from being prompted by selfish motives, divorce was being contemplated for spiritual reasons; that was how you became the best type of Christian, separated from the flesh and wholly spiritual.

Against this background, we may now seek to uncover the import of Paul's teaching more fully. Verses 10-11 are remarkable in several ways. First, they are remarkable with regard to the source of the teaching given. While Paul begins by stating that he gives the command, he immediately corrects himself by interjecting, "not I, but the Lord." Taken with the disclaimers in verses 12 ("I, not the Lord") and 25 ("I have no command from the Lord"), this seems clearly to mean that regarding divorces between Christians, Paul had knowledge of an actual pronouncement of Jesus, whereas Jesus had given no pronouncement on mixed marriages and "virgins." The command given by Jesus was: "A wife must not separate from her husband. . . . and a husband must not divorce his wife" (vv. 10*b,* 11*b*).[117] This is essentially the same as the saying of Jesus in Mark

---

117. It is important not to be misled by the use of the term "separate" in 1 Cor. 7:10. In later ecclesiastical as in modern civil law, separation is a legal state short of divorce. A superficial reading of verse 11*a* might seem to have this in mind, "But if she does (separate) she must remain unmarried or else be reconciled to her husband." However, the statement makes just as good sense if Paul is speaking of divorce, and the context shows clearly that this is the case. Thus, the parallel statement to verse 10*a* is verse 11*b,* "and a husband must not divorce his wife." Again, the word "separate" in verse 15 is clearly used in parallel to verses 12 and 13 where a word for "divorce" is clearly used. Moulton and Milligan say that "separate" (Greek *chorizomai*) "has almost become a technical term in connexion with divorce," citing 1 Cor. 7:10, 11, 15, besides

10:11-12. "Anyone who divorces his wife and marries another woman commits adultery against her. And if she divorces her husband and marries another man, she commits adultery."

The main differences in the Marcan form of the saying are threefold. First, it is not merely divorce that is forbidden but divorce and remarriage. Second, the Marcan saying states the consequence of such divorce and remarriage—namely adultery. It is especially notable that contrary to prevailing Jewish law in which adultery was an offense only against an adulteress's husband, Mark indicates that a husband's adultery is an offense against his wife. Third, it is striking that in the form of Jesus' saying in 1 Cor. 7:10*b* and 11*b,* the command against divorce is addressed to the woman first, precisely the reverse of the order in Mark.

What this amounts to is that while consciously dependent on the teaching of Jesus, Paul does not quote Jesus' words—either in their Marcan form or any other form in which they are found (e.g., Luke 16:18)—nor does he simply paraphrase them. Rather, he *applies* the teaching of Jesus to the situation confronting him. This is probably the reason why, of all the reports of Jesus' teaching on divorce, this is the only one in which the wife is addressed first, because the problem in the Corinthian church arose because a woman or women either had divorced or were contemplating divorcing their husbands in the interests of leading "holier" lives as ascetics.[118]

This leads directly to a second striking feature in these verses, namely, that no sooner has Paul laid down a command of the Lord than he immediately provides for its being breached in some measure. Paul quotes with approval the Lord's teaching, "A wife must not separate from her husband," and then promptly makes provision for a situation in which that very thing may happen, "But if she does . . ." (v. 11).[119] Further, Paul does not treat such persons—husbands

---

other literature (*The Vocabulary of the Greek New Testament, Illustrated from the Papyri and Other Non-Literary Sources* [London: Hodder and Stoughton, 1952], 696). For a full, up-to-date discussion, see Collins, *Divorce in the New Testament,* 16-22.

118. See Collins, *Divorce in the New Testament,* 22-24. Also Margaret Y. Macdonald, "Women Holy in Body and Spirit: The Social Setting of 1 Corinthians 7," *New Testament Studies* 36, n. 2 (April 1990): 161-81. Collins, however, while agreeing that a specific situation is in mind, questions whether the language is precise enough to refer to a single individual or to denote the purpose for which divorce is sought (*Divorce in the New Testament,* 25-29).

119. Fee comments, "To press for the ideal, and even to urge it as a command of the Lord, does not make it binding law; and the possibility that exceptions will occur is simply a concession to reality" (*First Epistle to the Corinthians,* 295, n. 24).

or wives—as automatically excommunicated from the church. He regards them still within the sphere of church discipline. Yet more noteworthy is that he does not order the divorcing party to return to his or her partner even though he lists that as an option. The courses open to such individuals are two, "She must remain unmarried or else be reconciled to her husband" (v. 11a).[120]

Paul was seeking to deal with the situation in a way that conformed as closely as possible to the teaching of Jesus, teaching that, as we have seen, forbids divorce. But Paul did not apply Jesus' teaching legalistically. Divorced persons are not outlawed, nor are they ordered to return to their divorced spouses, assuming that to be possible. They *are* instructed not to remarry, a directive readily understandable in the Corinthian situation in which remarriage following divorce for "spiritual" reasons could readily become an occasion for abuse on the part of those within the church and ridicule on the part of those without. This passage shows an application of Jesus' teaching in a situation in which it is not fully applicable. Paul's approach is not to conclude that since Jesus' teaching against divorce could not be applied fully, it should not be applied at all—an all-or-nothing approach that demanded total conformity or exclusion. Paul rather recognized that while the divine pattern was lifelong marriage and anything short of that was a departure from God's will, yet there were some situations where complete conformity with the divine pattern was not possible. The specific case he had in mind was one in which divorce had taken place or was contemplated and reconciliation was not possible.

At the same time, the divine standard was not irrelevant. On the contrary, each individual case was measured against it, and it remained the ideal to which the Corinthian Christians must seek to conform as closely as the individual case permitted.[121]

---

120. Heinrich Baltensweiler, noting that Paul does not apply the teaching of Jesus legalistically, suggests that he can allow divorce in these circumstances because it is a means to prevent something worse—the remarriage that the teaching of Jesus forbade but was commonplace in the Roman world (Baltensweiler, *Die Ehe im Neuen Testament,* 263).

121. David L. Dungan concludes, "Thus Paul seems to be a middle term containing within himself a veneration for the earliest tradition of the words of the Lord, as well as a lively innovativeness in applying them to guide the missionary Church" (*The Sayings of Jesus in the Churches of Paul* [Philadelphia: Fortress Press, 1971], 145. While at that point Dungan is referring to the Lord's command concerning support for the

Paul now turns to a fourth group in Corinth, who are labeled simply "the rest" (v. 12). Despite suggestions to the contrary, these are almost certainly to be understood as parties to mixed marriages between Christians and pagans.[122] Paul proceeds to address both Christian husbands and wives, as in the three types of marital status already treated, except that, as with the first two, he deals with the husband's position first. He begins by making clear that, in contrast with his instructions to the married, he cannot quote a word of the Lord on this case, "To the rest I say this (I, not the Lord)" (v. 12a).

Jesus was never confronted with the problem of mixed marriages and so never pronounced on it. Nonetheless, Paul does so as an authoritative, apostolic interpreter of the mind of Christ with every expectation that his directions will be complied with.[123] Accordingly, he adopts the imperative mood: "If any brother has a wife who is not

---

apostles, the same principle would hold regarding the Lord's command concerning divorce, which Dungan treats in Part II of his book. His reference in the quotation above to the missionary situation is illuminating in view of adjustments and adaptations sometimes necessitated there.

122. Various alternative understandings have been suggested. Dungan takes "the rest" to be nonbelievers, in keeping with Paul's usage elsewhere (e.g., 1 Thess. 4:13; 5:6) (ibid., 93-94). This is possible grammatically, but inasmuch as Paul proceeds to direct his counsel to the Christian partners, a wider sense seems to be required. P. J. Tomson argues that "the rest" are Gentile Christians involved in informal (but in Hellenistic law, legitimate) marriages to pagans (*Paul and the Jewish Law: Halakha in the Letters of the Apostle to the Gentiles: Jewish Traditions in Early Christian Literacy,* in *Compendia Rerum Iudicairum ad Novum Testamentum 3/1* [Assen: von Gorcum, 1990], 108-9, 118). This may be so since, as Tomson argues, a Jew would be unlikely to be married to a pagan. However, even if that were so, it is incidental to the point Paul appears to have in mind, which is to evaluate existing marital status from a Christian perspective. The material element in this grouping is that one partner is Christian and the other is not.

123. C. K. Barrett captures perfectly the import of Paul's statement, "I say, not the Lord," in commenting, "Paul distinguishes sharply his own judgment from a pronouncement traceable to Jesus, but this does not mean that he regards his charge here as having no authority, or even significantly less authority than that of verse 10" (*The First Epistle to the Corinthians* [London: A. and C. Black, 1973], 163). Throughout this chapter, Paul practices a mode of interpretation common among the rabbis. For an account, see Peter Richardson, "'I Say, Not the Lord': Personal Opinion, Apostolic Authority and the Development of Early Christian Halakah," *Tyndale Bulletin* 31 (1980): 65-86. Richardson writes, "The whole chapter functions as *halakah,* but lenient *halakah.* The attempt to distinguish between what is more and what is less authoritative—which was the starting point of the study—fails" (84). A much fuller and more recent treatment of Paul's interpretative method can be found in P. J. Tomson, *Paul and the Jewish Law,* chaps. 2 and 3. For a close examination of verse 12a against the rabbinic background, see Collins, *Divorce in the New Testament,* 42-43, 46.

a believer and she is willing to live with him, he must not divorce her. And if a woman has a husband who is not a believer and he is willing to live with her, she must not divorce him" (vv. 12-13).

The verse immediately following shows that again the Corinthian concern is prompted by an exaggerated concern for holiness, Would not a Christian be defiled by sexual relations with an unbelieving spouse? Paul replies that the "contamination" works precisely the other way around, "the unbelieving husband has been sanctified through his wife, and the unbelieving wife has been sanctified through her believing husband"—a principle Paul also extends to the children of such marriages (v. 14).[124] Thus far Paul's meaning is clear and consistent with the word of Jesus applied in verses 10 and 11. Indeed, strictly speaking, it is more consistent with it because in verse 11 Paul admits divorce as a possibility, but in verses 12 and 13 he provides no room for it and insists that the Christian is not to take any initiative to sue for divorce.

But suppose the unbelieving partner insists upon a divorce? Two critical questions clearly follow. First, is the believing partner to accept such a divorce as dissolving the marriage? Second, if so, does this bring the freedom to remarry? Paul, however, does not formulate the issues in precisely that way nor is his language wholly clear, at least on the surface. It will be best to follow the argument as he develops it and see how he addresses the questions indicated.

First, Paul spells out the believer's response. "But if the unbeliever leaves, let him do so. A believing man or woman is not bound in such circumstances" (v. 15*ab*). The word translated "leaves" is the same word rendered "separate" in verses 10-11, and it was shown there[125] that it means "divorce," a sense that is confirmed by verses 12 and 13, where refusing to "divorce" is the parallel response Paul enjoins upon believers married to unbelievers. But what is meant by the statement, "A believing man or woman *is not bound*" (v. 15, emphasis added)? At the very least this means that the believer is not bound to try to hold together a marriage that the unbelieving part-

---

124. Precisely what Paul means by such sanctification is debated. Most probably he is thinking in Old Testament terms in which a ritually holy object could transmit holiness to whatever it touched, like the altar coals on Isaiah's lips. When the cultic image is ethicized, it would mean that an unbeliever lives within the sphere of holy influence, and Paul believed that holy contagion was more potent than unholy contagion. For a somewhat different explanation, see Fee, *First Epistle to the Corinthians,* 299-302.

125. See n. 117.

ner wishes to dissolve. The term rendered "bound" means "bound as a slave." C. K. Barrett's translation and comment bring out the sense well: "In such cases the Christian brother or sister is not enslaved, that is, to a mechanical retention of a relationship the other party wishes to abandon."[126]

Second, the reason Paul urges Christian acquiescence in such forced divorces is that "God has called us to live in peace" (v. 15c). If "peace" is the opposite of being bound or enslaved, the meaning will be that the torment and tension of trying to maintain a relationship the pagan partner does not want and has brought to an end will be the reverse of the peace at the heart of the Christian calling. If, on the other hand, "peace" stands in opposition to divorce, then the meaning will be that the torment of divorce will be destructive of Christian peace. In view of the statement that the divorcing pagan should be allowed to leave, the former gives the better sense.

However, it is possible that verse 15c is to be taken with verse 16, so as to read, "God has called us to live in peace. For how do you know, wife, whether you will save your husband? Or, how do you know, husband, whether you will save your wife?"[127] The effect of this is to add a second reason to that given in verse 14 for the refusal of a Christian to divorce a pagan spouse, namely, continuance of the marriage creates the possibility that the unbeliever will be converted.[128] In that case, verse 15c not only provides a link with verse 16 but also resumes the thought of verse 14 by adding a second reason why divorce should not be resorted to. The statement about the unbelieving spouse's departure (v. 15ab) thus becomes a passing comment in a passage chiefly concerned with giving directions against divorce together with supporting reasons.[129]

---

126. *First Corinthians,* 166. The attempt to refer that to which the believer is "not bound" in such cases to the command against divorce in verses 10 and 11 (A. Robertson and A. Plummer, *A Critical and Exegetical Commentary on the First Epistle of St. Paul to the Corinthians,* in ICC [Edinburgh: T. and T. Clark, 1958], 143) can scarcely apply to a case where the unbeliever is doing the divorcing and believers have just been forbidden to do so (vv. 12-13).

127. The conjunction "for" links verse 15c with verse 16. However, it is left untranslated in NIV.

128. This assumes that verse 16 is to be understood in an optimistic rather than a pessimistic sense. For a recent review and evaluation of these options favoring the former, see Collins, *Divorce in the New Testament,* 60-62.

129. For a brief account of the hermeneutical arguments, see Collins, *Divorce in the New Testament,* 62-63. It is worth pointing out that if verse 16 is taken in an optimistic sense, it *must* refer back to verses 12-14; for if the unbelieving spouse has departed, the

The upshot of this is that, as in verse 11, Paul again accepts divorce as a possibility, in this case as the initiative of a pagan married to a Christian. But, again as in verse 11, he accepts it in the context of the insistence that divorce is not part of God's will and that the Christian partner in a mixed marriage should not take the initiative to secure it. The answer to the first of the two questions posed above then (whether the believing partner is to accept divorce as ending the marriage) is clearly yes.

This still leaves us with the second question, Does such divorce bring the freedom to remarry? Here we must return to verse 15b: "A believing man or woman is not bound in such circumstances." It was maintained above that, at the very least, this must mean the believer was not bound to try to hold a marriage together by force or, when it had been legally terminated, by pretense. However, some interpreters have contended that "not being bound" denotes much more than this; specifically, it implies the freedom to remarry.

In favor of this are several factors. First, in the earlier context where divorce is contemplated and permitted between Christians (vv. 10-11), specific limits are placed on the options of the divorcing wife, celibacy or reconciliation. It would be odd if nothing were said about remarriage where that question would have arisen with redoubled force, namely, in cases of divorce by a pagan partner. Second, perhaps it is this very question addressed in verse 15b, "A believing man or woman is not bound in such circumstances." It is true that the word rendered "bound" (Greek *douloō*) is not that normally used by Paul to denote the marriage bond (Greek *deō*, as in 1 Cor. 7:39; Rom. 7:2). If anything, it is a much stronger term, denoting enslavement,[130] so that whereas the normal term would have signified that

---

circumstances for his or her sanctification have been removed as has the opportunity for his or her being won to Christian faith by the conduct of the Christian spouse.

130. K. H. Rengstorf, noting that the term *douloun* means basically "to make a slave," "to enslave," and that the New Testament always uses it figuratively, comments, "In 1 C. 7:15 *douloun* expresses total binding by another." In further illustration of its meaning, he quotes Titus 2:3, "Teach the older women . . . not to be slanderers or addicted *(dedoulōmenas)* to much wine" (Rengstorf, "Doulos, etc.," TDNT, 2:279). It is hazardous to argue that since, in three other instances (Rom. 7:2; 1 Cor. 7:27, 39) Paul uses "bind" *(deō)* of the marriage bond, that his use of "enslave" *(douloō)* in 1 Cor. 7:15 to mean "not bound" denotes something less than the reversal of the marriage bond. Both terms tend to be used literally or metaphorically rather than legally. But when occasion requires it, they can carry legal overtones. *Douloun* seems to carry legal overtones in Gal. 4:3 (cf. 5). It would be odd if, within a single section of the Epistle, "free" meant "free to remarry" (as in v. 39) and "not bound" meant "free not to maintain the marriage" (15) but not "free to remarry."

the marriage bond was ended, the stronger term repudiates the existence of a continuing relationship dismissively. Moreover, the language of bondage and freedom Paul uses may very well be borrowed from his Jewish antecedents where it was used in this very sense, as the Mishnah makes plain: "The essential formula in the bill of divorce is, 'Lo, thou art free to marry any man.' R. Judah says, 'Let this be from me thy writ of divorce and letter of dismissal and deed of liberation, that thou mayest marry whatsoever man thou wilt.' The essential formula in a writ of emancipation is, 'Lo, thou art a freed woman: lo, thou belongest to thyself.'"[131] Paul thus appears to countenance divorce and remarriage in cases where a Christian spouse is divorced and deserted by a pagan.[132]

---

131. Gitt. 9.3, as in Danby, *Mishnah,* 319. Further contemporary evidence from Judaism is listed by Keener, *And Marries Another,* 171, n. 87. It accords well with such links to Paul's Jewish background if, as has been claimed above (see n. 123), 1 Cor. 7 is written as a piece of rabbinic *halakah;* and—in Richardson's phrase—"lenient *halakah.*"

132. Scholarship is divided on this point. Broadly speaking, three views are held. (1) Some scholars maintain that "not bound" cannot refer to remarriage, since this has already been excluded in verse 11, and beyond that, that remarriage would be inconsistent with Paul's general advice throughout the chapter, namely that "each one should retain the place in life that the Lord assigned to him and to which God has called him" (v. 17; cf. vv. 20, 24). Dungan concludes, "To judge from what Paul says explicitly, nothing more is permitted the Christian than accepting the unbelieving partner's wish for divorce" (*Sayings of Jesus in the Churches of Paul,* 97). Beyond these points, those who hold this view tend to appeal chiefly to the general biblical teaching on marriage and divorce. See, for example, Dupont, *Mariage et Divorce,* 57-61, and more fully Heth and Wenham, *Jesus and Divorce,* 140-44, whose arguments are restated by Heth in House, *Divorce and Remarriage,* 109-14. (2) A second group of scholars interprets the passage on some such lines as those indicated in the text. See for example, Murray, *Divorce,* 73-75; Keener, *And Marries Another,* 50, 61-62; Edgar in House, *Divorce and Remarriage,* 187-91; Larry Richards in House, *Divorce and Remarriage,* 239-42. F. F. Bruce understands the abandoned Christian as being "in a state of what amounted to widowhood. No compulsion should be exerted on the unbeliever to remain or return, and presumably remarriage would not be completely excluded for the believer" (*1 and 2 Corinthians,* 70). It is worth noting that, for all its absolute opposition to divorce, the Roman Catholic Church has always permitted the dissolving of a marriage that fell within the strict parameters of "Pauline privilege," as this has come to be called, even if the marriage has been consummated. For references, see Fee, *First Epistle to the Corinthians,* 302, n. 34. A recent statement from the Roman Catholic side is Crossan, *Bond of Marriage,* 26-29. (3) A third group of interpreters concludes that Paul does not address the issue of remarriage in 1 Cor. 7:15. There is a partial overlap between this view and that described in point 1 above. However, those in group 3, while holding that Paul says nothing of remarriage in this context, decline to conclude that he is opposed to it. Cf. I. H. Marshall, "What is not clear is whether in such a case the Christian partner is free

Before attempting to sum up Paul's teaching on divorce in the two sections in which he treats it directly, it may be worthwhile to look briefly at a third context in which some interpreters hold he also deals with it, namely, 1 Cor. 7:27-28. The NIV translates the verses: "Are you married? Do not seek a divorce. Are you unmarried? Do not look for a wife. But if you do marry, you have not sinned; and if a virgin marries, she has not sinned. But those who marry will face many troubles in this life, and I want to spare you this." The *Revised English Bible* is even more explicit, rendering: "Are you bound in marriage? Do not seek a dissolution. Has your marriage been dissolved? Do not seek a wife. But if you do marry, you are not doing anything wrong, nor does a girl if she marries; it is only that those who marry will have hardships to endure, and my aim is to spare you." If these, particularly the latter, are faithful translations, then we appear to have Pauline sanction for divorce and remarriage; for while he discourages both (and marriage too), it is not because they are inherently objectionable, but merely because marriage may occasion difficulties.

Nor does this view lack scholarly support. The translations quoted would themselves lead us to draw that conclusion. Craig Keener claims the word translated "unmarried" in NIV and "dissolved" in REB means literally not "free" but "freed." He continues, "The person who is 'freed' can therefore only be a person who was previously bound, and in the context this can only mean that the person was previously married. Given the fact that 'freed' in the first line refers to divorce, we must take it as referring to divorce in the second line as well; if Paul did not mean us to take the word the same way in

---

to remarry (the so-called 'Pauline privilege'). This particular situation is clearly not one of much contemporary relevance, but it does raise the question whether in the analogous situation of the so-called 'innocent party' remarriage is allowable. On this point, there does not seem to be any clear New Testament teaching" ("Divorce," in NIDNTT, 507). A fuller statement of this view can be found in Fee, *First Epistle to the Corinthians,* 302-3, where he concludes, "All of this is not to say that Paul *disallows* remarriage in such cases; he simply does not speak to it at all." Collins straddles groups 1 and 3, asserting that the apostle does not explicitly answer our question "whether Christians divorced by unbelievers may remarry." Noting that such persons are *agamoi* (unmarried) and that Paul permits others of that description to marry (vv. 8-9, 39), Collins concludes, "Given this situation it is quite likely that Paul would have expected a Christian who became *agamos* because he or she had been divorced by an unbelieving spouse to remarry" (*Divorce in the New Testament,* 63-64).

the same set of instructions, he could have indicated this easily enough by using a different word."[133]

However, this view is open to several objections. First, and generally, if this passage speaks of divorce and remarriage, it does so with an acceptance uncharacteristic of Paul's earlier references in the chapter (vv. 10-11, 12-16). There Paul has been concerned to hedge and restrict them; here he appears to take them in his stride. Second, if he is speaking of divorce and remarriage in general, it is hard to see how these are relevant in a context in which his argument has progressed to treating the problem of "virgins." By far the best sense to give to those thus labeled are persons betrothed but not yet married.[134]

If Paul's standard advice throughout this chapter, that all remain as they were when they became Christians, were applied to such individuals, this would mean that they would remain "in a state of permanent betrothal."[135] Paul repeats this advice (vv. 26-27, 29-35), adding, however, that it is no sin to decide otherwise and enter into marriage (vv. 27-28, 36-38). Now if this is a fair reconstruction of the context, one must ask how verses 27-28 relate to it. Verse 25 indicates that a new theme is being taken up,[136] namely, virgins; and while it is not impossible that Paul might begin with a generalized application of his principle (vv. 26-27) and then turn to the new topic, it is odd that verse 28 should read as a continuation of verse 27 and use the word "virgin" as though that had been the topic all the time.

This leads to a third problem with this view—which may also point to its solution—namely, that the language allegedly used in verse 27 to refer to divorce does not normally convey that meaning. On the contrary the term used for that purpose in verse 27, variously rendered "divorce," "unmarried" (NIV), and "dissolved" (REB), liter-

133. Keener, *And Marries Another,* 63. Cf. Colin Brown, "Separate, Divide," in NIDNTT 3, esp. 536-38. A more polemical statement of this view (in critique of Heth and Wenham) is William F. Luck, *Divorce and Remarriage: Recovering the Biblical View* (San Francisco: Harper and Row, 1987), 176-85.

134. The various options are reviewed evenhandedly by Fee, *First Epistle to the Corinthians,* 325-27. For a developed statement of the position adopted here, see J. K. Elliott, "Paul's Teaching on Marriage in I Corinthians: Some Problems Considered," NTS 19, 2 (January 1973): 219-25.

135. The phrase is F. F. Bruce's, *I Corinthians,* 73.

136. The formula "now concerning," which occurs at 7:1; 8:1; 12:1 occurs here also. In each place it appears to indicate the beginning of a reply to a question asked by the Corinthians in their letter to Paul.

ally means "loosed" (Greek *luō*), and there is no known instance of its being used in the sense of "divorce." On the other hand, there are numerous instances of its being used to denote release from the terms of a contract,[137] which is precisely the problem "concerning virgins" being dealt with here. Paul's advice is that a man betrothed to a woman should not break that commitment, but conversely, a man who has no such obligation should not seek a wife.[138] At the same time he insists that neither the betrothed man nor the virgin to whom he is betrothed will sin by choosing to marry, though he warns that they will endure hardship that he would wish them to be spared (v. 28).[139]

Now that we have examined the specific aspects of Paul's view of marriage and divorce, we may seek to summarize it and, at the same time, discern the principles that underlie it. We may begin with his understanding of and attitude toward marriage. It is of the utmost importance to keep in mind that nowhere does he expound his view of divorce in the context of a comprehensive statement of his attitude toward marriage. Everything that he writes of marriage in 1 Cor. 7 is written in response to the questions of the Corinthians, at least some of whom rejected marriage as unspiritual. His teaching about marriage is further complicated by the fact that he himself was celibate (v. 7) and, moreover, believed that celibacy facilitated greater freedom in the service of God (vv. 32-35). Interlinked with this, though distinguishable from it, was Paul's conviction that "the present crisis" (v. 26) was such that marriage could only be a source of stress to anyone committed to faith in Christ.

---

137. See the evidence in Moulton, *Vocabulary of the Greek New Testament,* 384.

138. This interpretation would imply that the word "woman" (Greek *gunē*) is used in two senses in verse 27. In its first two occurrences, it would mean "woman," while in the third it would more probably mean "wife." Elliott comments, "Throughout Paul's writings *gunē* (woman) is an ambiguous term . . . *gunē* seems only to mean 'wife' where the context is clear. Where the context is not clear *gunē* is qualified" (Elliott, "Paul's Teaching on Marriage in I Corinthians," 222). This interpretation would further imply that the word rendered "bound" (Greek *deō*) in verse 27, meaning "bound to a woman" and translated as "bound in marriage" in REB and as "married" in NIV, will likewise take its meaning from the context. Accordingly, Elliott understands it here to mean "bound by a *promise* of marriage" (223) (i.e., engaged). In other passages normally cited to show that it means "married" (e.g., 1 Cor. 7:39; Rom. 7:2), this is clear from the context.

139. That Paul finds it necessary to say that the marriage of engaged couples is "not sin" is occasioned by the claim of at least some Corinthians that it was and not by any ascetic proclivities of Paul. See Fee, *First Epistle to the Corinthians,* 332-33.

These factors are largely negative in their estimate of marriage. However, it is important to note that these positions are qualified significantly by other views expressed in the same chapter. Thus, Paul recognized not only the sexual urge but also its indulgence within the marriage bond as being perfectly normal (vv. 3-5, 8-9, 36-38). Further, he rejected the inference that marriage was a sin per se— even in the "present crisis" in which he believed it constituted an obstacle in God's service. Against this background we may now summarize the principles underlying Paul's teaching.

First, the baseline of his view was the lifelong character of the marriage covenant. This he founded on the teaching of Jesus: "To the married I give this command (not I, but the Lord): A wife must not separate from her husband. . . . And a husband must not divorce his wife" (vv. 10, 11c). This principle he reaffirms at the end of the chapter: "A woman is bound to her husband as long as he lives. But if her husband dies, she is free to marry anyone she wishes, but he must belong to the Lord" (v. 39). P. J. Tomson points out that in terms of prevailing views in Judaism, both Pharisaic and Sadducean, Paul's basic principle represented a departure from both.[140]

Logically, this would entail a total ban on divorce. Yet this is precisely what Paul does not do. On the contrary, he proceeds to apply the principle in ways that are formally at variance with it:[141] first, in recognizing the divorce of a Christian woman of her pagan husband (vv. 10-11); and second, in not only recognizing the fact of a divorce of a Christian woman by her pagan husband but also, apparently, freeing the Christian partner from the bond of marriage so that she is free to marry again (v. 15).

This exhibits a second principle in Paul's teaching. While he affirmed the law and specifically the teaching of Jesus, he did not apply it in a legalistic way. Indeed, this is virtually the pattern on which

---

140. "While he calls himself a former Pharisee (Phil. 3:5; cf. Acts 22:3) he formally transmits a *halakha* not supported either by the Hillelite or the Shammaite wing of Pharisaism. He explicitly ascribes it to a commandment of Jesus (1 Cor. 7:10f)" (*Paul and the Jewish Law,* 123).

141. Numerous writers make this observation. For example, Larry Richards, "Despite the exceptionless form of some of Paul's sayings in 1 Corinthians 7, his statements about remaining unmarried or else being reconciled, and even his command not to divorce, are not exceptionless at all" (House, *Divorce and Remarriage,* 241). Again Peter Richardson writes, "So Paul cites a word of the Lord, orders obedience to it, and immediately allows an exception to it against the clear intent of both what the Lord says and what Paul himself commands" ("I Say, Not the Lord," 82).

the whole of 1 Cor. 7 is written. Repeatedly, he states a principle, only to modify it as soon as he has written it. Thus, in verse 1 he affirms that sexual abstinence is good but at once modifies it by adding that this way of life is only for those so gifted (vv. 2-7). In verse 8 he affirms that the "demarried" should remain so but modifies it for those lacking self-control (v. 9). In verse 10 he quotes Jesus' ruling against divorce but promptly qualifies it by spelling out the terms on which divorce is admissible (v. 11). And so throughout the chapter.[142]

If we inquire as to why Paul follows this principle, the answer is not difficult to discern. It is clearly that the rigorous application of the law leads, in many cases, not to the upholding of the intention of the law, but rather to its subversion. The enforcement of sexual abstinence on those—married or "demarried"—who lack the gift of self-control will lead only to immorality, which is precisely the opposite of the law's purpose. The enforcement of the law against divorce will culminate, in many cases, not in the unity of the marriage relationship envisaged in the beginning, but in the shackling together by legal chains of those for whom an authentic marriage relationship has ceased to be a reasonable possibility. Hence a Christian spouse is not to regard himself or herself as being enslaved to an unwilling pagan partner.

There can be no doubt of Paul's commitment to the divine design of the permanence of marriage. His statements in verses 10-11 and 39 place this beyond all doubt. However, in a world of fallen creatures who not only make mistakes but willfully sin in marriage-related decisions and actions, the divine pattern is not always capable of realization. In such cases how could the law best be fulfilled? Richardson's statement seems to capture Paul's attitude well: "Paul's hermeneutic was based on his perception of spiritual insight, aimed at an undivided response to the Lord, in an interim time when the

---

142. Peter Richardson sees this as the employment by Paul of the rabbinic method of the development of *halakah*. See his account of it in "I Say, Not the Lord," 74-79, and his analysis of 1 Cor. 7 as an example of it on 79-84. Note his summary statement, "Paul assumes a kind of authority for himself—an apostolic authority— which includes the possibility of developing *halakah*. This apostolic *exousia*, however, has several sides: it contains within it the right to command, yet even when commanding it is lenient" ("I Say, Not the Lord," 85). For a still fuller treatment of Pauline *halakah*, see Peter J. Tomson, *Paul and the Jewish Law,* chaps. 2 and 3.

urgency of imitating Christ took precedence over a rigorous pursuit of the law."[143]

We may now endeavor to bring together the results of our study of the New Testament evidence. The first conclusion, which emerges unequivocally, is that the baseline of the New Testament understanding is that in the divine plan and intention, marriage is permanent and lifelong. Consequently, divorce is always a departure from the divine design. The New Testament data point decisively to Jesus as the Source of that view, a conclusion supported by an overwhelming majority of New Testament specialists.[144] The fullest accounts of Jesus' teaching on the subject (Mark 10:2-12; Matt. 19:3-12) show Him locked in conflict with currently held opinions, just as they also record His proclamation of a return to the creation ideal and the shock that that declaration evoked from His hearers.

Second, while Jesus' proclamation of the permanence of marriage is unqualified and unequivocal, there are distinct indications that this teaching was not applied in a legal, still less a legalistic, way. This is suggested, for example, by the wording of Matt. 5:32, which implies that a wife may be a victim of adultery ("causes her to become an adulteress"), whereas in Judaism men only were regarded as victims of adultery. Again, if Lövestam's interpretation of the exceptive clause is correct, then it is accepted that while a husband may have, in keeping with Jewish legal requirements, terminated his marriage on account of his wife's adultery, this does not contravene the spirit of Jesus' teaching.

This fidelity to the principles of Jesus' teaching while avoiding a

---

143. Peter Richardson, "I Say, Not the Lord," 86. D. L. Dungan cites 1 Cor. 9:14-15 as yet another illustration of this phenomenon, "The Lord has commanded that those who preach the gospel should receive their living from the gospel. But I have not used any of these rights (14b-15a)." Dungan comments, "He (Paul) did not seek to abolish or curtail it. Instead, he and his associates simply made a practice of setting this regulation aside whenever they encountered circumstances, where to have kept it would have made them an hindrance to the Gospel. But Paul does not react against the regulation itself" (*Sayings of Jesus in the Churches of Paul,* 141).

144. Not all scholars reach that conclusion by the same route. Some trace the exceptive clauses to Jesus directly and interpret them against a Jewish Christian background as has been done above. Cf. Isaksson, *Marriage and Ministry,* 74-115, 142-48; Atkinson, *To Have and to Hold,* 117-18; Laney, *Divorce Myth,* 66; and Lövestam (guardedly), "Divorce and Remarriage in the New Testament," 60, n. 67. More regard it as an apostolic application of Jesus' teaching to a specific situation in the same way that Paul does in 1 Cor. 7:10-11. Cf. Dupont, *Mariage et Divorce,* 69; Collins, *Divorce in the New Testament,* 217-18; Stein, "Divorce," in *Dictionary of Jesus and the Gospels,* 196a, 197b; Hagner, *Matthew 1—13,* in WBC, 124.

legalistic and wooden enforcement of them is most visible in Paul in 1 Cor. 7. As has been seen, Paul's ethical baseline in the matter of divorce is the teaching of Jesus: "A wife must not separate from her husband. . . . And a husband must not divorce his wife" (vv. 10*b*, 11*c*). However, he is apparently confronted with an instance of that very thing.

Two things are striking about his response. One is that he does not pronounce a sentence of excommunication. On the contrary, he treats the woman concerned as a member of the Corinthian church and therefore subject to Christian discipline. A second notable feature is that he interjects a remarkable qualifying clause: "If she [separates], she must remain unmarried or else be reconciled to her husband" (v. 11*a*). Formally, this conflicts with what he has just stated to be the teaching of Jesus: "A wife must not separate from her husband." He does not order her to return to her husband, though he does order her to remain unmarried if she will not be reconciled. Neither does he withdraw the basic guideline given by the Lord.

A third conclusion may be indicated. It is remarkable that both in summarizing Jesus' teaching as well as in applying it, Paul does not use the language of adultery to describe the consequences of breaking the Lord's command, even though it is used in the divorce sayings in all three Gospels.[145] His concern appears rather to be with restoration, and he quotes Jesus' teaching to exhort rather than to condemn. This in itself may suggest what the context of Jesus' sayings implies, that there is a proclamational note in His teaching. The overriding import of Mark 10:2-12 and Matt. 19:3-12 is the recalling of hearers to the creation design for marriage. The setting of Matt. 5:31-32 in the contrasting statements of the Sermon on the Mount in Matt. 5:21-48, where what is called for is an inward conformity with the will of God that will issue in a life of loving obedience (Matt. 5:43-48), merely underscores this. In the words of Bruce Vawter, "Jesus' command regarding divorce was not the promulgation of a divine law . . . it was and is a word addressed to the Christian conscience by divine grace."[146] The same may be said of Luke 16:18 whose context

---

145. This is the more striking in that Paul has already used such language in 1 Cor. 7:2, "But since there is so much immorality *(porneia)*, each man should have his own wife, and each woman her own husband."

146. Bruce Vawter, "Divorce and the New Testament," CBQ 39 (1977), 540.

has often puzzled commentators. But Lövestam points out that it stands in a setting where "the quality and character of the heart are contrasted with superficial righteousness, righteousness before man (v. 15)." Hence he concludes, "What applies in the divorce logia is thus not a new law with casuistic elements, nor a new pattern of behavior in the perspective of rights, but the attitude of the heart which faithfulness and selfless service in marriage on the one hand and divorce and remarriage on the other are evidence of."[147]

With this we come to the boundary between teaching as such and its implementation in the real situations of life.

---

147. Lövestam, "Divorce and Remarriage in the New Testament," 62.

4 ∽ Divorce and the Gospel

A STRIKING FEATURE in much of the Christian literature on divorce is that so rarely is consideration given to the implications of the gospel for divorce. This state of affairs is probably engendered, at least in part, by the watertight character of the main views advanced by Christian interpreters who—to change the metaphor—depict Christianity and divorce in nose-to-nose confrontation, with no room for adjustment on either side. One has only to reflect on the positions outlined earlier to see how this is so.

In one view marriage is held to be indissoluble in the strict sense of that term. The case is not simply that marriage *should* not be dissolved, but that it *cannot* be dissolved. Marriage, by definition, creates a relationship indelible and irreversible. Indeed, as was noted,[1] some scholars, basing on the laws of Lev. 18, maintain that the marriage relationship is a form of blood relationship that can no more be undone than bloodline family relationships. On this understanding divorce is a piece of fiction that purports to do what cannot be done. At face value this produces deadlock, placing all divorcés beyond the Christian pale.

A second view noted above held that divorce is permissible but only on the grounds of adultery. Adherents of this position base their claim on the exceptive clauses in Matt. 5:32 and 19:9, holding that these expressions specify adultery not only as the grounds on which divorce is permissible but also as the grounds justifying remarriage.[2] "It is surely reasonable to assume," writes John Murray, "that if the man may legitimately put away his wife for adultery, the marriage bond is judged to be dissolved. If divorce involves dissolution of the marriage bond, then we would not expect that remarriage would be regarded as adultery."[3] Adultery is the sole ground on which divorce,

---

1. See chap. 3, pp. 96-97.
2. See chap. 3, pp. 102-9.
3. Murray, *Divorce,* 42.

or divorce followed by remarriage, is admissible within the Christian framework. While this view differs in principle from the first, by conceding that the marriage bond may be broken, yet in practice it terminates in the same confrontationalism as the first. It cannot address, except in condemnation, those whose marriages have been dissolved under civil law for reasons other than adultery.

The third interpretation noted earlier understands marriage as being indissoluble in the divine intention. The exceptive clauses take account of situations peculiar to first-century Jewish Christians and have no relevance today.[4] The teaching of Christ affirms the permanence of marriage as the divine plan instituted at creation and reinstituted by Christ in His proclamation of the kingdom of God. This proclamation stands in judgment over any and all departures from it. Again, the element of confrontation is present.

All three views necessarily provoke the same questions: What if the divine plan is breached? Is there no remedy? Are those who have broken the divine standard beyond redemption? The questions are particularly pressing in the case of Jesus, who, on the one hand, declared the purpose of His coming to be the proclamation of the good news of the kingdom of God (Mark 1:14) and, on the other, cast aside current haggling over which grounds for divorce were permissible (Matt. 10:3-9) and reinstated the creation standard (Mark 10:6-9; Matt. 19:8-9), overturning even the Mosaic concession in the process. How are the two to be related? Or are there defined groups, specifically the divorced, for whom there is no good news? Are divorce and remarriage sins of such magnitude that they are beyond the reach of the grace of God, which was both proclaimed and imparted by Christ?

In coming to grips with this issue it is important to safeguard both sides of the question. If it is possible to treat the problem of divorce in abstraction from the good news of the gospel, as is frequently done, it is just as possible to press the message of grace to the point that the teaching of Jesus on marriage and divorce is disparaged and overridden. The one is as destructive of the reality of grace as the other. Throughout one must be guided as much as possible by the full range of the relevant biblical teaching.

What then are those aspects of biblical teaching and interpretation that bear upon this issue? The following would seem to be of prime significance.

---

4. See chap. 3, pp. 110-18.

The Good News of God's Mercy to Sinners Without Discrimination

The characteristic and unbroken thrust of the biblical message is God's grace to the undeserving. It is so much the theme of the Bible that it requires no detailed proof. In the Old Testament Israel is chosen from among the nations by the sheer love of God (Deut. 7:7-9) so that by her obedience and service she might bear the message of His love to all the nations (Isa. 49:1-6). In the same way, the tone of the New Testament proclamation is set by Jesus' insistence on consorting with the outcasts of His day: the social underdogs (Mark 2:15-16), the light-fingered (Luke 19:1-10), the women of ill repute (Luke 7:36-39; 8:1-3). He affirmed that ministering to these was the precise purpose of His mission (Mark 2:17). No one would dispute this. More directly to the point is the evidence that this grace is depicted as being applied in fractured marital situations. This is the case in both Testaments.

1. The Old Testament

It was noted in chapter 2 that the Old Testament prophets used the image of marriage and divorce to depict the relationship between God and Israel. Attention was drawn to the caution needed in interpreting such contexts, since the primary intent of the prophets was to convey teaching about religion, not teaching about marriage. Even so, a real analogy is presupposed for the illustration to be possible, and it was noted particularly that the foundational element common to both the relationship between God and Israel and the relationship between marriage partners was that of covenant.[5]

Against that background two examples are of particular interest. The first is that of Hosea whose relevance here is that his marital experience is part of the warp and woof of his message. Whether in fact he divorced his wife is uncertain, as we have seen.[6] What is not in doubt is that she was an adulteress and therefore was legally exposed to the penalty of death by stoning (Deut. 22:22). Further, her condition was of such a character that Hosea had to buy her freedom (Hos. 3:2)—probably from either concubinage or temple prostitution,[7] either of which would have rendered her open to divorce un-

---

5. See chap. 2, pp. 54-55.

6. See chap. 2, p. 57.

7. Commenting on Hos. 3:1-2, Craigie writes, "The implication of verse 2 is either that Gomer had become somebody's slave or concubine and thus must have her free-

der the ancient law recorded in Deut. 24:1.[8] Yet the prophet does not take recourse to the law. He neither seeks the penalty for adultery nor rids himself of his wife. Peter Craigie asks, "How can God ask Hosea to do what is prohibited in divine law?" He replies, "The question is phrased wrongly! Love always precedes law. If law took preeminence, there would be no gospel in either Old or New Testament. And as Hosea is asked to go beyond law in the pursuit of love, so too does he demonstrate God's purpose of love that transcends law. Here, in a nutshell, is the Gospel of Love in the Old Testament . . . law may follow love to give some structure to the forms of love, but it can never have preeminence."[9]

This does not mean that moral values are consigned to the scrap heap. Eichrodt stresses that such a conclusion is excluded both by the emphasis on the utterly paradoxical character of God's love and the reality of the divine anger against sin.[10] What it means is that the categories of law are inadequate for describing the relationship between human persons and God.[11]

The second Old Testament illustrative example of the range and depth of divine mercy is Jeremiah. The relevant passage is chapter 3, which has been dealt with earlier[12] and therefore need not be treated fully here. Again, the metaphor of divorce is being used to illuminate the religious infidelity of Judah, the first verse of the chapter echoing the divorce law of Deut. 24:1: "If a man divorces his wife and she goes from him and becomes another man's wife, will he return to her?" (NRSV). The answer to the question is clearly no.

---

dom purchased; alternatively, and more probably, she had become a slave or possession of the temple of Baal, where false religion prospered. There, she would have been engaged in the sexual practices of the fertility worship of Baal. From such enslavement, Hosea purchased her, the price paid (verse 2) being approximately the amount required to redeem a person from slavery" (*Twelve Prophets*, 1:27).

8. Ibid., 28.

9. Ibid. Von Rad likewise argues that in Hos. 3 there may be a suspension of the law of Deut. 24:1-4, since Yahweh does what the Law forbids. In von Rad's striking words, "In Hosea's view what is impossible for the law is done by God" (von Rad, *Deuteronomy*, 150). Cf. Wolff, *Hosea*, 63b.

10. "Hosea is outdone by hardly any other prophet in the ferocity of his threats and the savagery of his proclamations of punishment. *The wrath of love* is presented in all its paradoxical actuality" (Eichrodt, *Theology of the Old Testament*, 1:252-53).

11. Eichrodt again is careful to strike a balance, "This implies no depreciation or condemnation of the legal aspect of man's relationship to God, but its interpretation in accordance with the dominant fundamental principle of love" (ibid., 252 n. 1).

12. See chap. 2, pp. 59-61.

The law forbids such a thing as a source of pollution: "Would not such a land be greatly polluted?" (v. 1*b*, NRSV).

Yet the recurrent refrain of the chapter is God's repeated entreaty to Judah to "return," as had been His earlier plea to Israel (vv. 6, 10, 11, 14). The unfaithfulness of Judah, like that of Israel before her, is compared to adultery (vv. 1-2, 6-9). Moreover, Jeremiah explicitly takes the marriage metaphor a step further than Hosea may have done, stating that Yahweh did indeed divorce Israel (v. 8). On two counts, therefore, Judah stands under the penalty of the law: as an adulteress she stands under the penalty of death and as divorced she stands under the penalty of permanent rejection by Yahweh. Yet God, in defiance of His own law, entreats her to return to Him again.

What this amounts to is not merely that the covenant relation between God and Israel is viewed at its highest pitch in the Old Testament in terms of love,[13] but that that love is understood and exhibited in redemptive terms. The message of the prophets was that the covenant should never have been broken. Even though it had been broken, it could be restored—even against the letter of the covenant law. Of special significance to our interest is that they use the image of marriage to illustrate this—a strange choice if it could be replied not only that marriage law forbade such a thing but that marriage law was enforced with iron inflexibility.

2. The New Testament

The picture painted in the New Testament is similar to that depicted in the Old. As already observed, the banner suspended over Jesus' ministry by His critics was, "This man welcomes sinners and eats with them" (Luke 15:2; cf. Mark 2:16). The charge was wholly justified. Again, of particular relevance to our interest is that, prominent among those whom Jesus welcomed, were persons who had infringed the marriage laws. This is made clear in some of the general descriptions of the categories of people with whom Jesus kept company. In some instances the familiar expression "tax collectors and sinners" takes the form "tax collectors and prostitutes" (Matt. 21:31-32). The word translated "prostitute" (Greek *pornē*) together with its

---

13. Compare the comment of Eichrodt on Hosea, "The transition from the idea of the covenant to the conception of the marriage between Yahweh and Israel was made easier by the element of contractual obligation common to both, but it needed the shattering experience of the prophet, whose whole being was committed to Yahweh's service, to make the marriage-bond the supreme demonstration of God's attitude to Israel" (*Theology of the Old Testament,* 1:251).

derivatives (e.g., *porneia*), while capable of narrower definition where the context requires it, could also denote any kind of sexual activity outside the marriage bond.[14]

In Judaism at the time of Jesus such conduct was viewed as placing one beyond hope of salvation. A Jewish work of the second century B.C., titled "The Testament of the Twelve Patriarchs," reads, "From the words of Enoch the Righteous I tell you that you will be sexually promiscuous like the promiscuity of the Sodomites and will perish, with few exceptions. You shall resume your actions with loose women, and the Kingdom of the Lord will not be among you, for he will take it away forthwith."[15]

In contrast with such a view, Jesus is depicted as One not merely socializing with such outcasts but proclaiming to them the forgiveness of sins and opening the door to the kingdom of God. He makes the staggering claim that they are entering the Kingdom instead of the scribes and Pharisees (Matt. 21:31-32).[16] This does not mean that Jesus minimized sexual sin. On the contrary, as Hauck-Schulz says, "The New Testament is characterized by an unconditional repudiation of all extramarital and unnatural intercourse."[17] Sexual immorality and adultery are among the sins Jesus names as springing from the heart (Mark 7:21), and to squander his inheritance with prostitutes was the ultimate charge flung by the elder brother at the prodigal son (Luke 15:30). Without in any way condoning their sin, Jesus did not shun them or in any way signal that their sin was unforgivable and they were beyond redemption.[18] That this attitude persisted

---

14. See F. Hauck and S. Schulz, "*Porne,* etc.," in TDNT, ed. G. Friedrich (Grand Rapids: Wm. B. Eerdmans Publishing Co., 1977), 6:section C.1.

15. "Apocalyptic Literature and Testaments," in *The Old Testament Pseudepigrapha,* ed. James H. Charlesworth (New York: Doubleday, 1983), 1:827. Even more pungent is the declaration in the Book of Jubilees from the same century denouncing the sin of incest: "And you, Moses, command the children of Israel and let them keep this word because it is a judgment worthy of death. And it is a defilement. And there is no forgiveness in order to atone for a man who has done this, forever, but only to execute him and kill him and stone him and to uproot him from the midst of the people of our God" (33:13; cf. Charlesworth, *The Old Testament Pseudepigrapha* [1985], 2:119).

16. Jeremias argues convincingly that "instead of" rather than "ahead of" is the real meaning of the verb (J. Jeremias, *The Parables of Jesus,* 3rd rev. ed. [London: SCM Press, 1972), 125, with n. 48.

17. Hauck and Schulz, "*Porne,*" 590.

18. Cf. H. Reisser, "Whereas, however, according to Jewish law, prostitutes and tax collectors were excluded from the people of God and thus from salvation, Jesus proclaimed to them God's forgiveness on the basis of their faith and thus the way to salva-

in the New Testament church is attested in the writings of Paul, who condemned fornication in no measured terms (1 Cor. 5:1-5; 6:18) but could also in the same breath both denounce it and exult in the fact that within Christ's Church were those who had been cleansed from it (6:9-11).

The attitude expressed in terms of general principle in the passages noted comes to vivid and dramatic visibility in two episodes in the life of Jesus. The first is His anointing by the sinful woman in the house of Simon the Pharisee (Luke 7:36-50). The story stands last in the series of six units in Luke 7, illustrating the themes characteristic of Jesus' ministry. In particular the way is prepared for it by verses 29-30, which pointedly note the opposite reactions of the tax collectors, on the one hand, and the Pharisees and lawyers (scribes), on the other, to Jesus' praise of John the Baptist (v. 28). The way for it is even more immediately prepared with the reference to "tax collectors and sinners" in verse 34.

First of the points of relevance in the story for our concern is the character of the woman. She is described simply as "a woman . . . who was a sinner" (v. 37, NRSV). Suggestions that this may mean no more than that she was the wife of a nonobservant Jew are much less likely, in view of verses 48-49, than that she was a woman of the streets or an adulteress.[19] Second, the failure of Jesus to dismiss the woman, especially in view of her exhibitionist behavior, indicates to Simon that Jesus was not the prophet he had thought He might be. Had He been a prophet, He would have refused to have any dealings with the woman. Third, Jesus both affirmed that she had been forgiven and confirmed this by speaking to her words of forgiveness (vv. 47-48). Because she had received much grace, she showed much gratitude.[20] Again, Jesus brings forgiveness to those who had breached the boundaries of marriage.

The other episode in which Jesus is seen doing the same is that of the woman taken in adultery (John 7:53—8:11). It is widely recognized that the textual evidence is decisively against this passage be-

---

tion (Matt. 21:31f; Heb. 11:31; cf. Jas. 2:25). Their faith is held up as an example for the self-confident priests and elders of the people. This in no way softens Jesus' rejection of prostitution (Mk. 7:21 par.). It does mean that, along with other sins, it is no longer excluded from forgiveness" ("Discipline," *Porneuo,* in NIDNTT 1:499-500).

19. So Marshall, *Gospel of Luke,* 308.

20. For a discussion of the exegetical problems in verse 47, see Marshall, *Gospel of Luke,* 313.

ing part of the original text of John's Gospel.[21] It is almost as widely recognized that the passage is part of the authentic teaching of Jesus.[22] It testifies to the same clash of views between Jesus and the religious authorities of His day as do the passages noted earlier. The features of the story that relate to our study are that the woman had been apprehended "in the act of adultery" (v. 4). The force of the English expression "caught in the act" is reinforced by the original inasmuch as the Greek expression is a technical legal term *(ep' autophōrōi)*. The evidence is therefore irrefutable, and the verdict foreclosed. Next, the penalty prescribed by the Mosaic Law for adultery was death by stoning (Deut. 22:21-22; cf. John 8:5).[23]

A third and most important feature of the story is the nature of the dilemma into which Jesus has been maneuvered. It is almost certainly wrong to see Jesus as being forced to choose between Moses and Caesar. The stakes were much higher than that. Jesus, in effect, was being asked to choose between the law of God and His own proclamation. As Hoskyns puts it, "It would be more natural to suppose that the scribes and Pharisees, knowing the mercy of Jesus towards sinners, desire to set this mercy in direct opposition to the Law of God, in order that they may accuse him as a transgressor of the Law."[24] The issue is thus very sharply focused: God's law or Jesus' "good news"?

---

21. For a recent statement of the evidence, see G. R. Beasley-Murray, *John,* in WBC (Waco, Tex.: 1987), 36:143. The same view has been maintained by commentators of all stripes for the last century. See B. F. Westcott, *The Gospel of John* (London: James Clarke, 1880. Reprint, 1958), 125.

22. So Beasley-Murray, *John,* 144. A fuller discussion may be found in Edwyn Hoskyns and F. Noel Davey, *The Fourth Gospel* (London: Faber and Faber, 1947), 565-66. As to why the story was not incorporated into one of the Gospels earlier, R. E. Brown (following Riesenfeld) concludes that the most plausible explanation is that "the ease with which Jesus forgave the adulteress was hard to reconcile with the stern penitential discipline in vogue in the Early Church" (*The Gospel According to John I—XII,* in AB [New York: Doubleday, 1966], 334). For a recent statement of the case against the authenticity of the passage, see Daniel B. Wallace, "Reconsidering 'The Story of Jesus and the Adulteress Reconsidered,'" NTS 39, 2, April 1993, which is itself a response to the opposite point of view, argued by John Paul Heil, "The Story of Jesus and the Adulteress (John 7,53—8,11) Reconsidered," *Biblica* 72 (1991): 182-89.

23. There is some discussion as to whether stoning was indeed the mode of execution for adultery and whether, in Jesus' day, the Jews had the authority to impose the death penalty anyway. It appears that stoning was the penalty for a range of crimes, including adultery, and that, whether legally or otherwise, Jewish extremists found ways of imposing it when they wanted to. See the discussions in Hoskyns and Davey, *Fourth Gospel,* 568-69, and Barnabas Lindars, *John,* in *New Century Bible Commentary,* 309.

24. Hoskyns and Davey, *Fourth Gospel,* 569. Cf. Lindars, "The behaviour of Jesus

Jesus' response is to say nothing but instead write on the ground with His finger, "an essential feature of the story," as Lindars rightly says.[25] It is idle to speculate about *what* He wrote, and more to the point to inquire *why* He wrote. Whatever He wrote—if it was anything more than doodling—was presumably visible to His questioners and failed to satisfy them, for "they kept on questioning him" (v. 7).[26]

In short, the writing on the ground was a way of avoiding communication. He had been challenged to speak (v. 5*b*), but He did not speak to order. When finally He spoke, it was to return the dilemma to His critics: "If any one of you is without sin, let him be the first to throw a stone at her" (v. 7). R. E. Brown comments: "He is dealing here with zealots who have taken upon themselves the indignant enforcement of the Law, and he has every right to demand that their case be thoroughly lawful and their motives be honest. He recognizes that, although they are zealots for the word of the Law, they are not interested in the purpose of the Law, for the spiritual state of the woman is not even in question, or whether or not she is penitent."[27] Taking the point, albeit unwillingly, they make themselves scarce. In Lindars's words, "This means that, instead of trapping Jesus into an open denial of the Mosaic law, they have capitulated to His own teaching on the nature of God's Kingdom."[28] In a word, there is mercy for those who break the law—including the law of marriage.

Yet—and this is the focal point of emphasis—this does not

---

presented a direct challenge to the strict Jews, and it was theologically based on his preaching of the Kingdom" (*John,* 310). The contention that the scribes and Pharisees themselves were seeking a way to avoid the woman's execution has been argued ingeniously (though hardly convincingly) by Brad H. Young, "'Save the Adulteress!': Ancient Jewish *Responsa* in the Gospels?" NTS 41, 1 (January 1995): 59-70. Even if correct, Young's interpretation leaves the central issue of the narrative unchanged: Is there no escape from the rigor of the law?

25. Lindars, *John,* 311.

26. Westcott points out that both in verses 6 and 8, the verbs "to write" are in the imperfect tense and so represent the action as continuous (*Gospel of John,* 126).

27. Brown, *John I—XII,* 338.

28. Lindars, *John,* 312. Cf. Gail R. O'Day, "Both the Scribes and Pharisees and the woman are invited to give up old ways and enter a new way of life. Both stand under the power of old ways, the power of sin, to use the rhetoric of the text, but the present moment *(apo tou nun)* invites both to a new way of life . . . The Scribes and Pharisees and the woman are invited to leave behind a world of judgment, condemnation, and death and enter a world of acquittal and life" ("John 7:53—8:11: A Study in Misreading," *Journal of Biblical Literature* III, 4 [Winter 1992]: 637-38).

mean that the law is set aside or even disparaged. In the very act of pronouncing mercy Jesus affirms the standard of the law: "Neither do I condemn you. . . . Go now and leave your life of sin" (v. 11b). Wherever forgiveness is truly received, it brings moral renewal, but it is the proclamation of forgiveness rather than the mere enforcement of the law that does so. As Lindars says pointedly, "It is in his *exercise* of the divine compassion rather than in an admonition that he gives the real incentive for a better life in future."[29]

The passages reviewed are by no means the only ones in which Jesus is shown bringing good news of acceptance to those who had made marital shipwreck. His encounter with the woman at Jacob's well (John 4:1-42) is another that speaks loudly with the same voice as the prophets before Him and the apostles after Him to say that sins against God's marriage law do not place the sinners beyond the reach of God's mercy and forgiveness.

The Interrelation of Law and Gospel

A second factor that bears upon the question of what happens where the divine plan for marriage is broken is the interrelation of law and gospel. The immediately preceding section has touched on this issue at least in an illustrative way, insofar as it is present implicitly in Jesus' interaction with and proclamation of grace to the outcast. However, it may be useful to treat it directly in terms of theological principle.

The relation of law and gospel has been one of the five or six issues at the head of the theological agenda in recent years,[30] and the

---

29. Lindars, *John.* J. Ian H. McDonald observes, "Yet Jesus does not criticize the law or suggest that anything goes! The libertine or radical revisionist finds cold comfort here, as the final charge—conventional though it is—makes clear. What it shows is that in some situations, and perhaps with certain groups of people, the moral priority lies with the readiness to understand rather than condemn, with an unconditional acceptance of the sinner which looks to the future rather than the past (and who is without sin?), and with the liberation of the oppressed" ("The So-Called *Pericope de adultera,*" NTS 41, 3 (July 1995): 427). Hoskyns makes much of the Christological implications of verses 9-11, adding the summarizing comment, "She is faced by the call of God to righteousness, and sent forth as the object of the mercy of God, who has passed over her sin. Here then the mercy of God and His truth meet. For only in the mouth of the sinless Jesus can the full condemnation of sin, and the full demand for the righteousness of God, march with the authoritative pronouncement of His mercy and charity" (Hoskyns and Davey, *Fourth Gospel,* 570).

30. The beginning of the debate is usually traced to the appearance of E. P. Sanders, *Paul and Palestinian Judaism* (Philadelphia: Fortress Press, 1977).

most that can be said is that the debate continues.[31] The volume of literature generated is enormous and cannot possibly be reviewed here. The focal point of the discussion has been the place of the law in the teaching of Paul, as is indicated by the titles of many of the books that have appeared. In particular, it has been insisted that the antithesis between law and gospel as alternative paths to salvation that has been claimed to lie at the heart of the Pauline message particularly since the time of the Protestant Reformation is, in fact, a false antithesis. But in truth the issue is much wider than Paul, going back to Jesus himself and in the end involving not only the relation of law and gospel but the relation between the Old and New Testaments and the salvation proclaimed in each. The mere mention of these issues is enough to show that they cannot be dealt with here thoroughly, but something may be attempted at least insofar as the matter affects the subject of these pages.

Several misconceptions surround the understanding of law and gospel, at least at the popular level.[32] One is that law and gospel stand in opposite corners as paths to acceptance with God. The law was the means by which salvation was sought in the Old Testament. Failure to attain salvation by obedience to the law led to the displacement of the law by the gospel. Believers in Christ, therefore, are not under law but under grace (Rom. 6:14*b*). Implicit in this is the understanding that law is fundamentally something to be *done,* and failure to *do* it or *keep* it triggers the prescribed penalty.

Some of these conceptions—or misconceptions—of the significance of the law are applied to divorce and remarriage. In particular, the law is seen as requiring exact compliance—including Christ's ruling against divorce and remarriage—in such a way that any deviation from it involves a failure to obey God's command and, where the infraction cannot be reversed, a permanent falling short of God's will. This constitutes an irremovable impediment at the very least in one's usefulness in God's service. Some would go further and see it as a permanent disqualification from many, if not most, avenues of ministry within the Church.

It may help to place this matter in perspective if the fundamen-

---

31. See the recently published Frank Thielman, *Paul and the Law: A Contextual Approach* (Downers Grove, Ill.: InterVarsity Press, 1994).

32. That they are debated equally at the academic level is sufficiently demonstrated by Wayne G. Strickland, ed., *The Law, the Gospel and the Modern Christian: Five Views* (Grand Rapids: Zondervan, 1993).

tal features of the biblical understanding of law are set down (even if there is a degree of oversimplification, and many aspects are not addressed). First, law is always preceded by grace and set in the context of grace. This is nowhere more strikingly expressed than in the account of the giving of the law at Sinai. The Ten Commandments are prefaced by the historical prologue: "I am the LORD your God, who brought you out of Egypt, out of the land of slavery" (Exod. 20:2). The commandments follow as the ground plan for the life of God's redeemed people. As John Goldingay puts it: "The starting point for understanding it [sc. the law] is that the law belongs to the covenant relationship between Yahweh and Israel. . . . Further, the order of these two concepts is significant: the covenant relationship existed first, established on the initiative of Yahweh. The giving of the law followed Yahweh's establishing of his relationship with Israel. . . . Put theologically, grace is prior to law in the OT."[33] What this amounts to is that the law was never given as the means of salvation, rather it was given as the pattern of life for those who were already redeemed.[34]

This leads directly to the second observation; in character and purpose, the law sets out the guidelines for the life of the people of God, which is by definition a life of fullness and fulfillment because the Lawgiver is also the Lifegiver. An important function of the law is therefore to give guidance and direction. As is frequently pointed out, the Hebrew designation for the Pentateuch, or the first five books of the Bible, is "Torah," which, while commonly translated "Law," means more than that term denotes in English. "Instruction" gives a more adequate sense, as the contents of the Pentateuch suggest. For while law is a prominent element in the Pentateuch, there is also a significant proportion of narrative. Yet while all is not legislation, all gives instruction. An important function of biblical law is to give instruction, and it is misleading to confine its significance to the idea of regulations the English term "law" tends to suggest.

---

33. John Goldingay, *Approaches to Old Testament Interpretation,* rev. ed. (Downers Grove, Ill.: InterVarsity Press, 1990), 44.

34. Cf. Christopher J. H. Wright, "The law was never given as a means of salvation (again, even hypothetically), but as a gift of grace to those already redeemed. Thus a rigid separation of law and grace cannot be accepted as a valid way of categorizing the Old and New Testaments, still less of setting one against the other—except in terms of the specific argumentation of Paul against a *distorted* view of both" ("The Ethical Authority of the Old Testament: A Survey of Approaches, Part II," *Tyndale Bulletin* 43.2 [November 1992]: 226).

This has important implications for the interpretation and application of biblical law today just as it did in biblical times. Christopher Wright criticizes those who would argue for the large-scale application of biblical (including Old Testament) law in contemporary society, claiming that they overlook two important factors. First, "in biblical ancient Israel and contemporary cultures, law was not always in the form of hard and fast statutes intended to be applied to the letter in formal courts. Judges operated with precedents and paradigms guided by *torah* which means 'guidance' or 'instruction.' . . . The emphasis was on the imperative to do justice and act fairly without bribery or favoritism, but much was left to the discretion and judgment of those responsible (Deut. 16:18-20; 17:8-13)."[35] Wright's second criticism is that the approach he refers to

> attaches too much importance to the literal (and literary) form of the biblical penalties and fails to reckon with two points: *(a)* that in many cases it is probable that the penalty specified was a *maximum* penalty which could be reduced at the discretion of the elders or judges handling the matter. . . . Wenham has suggested that the death penalty for adultery may have been allowed to be commuted to monetary compensation, though would-be adulterers should not count on it (Prov. 6:32-35); *(b)* that what is important about the penal system of Israel's law is the scale of values it reflects rather than the literal prescriptions themselves. Careful study of Israel's penology shows that the range of offenses for which the death penalty was applied were to do with central concerns of protecting the covenant relationship and the family/household unit within which the relationship was preserved and experienced.[36]

It is significant that Jesus' attitude to and application of the law seems to have been governed by principles such as these. Reference has already been made to His association with the outcasts of society to the extent of eating with them (Mark 2:15-17). The objection to this was not social—association with those of a lower class—but religious, association with those who were ceremonially unclean because they did not observe the purity laws. This charge was also leveled against Jesus' followers (7:1-5). But a particular source of irritation to Jesus' critics was the failure of himself and His followers to observe the Sabbath law (2:23-28; 3:1-6).

---

35. Ibid., 217.
36. Ibid., 217-18.

The principle to which Jesus appeals in response to each of these charges is the same, that the intent of the law was to give life, not to provide a regulation to be kept. His defense for eating with sinners was that He had come to cure the sick, not to keep himself apart from the needy (Mark 2:17). His response to the criticism of His followers for eating with ritually unclean hands was that the intent of the law was to point to the need for inward purity (7:14-23), and to stress outward conformity at the expense of inward acceptance was, in truth, to abandon the law (vv. 6-13). Similarly, to observe the Sabbath law at the expense of hunger (2:25-26) or suffering (3:4) was a blind perversion of the purpose for which the Sabbath law was given, namely, for humanity's good (2:27). In a word, Jesus recognized that it was possible to enforce the law in such a way as to defeat its purpose and subvert its intent.

This point needs to be kept in mind regarding the application of other biblical laws. The law against murder is a good example. To take the life of another is uniformly presented in the Bible as a crime of the utmost seriousness. It is a crime against God, whose law declares, "You shall not murder" (Exod. 20:13). It is a crime against the victim who is a fellow member of the human family: "Your brother's blood cries out to me from the ground" (Gen. 4:10). The penalty for intentional murder is death (Num. 35:20-21); no substitute or satisfaction is acceptable (v. 31). "No murderer has eternal life in him" (1 John 3:15). On the contrary, all murderers will be consigned to eternal death in the lake of fire (Rev. 21:8). No word specifically declares murder to be a forgivable sin.

In many respects murder is like divorce. It is a sin against the covenant bond, that is, the bond between all members of the human race. It is a sin against society inasmuch as it weakens the bond that protects the value of human life. It is irreversible: the victim cannot be brought back to life, and the murderer can never become a non-murderer. Yet while the law made no provision for remission of the death penalty, God in His grace provided mercy. David murdered Uriah the Hittite (2 Sam. 12:9), a crime for which we have seen the law provided no remission; yet the prophet Nathan assured David of forgiveness in response to his penitence (v. 13). Both Jesus and His disciple Stephen prayed for the forgiveness of those who were killing them, even while the act was being carried out (Luke 23:34; Acts 7:59-60). All of this must be kept in mind in determining how the New Testament teaching on divorce is to be applied.

It is noteworthy that one of Jesus' sayings on divorce—in Matt.

5:31-32—stands in a context that is in some sense legal. Whether or not the Sermon on the Mount is to be viewed as the Christian equivalent of the law given on Mount Sinai, there can be little question that it is concerned to propound a Christian understanding of law.[37] The robust denial of any intent to overthrow the Old Testament law, coupled with the claim to fulfill it (vv. 17-20) and followed by the series of six contrasts between what had been said in the past and what Jesus himself said (vv. 21-48), is sufficient evidence of this.

The Christian understanding of the Old Testament law appears to be conditioned by at least two factors. The first is that the context of Christ's proclamation of the law is the coming of the kingdom of God in and with himself. In Matthew's Gospel the backdrop of the Sermon on the Mount is Jesus' proclamation of the Kingdom (4:17) and His ministry of preaching and healing in its power (vv. 23-25). What this implies in practice has been well stated by George Eldon Ladd: "The unique element in Jesus' teaching is that in his person the Kingdom of God has invaded human history, and men are not only placed under the ethical demand of the reign of God, but by virtue of this very experience of God's reign are also enabled to realize a new measure of righteousness."[38] That is to say, the power of the kingdom in Christ means that the law is present not only in demand but also in enabling strength.

The second factor conditioning the Christian interpretation of the law is that the touchstone of its fulfillment is located in motive and inner attitude as much as in outward performance. The "fulfilling" of the law spoken of in Matt. 5:17 and the "greater righteousness" of verse 20 are evidently expounded and illustrated in verses 21-48 where the law against murder is fulfilled in the avoidance of anger; the law against adultery, in the avoidance of lust; the law of love of neighbor, in love of all, including enemies. Putting these two factors together, Ladd concludes: "Thus the essential righteousness of the Kingdom, since it is a righteousness of the heart, is actually

---

37. Davies writes, "The case would seem to be that, while the category of a New Moses and a New Sinai is present in v-vii, as elsewhere in Matthew, the strictly Mosaic traits in the figure of the Matthaean Christ, both there and in other parts of the Gospel, have been taken up into a deeper and higher context. He is not Moses come as Messiah, if we may so put it, so much as Messiah, Son of Man, Emmanuel, who has absorbed the Mosaic function. The Sermon on the Mount is therefore ambiguous: suggestive of the Law of a New Moses, it is also the authoritative word of the Lord, the Messiah: it is the Messianic Torah" (*Sermon on the Mount,* 27).

38. George Eldon Ladd, *Jesus and the Kingdom* (New York: Harper, 1964), 286.

attainable, qualitatively if not quantitatively. In its fullness it awaits the coming of the eschatological Kingdom; but in its essence it can be realized here and now, in this age."[39]

In such a setting, law ceases to be mere regulation and becomes instruction also, ceases to be mere demand and becomes promise, ceases to be only law and becomes gospel. As such, the ban against divorce is part of Jesus' proclamation to be treated no different from other aspects of His proclamation with which it is here grouped: hatred, lust, love of enemies. "Jesus' saying about divorce," writes W. D. Davies, "was, when first delivered, probably intended to be more haggadic than halachic; that is, its purpose was not to lay down the law but to reassert an ideal and make divorce a sin, thereby disturbing then current complacency."[40]

This is confirmed by the way Jesus' teaching on divorce is reproduced in other parts of the New Testament. Thus on the one hand, in Mark 10:2-4, the Pharisees are intent on squeezing every centimeter of leeway they can extract from the Mosaic legal acceptance of divorce in Deut. 24:1-4. This Jesus brands as "hardness of heart," because it is concerned more with what the law will allow than with what God intended. Accordingly, He sweeps every concession aside with the appeal to God's creation design and asserts affirmatively, "Therefore what God has joined together, let man not separate" (Mark 10:9). Hugh Anderson comments: "It is most important to remember that here in Mark 10:6-9 Jesus is not absolutely prohibiting divorce *by way of a binding legal enactment,* but is absolutely elevating marriage (as an indissoluble union) by way of leading men to understand it, not as a remote ideal, but as a gift of God's creation, to be received gladly and celebrated naturally and spontaneously. . . . Here too Jesus' teaching may be construed as an invitation to accept God's gift and a call to the sacrifice for the sake of others that is necessary for its reception. Accordingly, from the Marcan viewpoint, the first responsibility on the Church is always to affirm that invitation and that call."[41]

Paul likewise applies the same teaching of Jesus in the Corinthian situation: "To the married I give this command (not I, but the Lord): A wife must not separate from her husband. . . . And a hus-

---

39. Ladd, *Jesus and the Kingdom,* 290.
40. Davies and Allison, *Matthew,* in ICC, 1:532.
41. Anderson, *Gospel of Mark,* 243.

band must not divorce his wife" (1 Cor. 7:10-11*b*). Yet in the church in Corinth, the former is precisely what has happened. Upon which Paul's comment is, "But if she does, she must remain unmarried or else be reconciled to her husband" (v. 11*a*). In a word, the divine design of the permanence of marriage is affirmed, but it is not enforced as a law. The wife is not ordered to return to her husband. What we appear to have throughout the New Testament is repeated affirmation of the divine plan of the permanence of marriage. Where, as a matter of fact, there is falling short of it, the principle is applied as far as may be possible, without in any way renouncing it.

Law and gospel are thus interrelated and interact upon each other. That relatedness and mutual interaction must not be broken. Gordon Fee writes: "Some find Paul and Jesus too harsh and try to find ways around the plain sense of the text. Others turn the text into law and make divorce the worst of sins in the church. . . . Paul does not raise this norm to law. Divorce may happen, and such a person is not ostracized from the community."[42] Law that defines limits can preserve standards but has no word of hope to speak to those who have transgressed them. Gospel that accepts everything has undermined its own existence, for where everything is acceptable, there is no need for grace. It is only as both are held together as the single whole that they are that justice can be done to the everlasting holiness of God, as well as to His everlasting mercy to sinners. Transgression of God's plan and intention for marriage is not an exception to this.[43]

The Effect of Repentance

A third factor not to be overlooked in viewing divorce in the context of the gospel is the meaning and significance of repentance. Its presence may be glimpsed in the earlier part of the chapter

---

42. Fee, *First Epistle to the Corinthians,* 296.

43. John Goldingay writes helpfully of this tension between grace on the one hand and behavior on the other. "It seems to me that we have to accept a dialectical 'yes—and—no' to the law, as we have to say yes—and—no to the question of whether man's commitment to God's ways is important to his relationship with God (and as God has to say yes and no to man: see Ho. 11)." He then proceeds to distinguish an "ethic of contexts" from "an ethic of norms," both assuming a soteriology of grace, but the former concerned to redeem persons as they are, the *latter* to stress how redeemed persons ought to be. "These two approaches need to be held in tension if neither is to fall into the other two positions (classically antinomianism and legalism) which lie just beyond them" (*Approaches to Old Testament Interpretation,* 50).

where the undiscriminating offer of God's mercy to sinners is spoken of; however, it deserves specific treatment.

The roots of the New Testament understanding of repentance lie in the Old Testament, and accordingly, it is there we must begin. While the Old Testament has no special terms for repentance, its concept of repentance is distinctive. Put at its broadest, it means the fundamental alteration of the relationship with God. This could be brought about in two distinguishable (though not necessarily separate) ways. On the one hand, repentance could be expressed through the medium of ritual: fasting, weeping, mourning, and sacrificial offering. Of particular note is the sharp distinction between willful and unintentional sin and the insistence that sacrifice was effective only for the latter.[44] In cases of willful sin, such as David's murder of Uriah and adultery with and later marriage of Bathsheba, repentance "converted" willful sin into unintentional sin, for which forgiveness was available.[45] The seriousness of presumptuous sin (or "sin with a high hand," as the Hebrew phrase translates literally) is thus maintained, but so also is the critical effect of repentance.

On the other hand, repentance could be expressed in confession and prayer, without any accompanying sacrifice. This idea comes to particular expression in the verb "to turn" (Hebrew *shūb*). Eichrodt writes, "The metaphor was an especially suitable one, for not only did it describe the required behaviour as a real act—'to make a turn'—and so preserve the strong personal impact, it also included both the negative element of turning away from the direction taken hitherto and the positive element of turning towards."[46] It was used intensively in the preaching of the prophets and especially by Hosea and Jeremiah. Hosea waits for the day when Gomer will say, "I will go and return [*shūb*] to my first husband" (Hos. 2:7, NRSV; 2:9,

---

44. See Num. 15:27-31.

45. Various theories are held among Old Testament scholars. Some hold that willful or presumptuous sin could be atoned for directly but only annually on the Day of Atonement in the holy of holies. So J. Milgrom, "Sacrifices and Offerings, OT," *Interpreter's Dictionary of the Bible,* Supplementary Volume (1976), 767. Some maintain that while the sacrificial law provided no sacrifice for deliberate sin, the sinner could find forgiveness by casting himself upon the mercy of God (e.g., 2 Sam. 12:13). So H. H. Rowley, *The Faith of Israel* (London: SCM Press, copyright 1956, 1979 printing), 88, 91 ff. Yet others hold that willful sin means *unrepented* sin, and that where repentance was forthcoming, pardon was given. See Victor P. Hamilton in *A Spectrum of Thought,* ed. Michael L. Peterson (Wilmore, Ky.: Asbury Press, 1982).

46. Eichrodt, *Theology of the Old Testament,* 2:466.

Hebrew); and in the same way, he foresees Israel's return to the Lord (3:5) and urges her to do so (10:12; 14:2ff.). In Jer. 3, already referred to, the prophet's message revolves around the idea that the "returning" of a divorced woman to her first husband is a violation of the law (v. 1), and yet that is precisely what he urges the nation to do in the name of the Lord (vv. 12, 14).

All of this points to the essential content of repentance. It is more than regret or remorse, though it includes these. It is more than a change of mind, though it includes that also. Forgiveness is also part of it, though as more than simply the legalistic remission of punishment. Since, as was noted earlier, "turning" has a positive as well as a negative side, both aspects must find place in any adequate understanding. Repentance thus incorporates the ideas of a renewed relationship with God, a fresh start, a fellowship such as existed before sin intruded.[47] Hosea's concluding oracle expresses it well: "I will heal their waywardness and love them freely, for my anger has turned away from them. I will be like the dew to Israel; he will blossom like a lily. Like a cedar of Lebanon he will send down his roots; his young shoots will grow" (14:4-6a).

When we turn to the New Testament, we find substantially the same concept in terms of general form and content. This is not surprising, since the New Testament terms are heavily influenced by the crucial Old Testament word "turn" (Hebrew *shūḇ*). However, the New Testament concept is shaped in specifics by the factors distinctive of its "new" situation, namely, the inauguration of the kingdom of God through the coming of Christ.

As to terminology, three words are used to convey the idea or some aspect of it. Most important is the word "turn" (Greek *epistrephō*), which, while found in a literal sense, is used figuratively in 23 of its 40 occurrences. A second term is "repent" (Greek *metanoeō*), which is often used in harness with "turn" and is found most frequently in the Synoptic Gospels and Acts.[48] A third term, also translated "repent" (Greek *metamelomai*), occurs only six times in

---

47. Cf. F. Laubach, "He who returns to God receives forgiveness (Isa. 55:7), remission of punishment (Jas. 3:9-10), fertility and prosperity (Hos. 14:5ff [Massoretic Text 6ff]) and life (Ezek. 33:14ff)" (Laubach, "Conversion," in NIDNTT, 1:354).

48. Of the 56 examples of the verb and the noun (Greek *metanoia*) in the New Testament, 25 are found in Luke and Acts. Against this Paul uses the word-group only five times.

the New Testament to denote something of which God or man would not repent (i.e., feel differently or sorry about). It tends to denote a change of feeling (Matt. 21:29, 32; 27:3; 2 Cor. 7:8) and does not enter largely into the defining of the concept.

The features given particular prominence in the New Testament picture of repentance are as follows. First, repentance involves a radical turning toward God. While a negative aspect is implied, the emphasis falls on the positive side. This is true of both terms just discussed: "turn" (Acts 26:18, 20; 1 Pet. 2:25) and "repent" (Acts 20:21). In some contexts they are used together (Acts 3:19; 26:20), with "repent" possibly expressing the negative side—departing from evil. But the fact that "repent" becomes the dominant term in the New Testament seems to be explicable chiefly in the depth of the turning involved, a change in the ways of thinking and willing.[49]

Second, while having God as its object, repentance takes place in view of the coming of Christ and the kingdom or rule of God that comes with Him. John the Baptist summoned the nation to repentance in view of the imminence of the Kingdom (Matt. 3:2) and in particular of the impending appearance of the Coming One who would sort out those who had repented from those who had not (3:8-12). Jesus sounded the same summons as the keynote of His proclamation (Matt. 4:17; Mark 1:14-15), even if the content of repentance differed in part from that of the Baptist's preaching. In particular, He saw in himself the beginning of God's decisive intervention (Matt. 12:28), so that repentance consisted in acceptance of Him and His way (vv. 41-42). In Goetzmann's words: "Repentance is now no longer obedience to a law but to a person. The call to repentance becomes a call to discipleship."[50] It is no surprise, therefore, that in the primitive Christian preaching the call to repentance is coupled with a call to faith in Christ (Acts 11:21; 19:4; 20:21).

A third feature given prominence in the New Testament picture of repentance is the consequences that flow from it. Paramount among these is the forgiveness of sins. In the Baptist's proclamation,

---

49. Cf. J. Goetzmann, "The change in the choice of words *metanoeō* instead of *epistrephō*—shows that the NT does not stress the concrete, physical concept implied in the OT use of *šûb*, but rather the thought, the will, the *nous*" ("Conversion," in NIDNTT 1:357).

50. Goetzmann, "Conversion," 358. Goetzmann notes that in consequence "there are many passages in which the term *metanoeō* does not appear, but in which the thought of repentance is clearly present." Among the passages he cites are Matt. 18:3; Luke 14:33; Matt. 5:3 (ibid., 358-59).

which called for the visible expression of repentance in baptism in water, baptism is defined as a repentance-baptism leading to the forgiveness of sins (Mark 1:4). Repentance and forgiveness are conjoined in the message Jesus' followers are commissioned to proclaim (Luke 24:47), and it is this very proclamation that stands at the heart of the apostolic preaching (Acts 2:38; 3:19; 5:31). However, repentance is taken to have positive implications as well as negative. Besides involving the remission of sin, it also brings with it a new quality of life, so that it is sometimes described as "repentance unto life" (11:18), a life characterized by light and lived in the light of God and the strength of God (26:18; Eph. 5:8). Such a life—in Laubach's words—"receives a new outlook and objectives. God's original purpose in creating man is realized in the new life."[51]

If the foregoing is sound—that the good news of forgiveness is for all; that while the law stands as the declaration of the eternal will of God, yet it comes as a gift of grace to sinners, not merely as a list of requirements; and that where there has been a falling short of God's will, as is the case with everyone (Rom. 3:23), repentance brings restoration—then one must ask what is the implication of this for divorcés. The Bible speaks of only one sin as unpardonable, and it is not divorce. The Samaritan woman had had five husbands (John 4:17-18), but this did not prevent her from coming to faith in Jesus as Messiah (v. 29) and bringing others also to faith in Jesus as Savior (vv. 39-42). Paul, likewise, having listed various sexual sins, including adultery, as grounds of exclusion from the kingdom of God, goes on to say of some of his Corinthian readers: "And [this] is what some of you were. But you were washed, you were sanctified, you were justified in the name of the Lord Jesus Christ and by the Spirit of our God" (1 Cor. 6:11).[52]

Paul's confidence is not always as prominent among his professed followers as it might be. Heth and Wenham, whose view of the whole matter is that "it seems safest to say that Jesus gave an absolute prohibition of divorce and remarriage,"[53] courageously confront the question about what is to be said to those already remar-

---

51. Laubach, "Conversion," 1:355.
52. Even von Allmen, arguing that every sexual union constitutes a couple, nevertheless concedes that, in the case of casual liaisons "it would be very wrong, however, to imagine that couples formed in this manner necessarily endure indefinitively. In fact, according to Paul, there can be pardon for fornicators who repent" (*Pauline Teaching on Marriage,* 34). See his preceding discussion on 32-33.
53. Heth and Wenham, *Jesus and Divorce,* 198.

ried after divorce. Their response to such persons is: "We believe that you should see that your present marriage is now God's will for you. You should seek to be the best husband or wife you can be, rendering to each other your full marital duty. If you come to the realization that Jesus calls remarriage after divorce the sin of adultery, then call sin 'sin' rather than seek to justify what you have done."[54]

While forgiveness is implied in such a statement, it is hardly the dominant reality nor is its application in such situations worked out with any precision. The impression that remains is of a somewhat grudging acceptance, which is permanently overshadowed by a relationship that is and will always remain wrong. Such a position seems inevitable on the view of marriage held by Heth and Wenham—that of covenant kinship—in which marriage creates a bond that is as binding as a blood relationship and therefore as indissoluble. When marriage is conceived in mechanistic terms, so that it becomes irreversible, then any breach of it, and particularly remarriage following divorce, would seem to be morally irretrievable. If marriage is incapable of being dissolved, divorce is an empty word and remarriage a synonym for adultery. No other option seems to be available.

It is difficult to see how Heth and Wenham can find it possible to say of such a remarriage that it "is now God's will." This accounts for the ambivalence conveyed by the quotation above. The impression given is that while the guilt may be pierced by an occasional shaft of the light of forgiveness, no one should expect that it will be dissipated by it completely.

Yet this is hardly the characteristic note of the New Testament. Paul was not slow to confess his past sins, including his persecution of the Church and complicity in the judicial murder of Stephen (Acts 22:19-20; cf. 7:57—8:1). However conscience-stricken Paul's confessions are, they always resound with the affirmation of the triumph of grace. "For I am the least of the apostles and do not even deserve to be called an apostle, because I persecuted the church of God. But by the grace of God I am what I am, and his grace to me was not without effect" (1 Cor. 15:9-10a). "I thank Christ Jesus our Lord, who has given me strength, that he considered me faithful, appointing me to his service. Even though I was once a blasphemer and a persecutor and a violent man, I was shown mercy" (1 Tim. 1:12-13a).

---

54. Ibid., 200.

It does better justice to biblical teaching to say that God takes us where He finds us. Not only have all fallen short of His design, but some have departed from it in ways that ensure that it will never be fully reproduced in their lives, the fullness of God's grace notwithstanding. Those who have divorced and remarried can never conform to God's plan for marriage as permanent and lifelong, but while forgiveness can never obliterate the *fact* of a past wrong, nor the responsibility for any ongoing consequences of such a wrong, it can assuredly obliterate the *guilt* of a past wrong. When the guilt of a past wrong is remitted, a new situation is created in respect of the wrong in question. What no longer carries guilt in the sight of God has lost its power to survive as an impediment in the relation of the soul with Him.

It is hardly for the Church to erect obstacles where God has removed them. That the old life stands under condemnation is sure, but that the condemnation of sinners for their past life is removed is just as sure. Both realities must be acknowledged, and the Christian name for such acknowledgment is repentance, which confesses the wrongness of the old life with the same readiness with which it accepts the gift of the new.

5 ❧ Divorce and Remarriage in the Church Today

IN THE END, all of the problems and questions about marriage, divorce, and remarriage present themselves in human form every time the church meets for worship. The pastor likewise confronts them at close quarters when parishioners come for counsel, as also do Christian parents to whom divorce has always been unthinkable but who are stunned to find that it has penetrated their own family. What is the church to do? What is the pastor to advise? How are the Christian parents to respond?

If the biblical understanding of marriage and the bearing of the gospel on marital breakdown have been correctly expounded above, then the one thing that is clear is there is no rule of thumb to be applied mechanically in all cases, no one-size-fits-all solution, no ready-made list of "grounds" on which divorce is to be permitted or denied. The constraints of the Church's situation arise directly from the teaching of the Church's Lord. On the one hand is God's design and intention that marriage is for life and is not to be ended for any reason other than death. On the other hand is the Good News, whose proclamation, a prime reason for the Church's existence, affirms that God's grace extends to every sinful breach of God's will, including His will regarding marriage. If there is one guiding principle to be insisted on and followed, it is that neither of these aspects is to be enforced in such a way as to nullify or obliterate the other.

Holding the two together, however, is not always easy. This is the Church's dilemma, a dilemma that it has not always successfully resolved, as is admitted by many Christian communities. For example, the Church, attempting to be faithful to the biblical teaching of the permanence of marriage, has frequently closed its doors to the divorced, in practice if not also in theory. The degree to which this has happened has varied from one communion to another, depending on whether divorce was accepted at all (in which case the party adjudged innocent continued to be admitted to the Lord's Table), or whether it was outlawed altogether (in which case exclusion was complete), or whether remarriage following divorce was permitted or denied (with consequences similar to those just noted).[1]

As attempts to maintain a high view of marriage such responses are admirable. However, whatever success they may have enjoyed in achieving that end, their impact upon the Church's capacity in both evangelism and pastoral ministry has been called in question by steadily rising divorce rates. From the 1960s through the 1980s these rose dramatically, so that while they plateaued in the 1980s, they involved between 40 to 50 percent of all marriages.[2] The net effect of this state of affairs was that churches that maintained a high view of marriage were automatically distanced from a growing percentage of the population, a distancing increased by the fact that five out of six men and three out of four women remarried shortly after divorce.[3] What this amounted to was that a large and growing segment of the population was placed beyond the Church's ministry.[4] They had done a deed that, in principle, was irreversible. For them there was no gospel. For all practical purposes they were outcasts.

Now it is not the responsibility of the Church to reshape the gospel to suit the taste of the marketplace, but it assuredly is the responsibility of the Church to ask itself if the gospel is being emptied

---

1. For example, the Roman Catholic Church, which has been a stout defender of the indissolubility of marriage, while not excluding the divorced from the Eucharist, enacted the penalty of excommunication upon those who remarried following a civil divorce. For details, with special reference to the United States, see Gerald D. Coleman, *Divorce and Remarriage in the Catholic Church* (New York: Paulist Press, 1988), 57-62. As Coleman indicates (and we shall see), that position, which was based on the 1917 Code of Canon Law, has now been changed.

2. For statistics (with references), see Jack Dominian, "The Consequences of Marital Breakdown," in *Divorce and Remarriage, Religious and Psychological Perspectives,* ed. William P. Roberts (Kansas City: Sheed and Ward, 1990), 128.

3. Dominian, "The Consequences of Marital Breakdown," 131; Coleman, *Divorce and Remarriage in the Catholic Church,* 8.

4. The point is illustrated vividly by the statistics for divorce and remarriage among Roman Catholics. Divorce rates among Roman Catholics are approximately the same as those among the population at large. Coleman writes, "It is a conservative estimate that there are at least six million U.S. Catholics who have been divorced; and since 1978 U.S. Diocesan marriage tribunals have processed approximately forty thousand annulment petitions each year. It is further estimated that seventy-five percent of divorced Catholics in the United States have remarried or will eventually do so, most without benefit of annulment and without a Catholic celebration of these new marriages" (*Divorce and Remarriage in the Catholic Church,* 5-6).

of its meaning by the implicit claim that there are situations in which it has no word of grace to utter. Doubtless it is easy to make sweeping generalizations on both sides of this issue, and this precisely defines the Church's dilemma. The Church affirms both the permanence of marriage and the message of grace, yet in many concrete situations it is impossible to attain both. What, then, is to be the Church's response?

Denominations have reacted differently. Some, while steadfastly refusing to permit the remarriage of divorcés in church, have made provision for a service of blessing of such marriages following a civil ceremony. For many years this was the practice of the Church of England, though it has been trenchantly criticized by Anglican theologians of all stripes as being logically and theologically absurd and even hypocritical.[5] More recently, the Church of England has agreed that in certain circumstances divorcés might be remarried in church.[6] Of particular relevance here is the recognition by Anglican theologians of the importance in such remarriages of giving clear expression both to the truths of the permanence of marriage and the forgiveness of the sinner. John Stott writes: "It could express this ambivalence either by permitting the remarriage in church (emphasizing the gospel of redemption), while adding some kind of discipline (recognizing God's marriage ideal), or by refusing the remarriage in church (emphasizing the ideal), while adding some expression of acceptance (recognizing the gospel). I myself incline to the former."[7]

The Roman Catholic Church, which, in an earlier age, pronounced the penalty of excommunication on all who remarried following divorce, has also sensed that such a position did scant justice to the note of grace in the gospel. Contemporary Roman Catholic theologians therefore lay great stress on Pope John Paul II's exhortation "Community of the Family," promulgated on November 22, 1981, which made the following points (among others). "First, Catholics who are divorced and who have not remarried enjoy full and complete union with the Church. They are not excommunicated. They may receive the Eucharist. Second, Catholics who are divorced and

---

5. See Andrew Cornes, *Divorce and Remarriage* (Grand Rapids: Wm. B. Eerdmans Publishing Co., 1993), 482-84.

6. For a brief account, see John Stott, *Decisive Issues Facing Christians Today,* 2nd ed. (Old Tappan, N.J.: Fleming H. Revell, 1990), 304-5.

7. Ibid., 305.

remarried should 'not consider themselves as separated from the Church, for as baptized persons they can and indeed must share in its life.' These persons, in other words, are not excommunicated and should consider themselves members of the whole community of the faithful. Third, Catholics who are divorced and remarried may not participate in the Eucharist because their new relationship, the new marital bond, objectively contradicts the first marital union, which the Church always desires to protect."[8] Here again we see an attempt to be faithful both to the divine pattern of marriage as permanent as well as to the good news of grace and forgiveness.

These examples are sufficient to show the difficulty of holding together God's design for marriage as lifelong and the word of pardon and grace to those who have failed in this design. They are also sufficient to show the necessity of holding these two together if the Church is to be a faithful and audible voice in a generation riddled with marital chaos.

We may now turn to some of the specific issues that give rise to or are leading problems in the current situation, as well as consider how they may be approached on the basis of the conclusions reached in the earlier chapters of this book.

Marriage as an Institution Today

Marriage in Western society at the end of the 20th century is vastly different from what it has been at any time in the recent or distant past. Even into the 19th century "arranged marriages" were far from unknown, the couple having very little if any say in the decision. Indeed, this aspect of marriage culture survives in many marriage services in the form of the ritual of the "giving" of the bride, the implication being that she is her father's property, to be disposed of as he considers best.

If the 20th-century mentality differs from that of recent centuries, it differs still more from the cultural mind-set of the centuries during which the Bible was written. In large areas of the Old Testament world, marriage was viewed as much in terms of possession of property as of moral purity, so that in the 10th commandment a neighbor's wife is bundled together with the rest of his property— his cattle and asses—upon which one must not cast a covetous eye

---

8. As summarized by Coleman, *Divorce and Remarriage in the Catholic Church,* 10-11.

(Exod. 20:17). This is why in Old Testament law while a wife could commit adultery against her husband, the reverse was not possible, since she was his property and he was not hers. A man could commit adultery only against another man by taking his wife (Lev. 20:10).

In the New Testament much of this is set aside. Jesus affirmed the equality of male and female, thereby giving the wife equal sexual rights over her husband (Mark 10:7-12), a view echoed by Paul (1 Cor. 7:4). However, in dealing with specific problems in local situations, some New Testament writers make concessions to existing social structures where the application of the teaching of Jesus in undiluted strength would have brought about the suppression of the Church altogether. The most obvious example of this is slavery, which is totally incompatible with the New Testament view that all God's creatures are made in His image.

Marriage likewise in its full meaning as reflected in the teaching of Jesus and Paul is sometimes presented in truncated form, apparently in the recognition that it must make its own path step-by-step in the old mind-set of the old world.[9] Thus even when enjoining mutual subjection of all Christians to each other (Eph. 5:21), Paul still speaks of the wife-husband relationship in terms of submission and headship, and—astonishingly—while exhorting husbands to love their wives (v. 25), never once exhorts wives to love their husbands! Again, the picture of the family (including the wife) presupposed in Col. 3:18—4:1 is strictly hierarchical.[10]

---

9. Richard N. Longenecker characterizes this understanding as "the developmental nature of Christian thought and expression as portrayed in the New Testament" (*New Testament Social Ethics for Today* [Grand Rapids: Wm. B. Eerdmans Publishing Co., 1984], 84). He continues, "We need to be conscious of the fact that in seeking to work out the principles of the gospel for his day, Paul and his colleagues seem to have been working from two important categories of thought: that category of thought which emphasizes what God has done through creation, wherein order, subordination and submission are generally stressed, and that category which emphasizes what God has done redemptively, wherein freedom, mutuality, and equality take prominence." Earlier, he has affirmed that the baseline of the New Testament view of society is Gal. 3:28 where Paul speaks "without any qualification or reservations" (75). He quotes approvingly F. F. Bruce's comment on this verse, "Paul states the basic principle here: if restrictions on it are found elsewhere in the Pauline corpus, . . . they are to be understood in relation to Gal. 3:28, and not '*vice versa*'" (84).

10. On account of such elements, some scholars have concluded that biblical sexual ethics have very little relevance to life today. Cf. L. William Countryman, *Dirt, Greed, and Sex* (Philadelphia: Fortress, 1988). Using a distinctly reductionist approach, Coun-

In today's world, however, the expectations of marriage are very different from those presupposed in such passages. In a paradoxical way one may say that the popular hopes and expectations of marriage come closer to the biblical picture of marriage at its best: mutual caring and lifelong fidelity. Yet this expectation is cherished at the very time when there is the least moral commitment for the attainment of that vision. But this is the vision that draws people to marriage. Sociologists agree that despite the high divorce rate, there is no loss of interest in marriage as an institution. This is confirmed by the fact that almost half of all remarriages take place within three years of divorce, and 75 percent of the divorced form a new attachment within the first year of separation and 90 percent at the end of the second year.[11] "It is important to state," writes Coleman, "that all reliable data supports the conclusion that for Americans . . . the importance of marriage and family life has not in any way decreased, and expectations about marital permanence and stability continue to remain very high, even among young people."[12]

Contemporary marriage is thus called upon to deliver most at a time when its moral capacity enables it to deliver least. This is perhaps the greatest challenge confronting Christian marriage today. In particular, the search for personal fulfillment, security from loneliness, the consciousness of belonging in a faceless world, and the deep desire for peace amid life's rush and restlessness—all come to expression in the desire for communion in the intimacy of marriage. It is possible to brand this as "selfishness," as John Stott does,[13] and in some cases it may be so. It may also be part of that yearning for the society of another that marriage was created to fulfill (Gen. 2:23-24). It is a probable confirmation of this that Roman Catholic theology—which in an earlier day named procreation of children as the primary purpose of marriage, and the mutual help of the spouses as only the secondary end—decisively rejected such a distinction at the Second Vatican Council.[14] "Childless marriages are still fruitful marriages," writes Lawler, interpreting the council's teaching, "made

---

tryman derives at most broad guidelines for Christian sexual life (241-65). Such an approach does scant justice to the vision of marriage as covenant loyalty that represents the loftiest teaching of both testaments.

11. Coleman, *Divorce and Remarriage in the Catholic Church,* 8.

12. Ibid., 6.

13. Stott, *Decisive Issues Facing Christians Today,* 287.

14. For an account, see Lawler, *Marriage and Sacrament* (Collegeville, Minn.: Liturgical Press, 1993), 70-71.

fruitful by the life of communion between the spouses generated and nurtured in them. . . . The generation and the loving nurture of children frequently enhances the life of communion between the spouses, but if there is communion generated and nurtured between them—mutual love, mutual care, mutual concern, mutual joy, mutual enhancement of life—their marriage is already immensely fruitful even if childless."[15]

All of this confirms the accuracy of Jack Dominian's conviction that we are now witnessing "a profound change in the nature of marriage." "The name remains the same, but its inner world is changing from being primarily a permanent contract, in which children and their welfare were its main concern, to a relationship intended to be permanent, in which companionship, equality and personal fulfillment are becoming just as important as the welfare of children."[16] If there is something in this that is profoundly consonant with the biblical pattern of marriage, there is also something profoundly challenging to the Church in the failure of married couples, both within the Church and outside of it, to achieve it.

How then is the Church to address the current travail? In particular, given the conclusion reached earlier that lifelong marriage is God's design, but there is grace where there has been failure, how is this to be put into practice in the hard reality of life situations? How is the Church to do justice to both sides of its responsibility? It is easy enough to do justice to one side, but the Church's commission is to preach and practice both. How is this to be done?

Some General Guidelines

Before coming to specific issues, it may help to clear the ground by attempting to formulate some principles to guide the overall approach. The operative word here is "principles." As indicated above, there is no set of rules or litmus tests to be applied in all cases. That appears not to have been the intention of the biblical teaching in any case, not least the teaching of Jesus. Moreover, the causes and consequences of broken marriages are too complex and diverse to be treated with a single-gauge approach. However, some guidelines must be established, if only in broad terms, to ensure that both of the Church's interests are not only safeguarded but actively contributing to each individual situation.

---

15. Ibid., 102-3.
16. Quoted in Stott, *Decisive Issues Facing Christians Today,* 287.

First, it must be laid down that no solution is consistent with the biblical teaching that does not admit that divorce is a departure from God's intended design for marriage. To say that divorce is always wrong, or even more that it is sinful, is to make a statement that is too sweeping to be true and too hurtful to be gracious, as will be discussed more fully below. There must be a recognition that it is a serious breach of God's plan for His creatures, and that the mind-set that it is acceptable to change spouses when things get "too difficult" is not one that is reconcilable with the Christian understanding of marriage. It was this very mentality that prompted Jesus to make His swingeing attack on divorce in Matt. 19:3-9.

Second, bound up with the recognition of the seriousness of divorce as a breach of God's design must be repentance commensurate with the responsibility for the breach. Again, this will vary from case to case. In instances where individuals have had unwanted divorce thrust upon them, a sense of failure will be more likely than a sense of sin. The consciousness that God is the ultimate victim of our sin (Ps. 51:4) is a truth that will give repentance focus and depth.

Third, where marriage has broken down beyond repair, the Christian guideline must be the closest approximation possible to God's original design for marriage. Again, this will vary from one case to another, though in no case will it make possible the fulfillment of God's original intent. In that respect, however, the divorced are in principle like all other penitent sinners: exhibitors of God's grace despite the scars sin has left upon them. As to its practical outworking, some will choose a life of celibacy, using the freedom such a state brings for the greater service of Christ. Both Jesus and Paul spoke of it in such terms (Matt. 19:10-12; 1 Cor. 7:32-33). Other factors also demand a hearing. Among these are the reality of sexuality, which is not extinguished by divorce (1 Cor. 7:1-9), the desire for a stable Christian home for children, as well as the longing for a life of fulfillment and Christian service. These are not ignoble or sub-Christian considerations. Nor should such marriages be regarded as substandard. Sometimes we are not given a choice between good and evil but only between lesser goods and lesser evils. The function—and the power—of grace is precisely to create good out of evil and to transform the ruins of human life into restored exhibits of redemptive grace.

With these general guidelines in mind, we may now take up in a more particular way some specific areas where the question of divorce and remarriage confronts the Church today.

The Divorce and Remarriage of Christians

If divorce is a breach of God's plan and will, then how can it ever be an option to which a Christian can have recourse? Within what frame of reference may a Christian resort to it? Even if these questions can be answered satisfactorily within a biblical framework, what of the question of remarriage after divorce?

At least two sets of considerations must be taken into account, one practical, the other theological. The two categories are not completely watertight, as might be expected. The practical considerations have theological implications, just as the theological considerations have practical bearings, but the distinction has broad validity and is useful for purposes of classification. Moreover, care must be taken not to insulate the two categories from each other in a way that effectively neutralizes either one. For example, it is fatally easy, in a pragmatic age such as ours, to convince oneself that a marriage is no longer "workable" when what is really needed is honest effort and openness to the reconciling grace of God. On the other side, it is just as easy to use theological considerations to manacle together a marriage that has long since ceased to be a marriage in any meaningful sense or to have any hope of becoming one. Keeping these dangers in mind, we may now turn to the two sets of factors involved.

1. Practical Considerations

We may move from those where the case is clearer and less disputable to those where a finer calculus is called for and the issues more difficult to judge.

First, there are situations in which divorce is virtually the only course to secure the physical, emotional, and material well-being of a spouse and/or children. Physical violence, emotional terror, sexual abuse of spouse or children are forms of maltreatment unjustifiable and unacceptable in terms of any theology that deserves to be called Christian. No serious Christian will want to rush to judgment on these matters. At the same time, no one can be asked seriously to accept as a way of life a relationship in which fear for survival or the warping of the lives of young children are abiding and deadly realities. It would be argued by some that all of these ends can be secured by legal separation. Where this is so, it should certainly be followed. Divorce should always be the course of last resort. At the same time, the law at its best is a blunt instrument, and there undoubtedly are cases where divorce provides the best if not the only way of securing a shield against treatment whose effect is destructive of human life and values.

Second, there are situations in which the capacities that make marriage possible are claimed to be absent (or never to have been present), and marriage is renounced not merely as unwanted but as unsustainable. Examples of this would be those in which a spouse would claim a homosexual or lesbian orientation with an intent to pursue the accompanying lifestyle. In some Christian traditions as well as some legal systems such unions would be treated as never having been marriages, so that a declaration of nullity rather than divorce would be pronounced to dissolve them. However, in many such cases parenthood is involved, which, with its ongoing responsibilities, makes the claim that there has never been a marriage look somewhat theoretical. However that may be, it is hard to maintain that legal termination of the relationship should be excluded.

Third, there are situations in which marriage has effectively ended in respect of all of those elements that make marriage what it is: mutual commitment, mutual support, companionship, affection, common pleasure. In short, the question is, Is such a marriage a real marriage, and if not, has it any hope of becoming one? One must move very carefully at this point. All marriages have their problems, and it is fatally easy to seize upon a given problem and use it as an excuse for seeking divorce when it is simply an idle and sinful evasion of the responsibility of paying the price of keeping one's covenant.[17]

The Christian's first responsibility in marital crisis is always to seek reconciliation and to continue seeking it until all reasonable expectation of it has disappeared. It is true that some argue that we

---

17. Such an attitude has been fostered by the legal doctrine (now the law in many countries) that the sole ground on which marriages can be dissolved is that of irretrievable marriage breakdown. Some recent Roman Catholic theology appears to be moving in the same direction. Michael Lawler writes, "A sacramental marriage becomes indissoluble only when the marital love on which it is founded attains its practical fullness as communion that is mutually faithful and loyal, that is mutually giving way and that is mutually servant. Even sacramental marriage acquires indissolubility only when, and because, the marital love that grounds it has become faithful and indissoluble" (*Marriage and Sacrament*, 105; see the entire section on "Indissoluble Marital Love and Indissoluble Marriage, 104-6). Insofar as this means anything, it appears to mean that indissoluble marriage is marriage that does not break down. There is no explicit affirmation that, in God's design, marriage is not intended to break down, and when it does an essential element in Christian marriage is breached. Lawler's treatment of what is known in Roman Catholic Canon Law as divorce by "internal forum" (i.e., on the basis of good conscience where objective evidence is lacking) is more adequate in this respect (*Marriage and Sacrament*, 109-11, especially 111).

can never know when a marriage is broken beyond possibility of repair, and therefore there can never be a time when a Christian may justifiably sue for divorce. Indeed, this argument against divorce was used by some of the church fathers.[18] Yet it is hard not to conclude that in some cases, actions so destructive of confidence and attitudes built up and calcified over years have so distorted personalities, reactions, and outlooks that reconciliation is very unlikely.[19] This conclusion must be reached by Christians in that situation in good conscience, with the recognition of failure, rather than with the desire to "get their freedom."

It is worth noting that in 1 Cor. 7:11, where Paul is apparently addressing a wife who has separated from her husband, he implicitly accepts the impossibility of reconciliation as an option in that case. He does not *order* her to be reconciled to her husband, presumably because reconciliation is not something that can necessarily be produced to order.

The factor common to all of these situations is that the covenant of marriage has been broken. This does not end a marriage automatically, but it creates a situation in which the marriage can be saved only if the covenant is restored through repentance and reconciliation. This brings us to the theological considerations involved.

2. Theological Considerations

Given, then, that a Christian comes in good conscience to the point that divorce seems to be the only option in an insupportable situation, what theological considerations call for attention?

First, the act of divorce must function as a vehicle of penitence. The place of repentance was commented on above but merits mention again. It is not necessarily true that blame rests equally upon both partners in a failed marriage. Nor is it true that there is no such thing as an innocent party in a divorce. No doubt things may have been said and done on both sides that did nothing to contribute to the survival of the marriage, but these can scarcely be equated with the material causes that led to breakdown. To refer to an example already cited, where a hitherto unrecognized or concealed sexual deviation

---

18. See for example Hermas, *The Shepherd, Mandate* 4.1. (For discussion, see the Appendix: "Marriage and Divorce in the Early Church to the Time of Augustine," Section 1.)

19. Some cases, indeed, call not just for supernatural grace for the spirit but supernatural healing for the psyche.

comes into the open together with the declared intention to indulge it, it is difficult to see how the other partner can be held at fault.

Nevertheless, there will very frequently be fault on both sides, and in the cases where that is not so, there will be a sense of grief at having fallen short of God's pattern for marriage. It is worth noting that in Matt. 5:32, the husband who divorces his wife is held to be guilty along with his divorced wife, who alone is described specifically in the setting of remarriage. In short, divorce by itself stands under condemnation because it is a departure from God's will that a husband "cleave" or "cling" or remain "united to" his wife (Gen. 2:24). All of this comes to expression for the Christian in the act of divorce. In the words of Eduard Schweizer: "Divorce *can* be a sign of repentance by which two people face up to their failure. It *can* be a confession that they have not succeeded in living according to God's will, i.e., on the basis of His gift. Divorce *can,* therefore, set one free to experience anew the mercy of God."[20]

Second, by formalizing the end of the covenant (already broken, in fact), divorce also formalizes the end of the marriage. It was argued above[21] that a central element in the biblical understanding of marriage is the element of covenant-commitment. Where that commitment is withdrawn or canceled, the covenant to which it is attached—in the case under consideration, marriage—is ended. It is maintained by some that since in the Old Testament (especially Ezek. 16) God's covenant with Jerusalem is spoken of in terms of marital faithfulness and is never broken despite Judah's infidelity (v. 60), therefore the marriage covenant is also unbreakable.[22] But this is to overlook that human marriages are made between two sinful human beings, not between the infinite, holy, and loving God and a wayward partner. While the divine purpose, inherent in the very meaning of marriage, is that it be lifelong, yet the effects of sin, moral and nonmoral, upon that relationship can be so grievous that the covenant loses all meaning and therefore is ended.[23] Divorce is the recognition of this.

---

20. Eduard Schweizer, *The Good News According to Mark,* ET Donald H. Madvig (Atlanta: John Knox Press, 1976), 206.

21. See chap. 1, especially the section "The Ideal of Marriage in the Old Testament."

22. Stott, *Decisive Issues Facing Christians Today,* 302. Stott goes on to concede that the marriage covenant can, in fact, be broken but only by "fundamental sexual unfaithfulness" (302). This he bases on the exceptive clauses in Matt. 5:32; 19:9.

23. John Murray writes, "Granting the basic and original principle of the indissolu-

Third, should remarriage come to be envisaged, it must be in the light of the recognition of the previous failure, as well as in solemn and sincere commitment to the Christian view of marriage as lifelong. As to the former, penitence should already have been a factor at the time of divorce. In the words of D. S. Bailey: "The failure of love can destroy *henosis* (oneness), and civil divorce can annul the marriage, but only repentance can sever the bond of guilt for their failure which still unites husband and wife to one another. Without that repentance and all that it must cost, they are tied together and cannot escape. . . . Nor, when the penitence is not on both sides, is the repentant one bound to the unrepentant; it is for each individual to sever the connection with the dead but persistent marriage, the sinful and tragic past. For the impenitent, then, it is clear that there ought to be no permission to remarry, but the case of the repentant is different; there it seems that with proper safeguards a second union might be allowed."[24]

This leads to the second prerequisite: honest acceptance of and commitment to Christian marriage as permanent. Promises come easily, especially to those contemplating marriage. The responsibility therefore rests heavily upon pastors, who are the frontline defenders of Christian marriage, to urge the probing of conscience that reveals the real depth of such declarations as far as may be, so that the moral issues do not become lost in the emotion and glitter of a wedding ceremony.

Remarriage for Divorced Ministers?[25]

Whatever be the case with others, it is frequently concluded that remarriage for divorced ministers is explicitly and definitively exclud-

---

bility of the marriage bond, yet, by reason of sin, are there any conditions under which the marriage tie may be dissolved with divine sanction and authorization? When we are asked this question we must never forget that the sinful situation which compels us to raise the question is one that rests under the divine judgment . . . Yet presupposing divine condemnation of the sinful situation in its totality and of the specifically sinful condition that might provide the ground for divorce, it is still possible to envisage a divinely authorized and instituted right of divorce. It is quite conceivable that while the reason for divorce is sinful the right of divorce for that reason may be divine" (*Divorce,* 2). Murray, as noted above (chap. 3, pp. 100-110), holds that the divinely authorized reason is sexual infidelity. I have argued that it is the divine grace that forgives any sin where there is repentance.

24. Bailey, *Mystery of Love and Marriage,* 83-84.

25. Throughout this section I am greatly indebted to the perceptive and well-documented treatment of the issue in Keener, *And Marries Another,* chap. 7.

ed by the plain words of the Pastoral Epistles. In particular, one of the qualifications for bishops or overseers (1 Tim. 3:1-2), deacons (v. 12), and elders (Titus 1:6) is that they be "the husband[s] of one wife" (KJV), which, on the view referred to, is taken to mean "never divorced and remarried." However, this is not the only possible interpretation of the expression in English and Greek. It could just as easily mean "the husband of one wife at a time," in which case its force would be to ban polygamy. This is the meaning suggested by the NIV rendering, "the husband of but one wife." Or again, the phrase might mean "one wife per lifetime," forbidding remarriage not only after divorce but after the death of a wife. This is the meaning suggested by the NRSV rendering, "married only once."

To review these different options is to raise the question, If the phrase by itself can bear so many meanings, how is the correct one to be identified? Guidance may be sought from several sources, particularly the relevant contexts in which these passages stand. These are three: the comparative, the cultural, and the local contexts.

First, the components of the comparative context—that is, the passages in the two Epistles in which the expression occurs—differ in many respects. Titus 1:4-9 is not only much briefer than 1 Tim. 3:1-7 (though both deal with the qualifications for bishops)[26] but much less specific. This implies that the list of qualifications was not standardized and that—in Keener's words—"Paul is establishing some new rules for some new situations."[27] If this is so, then the qualities enjoined are likely to relate in the first instance to the immediate situation, rather than have universal application.[28]

This conclusion is reinforced by the second context, namely, the cultural. It is entirely improbable that polygamy is in mind, for this was banned in Roman law; and while it remained theoretically legal in Jewish law, its practice is difficult to document. Indeed, Jews living in the Diaspora, where Timothy and Titus were working, conformed

---

26. Unless Titus 1:5-6 deals with bishops and verses 7-9 with elders. This seems unlikely, however, since the two pairs of verses are linked by the conjunction "for" (Greek *gar*). J. N. D. Kelly suggests that bishops were drawn from the ranks of the elders so the qualifications for both were the same (*A Commentary on the Pastoral Epistles* [Peabody, Mass.: Hendrickson Publishers, 1987], 13-14, 231-32.

27. Keener, *And Marries Another*, 86. Cf. also, "The fact that the two lists diverge slightly also indicates that the list was not an invariable standard for all situations" (101).

28. As Keener again points out, "Had the list already been standard, leaders like Titus—and certainly Timothy—would have already known its content, because they had been with Paul and had seen him appoint church leaders before" (ibid., 101).

to the practice of their Greek neighbors. Polygamy therefore is very unlikely to have been the target of this directive.

There is more to be said for the proposal that "one wife per lifetime" is in mind. This is particularly so in view of the complementary expression "the wife of one man" in 1 Tim. 5:9 (KJV), rendered in NRSV as "married only once" (though the marginal rendering of the Greek is given as "the wife of one husband"). There is abundant evidence from Roman, Greek, and Jewish sources that women who did not remarry following bereavement were held in high esteem.[29] This is the view held by some interpreters to be enjoined here, and since the parallel expression is used in reference to bishops in 1 Tim. 3:2 and Titus 1:6, it is concluded that the rule for both men in ministry and widows serving the church and in turn being supported by it was that they should marry only once.[30] There are those who transfer this into the contemporary church without modification.[31]

However, there is no clear evidence of the use of the term "wife of one husband" (Latin *univira,* Greek *monandros*) by Christian writers until the second century, where asceticism began to make serious inroads into the Church as an ideal.[32] Moreover, it would be surprising to find anything that smacked of asceticism commended in the Pastoral Epistles where asceticism, far from being part of the solution, appears rather to have been part of the problem. This brings us to the third context to be considered, namely, the local context. It is noteworthy that in all three contexts under consideration the emphasis falls on having been a good parent and spouse (1 Tim. 5:10; 3:4-5; Titus 1:6).

On the other hand, there is specific condemnation of those who reject marriage or demean it (1 Tim. 4:1-3). It is more likely, therefore, that the expression "wife of one husband" in 1 Tim. 5:9 means "faithful to her husband" as it is rendered in the NIV and that the complementary phrase "husband of one wife" carries the corresponding meaning.[33] In short, marriage is being enjoined as a qualification for

---

29. Ibid., 92-94.

30. Kelly states bluntly that "this is the plain meaning" of the expression and proceeds to rule out alternatives (Kelly, *Commentary on the Pastoral Epistles,* 75). Likewise, J. H. Bernard, *The Pastoral Epistles* (Grand Rapids: Baker, reprint 1980), 52.

31. So Cornes, having discussed the meaning of the passages under consideration (*Divorce and Remarriage,* 272-76), draws as a conclusion for today (282) that "elders and deacons should not remarry after the death of a partner" (283).

32. So Keener, *And Marries Another,* 94.

33. Perhaps the rendering that best brings out the force of the original is that of

leadership in the Church against those maintaining the opposite and, as part of that, faithfulness within marriage. There is therefore a strongly local conditioning to this requirement.[34] In a situation in which marriage was under attack as an inferior state, Paul urges to the contrary that leaders be married; and in a world in which infidelity was commonplace, he insists on marital faithfulness.

The issue of divorce and remarriage is not therefore directly addressed, as if Paul had laid down a regulation for all time that church leaders must be married. No doubt his enjoining marital faithfulness has implications for divorce; it implies that Paul was at one with the rest of biblical teaching that divorce was departure from God's intention that marriage be lifelong. But this is not the same as saying that divorced persons are, for that very reason, permanently excluded from the ministry. Paul is simply not addressing that issue here. When the issue does arise, it should be dealt with in the light of the same holy grace of God that the gospel applies to everyone else.

The Pastoral Care of the Divorced

It lies beyond the scope of this book to deal with the pastoral side of the problems attendant on divorce. However, it may be worthwhile to draw the pastoral guidelines that follow from the general drift of the argument. Two may be mentioned.

---

the *New English Bible,* "faithful to his one wife" (1 Tim. 3:2, 12; Titus 1:6); "faithful in marriage to one man" (1 Tim. 5:9). C. H. Dodd comments, "The natural meaning . . . is surely, as Theodore [of Mopsuestia], says, 'a man who having contracted a monogamous marriage is faithful to his marriage vows,' excluding alike polygamy, concubinage and promiscuous indulgence" ("New Testament Translation Problems II," *The Bible Translator* 28 [1977]: 115). Gordon Fee, who agrees with this in regard to 1 Tim. 3:2, 12; Titus 1:6, holds that in regard to widows (1 Tim. 5:9) the reference is to second marriage" (*1 and 2 Timothy, Titus,* in *The New International Biblical Commentary* [Peabody, Mass.: Hendrickson Publishers, 1988], 80-81, 119). But the idea that a needy widow (which is what 1 Tim. 5:3-16 is concerned with) should be denied assistance because of having married seems odd by any standard. Dibelius and Conzelmann reject the suggestion, quoting Theodore of Mopsuestia's interpretation, "If she has lived in chastity with her husband, no matter whether she has had only one, or whether she was married a second time" (*The Pastoral Epistles,* in *Hermeneia* [Philadelphia: Fortress Press, 1972], 75).

34. Many of the other qualifications of the church leader presuppose not only a specific local situation but also the prevailing cultural setting of that time. For example, the requirement that he must manage his own family well (1 Tim. 3:4), which in Titus 1:6 becomes a requirement that his children be believers, presupposes an understanding of the family that belongs to the Greco-Roman world of the first century rather than the Western Hemisphere in the 20th century. For a much fuller discussion, see Keener, *And Marries Another,* 95-100.

First, the Church's attitude to the divorced must be inclusive and welcoming, not exclusive and discriminatory. James Denney said we must preach the gospel in the spirit of the gospel, and the divorced—including divorced Christians—are not excluded from hearing the Good News in its character as Good News. The Church has not exactly earned a title to fame in this respect. Book titles such as Richard Lyon Morgan's *Is There Life After Divorce in the Church?*[35] or Michael A. Braun's *Should Divorced People Be Treated like Second-Class Christians?*[36] tell the story only too eloquently. Morgan quotes Wayne Oates as saying of divorced people in the church, "They are like men [and women] without a country or lost sheep of the house of Israel as far as their relationship to the churches is concerned. The majority of divorced people find new meaning in remarriage. This has become the prevailing pattern in our society. But it puts them in opposition to the church, whose teachings hitherto allowed these people no room."[37] It is in this connection that one frequently encounters the bitter comment that "the Church is the only army in the world that shoots its own wounded."

The Church's actions will not change until its attitude changes, and its attitude will not change until its understanding changes. A duty therefore rests upon all pastors to lead their congregations to a biblical understanding of divorce that, while frankly admitting that it is a falling short of God's design, nonetheless does not constitute an automatic passport to the outer darkness. In the words of Dwight Hervey Small: "Let the church be bold in grace! Let the divorced and remarried feel fully accepted in the community of sinners saved by grace, for we are sinners all. . . . Set the remarried free to find their place of service in the church, alongside those whose experience of the forgiving grace of God may have been in less conspicuous areas of life's struggle."[38]

A second pastoral guideline indicated by the foregoing argument is that the Church's ministry to the divorced and the remarried must be to seek to bring restoration and healing. This is possible meaningfully only on the understanding of marriage as a moral real-

---

35. Atlanta: John Knox Press, 1985.
36. Downers Grove, Ill.: InterVarsity Press, 1989.
37. Quoted in Morgan, *Is There Life After Divorce in the Church?* 106.
38. Dwight Hervey Small, *Remarriage and God's Renewing Grace: A Positive Biblical Ethic for Divorced Christians* (Grand Rapids: Baker, 1986), 74-75.

ity—moral, that is to say, rather than physical (as implied by the blood-relationship view) or metaphysical (as implied by the view that marriage is absolutely indissoluble by nature). Neither of these views does justice to the moral element in the biblical view of marriage as covenant, because each assumes that when assent is truly given to the marriage covenant, it can never be undone.[39] The effect of this can only be to remove marriage from the moral sphere.[40] But where marriage can be the subject of moral breakdown, it can also be the subject of moral restoration, and only within such a context can there take place both the healing of the wounds that result from divorce and—where it occurs—the restoration of broken relationships or the forging of new ones.

Within such a framework, the pastoral care of the divorced will be directed to at least three distinguishable ends according to individual circumstances. First must stand the objective of mending broken marriages. Clearly this will extend beyond those already divorced to those separated but not yet divorced to those contemplat-

---

39. The point at issue is well expressed by Atkinson, "The covenant model for marriage places the question of divorce in the area of moral responsibility. The theology of the 'absolute indissolubility of marriage by natural law' seems to deny the above affirmation that men can and do choose whether or not to remain faithful to their covenant obligations. To argue that divorce is impossible is neither biblically warranted nor pastorally realistic. God's law for marriage is a moral law, and therefore it is possible to conceive of exceptions on the basis of handling situations of moral offence without pretending that some metaphysical relationship exists whatever moral choices we make and however irreparably broken in practice relationships may become. It does not, however, minimize the responsibility of the partners—and of society—before God to be answerable for the way the moral obligations of the permanence of marriage are handled" (*To Have and to Hold*, 152-53).

40. This is well illustrated by the tortured attempts of those who adhere to a quasi-mechanistic view of marriage (once done it cannot be undone), to describe the place and effect of forgiveness in those who have divorced and remarried. Thus Cornes writes of a second marriage following divorce, "Yes, it was a sin, it was disobedience to Christ, to enter into this new marriage. That sin, however, like any other can be entirely forgiven" (*Divorce and Remarriage*, 399). "But how should the couple regard themselves when one or both are divorced? Are they, in God's eyes, married or not?" (401). The answer given is that they are. However, though valid, their marriage is illegitimate. "In other words, they should not have married, but they are married. This of course does not dissolve their first marriage; only death can do that. It therefore means that they are in a similar position to those who practice polygamy" (402; Cornes's full treatment should be read). Is not this attempting to have it both ways? It is difficult to see how a marriage can be sinful, entirely forgiven, valid, illegitimate, and polygamous all at the same time. What Cornes has done is to subordinate moral categories to mechanistic ones, or rather, to insulate the latter from the former, creating two universes of meaning where, in reality, there is only one.

ing separation. The Church is the community of the reconciled, and its mission is to bring reconciliation wherever it is lacking. Beyond that, marriage is a covenant relationship to which the two parties have freely committed themselves before God and society. "The centre of the meaning of marriage," writes David Atkinson, "(not what it is *for,* nor how it is made, but what it *means*) is the expression of a bond of moral troth (that is, covenant faithfulness) in which two people marry each other before God, and pledge to each other loyalty, trust, devotion and reliability."[41] The first pastoral duty in marital breakdown is to seek to avert or reverse it on the basis of the original moral commitment.

This will not always succeed. Sometimes it has already been rendered impossible by the remarriage of one of the parties; sometimes it is rendered impossible by the refusal of one of the parties to contemplate reconciliation; sometimes the damage resulting from a devastated relationship is too great for reconciliation to be viewed as a serious possibility. The pastoral task then becomes that of seeking to bring healing where mending is foreclosed. The only secure base upon which healing can take place is a moral base. This is not to underestimate the emotional trauma sustained by the divorced. Only those who have experienced divorce know the pain, the anguish, the anger, the grief, the loneliness that belong to that condition. No responsible person would want to add to that emotional burden. Yet it is possible to try to heal human hurts too lightly, and this can easily happen where wounded emotions are addressed directly rather than in terms of the moral causes that have given rise to them. To treat the symptoms rather than the disease is merely to prolong the pain.

The primary moral reality where marriage is ended by divorce is broken covenant. The attempt to apportion blame is probably the wrong way to approach the issue. This is not to say that blame is always to be distributed equally or that there is never an innocent party. It is simply to say that the first step toward healing is not the apportioning of blame but the recognition of failure. Dwight Hervey Small writes: "All divorce is failure, and failure itself represents a breach of God's intent . . . this does not mean that divorce is always a direct result of sin on the part of one or both partners. In some in-

---

41. Atkinson, *To Have and to Hold,* 85. Atkinson goes on to develop the idea of covenant faithfulness as involving faithfulness to a vow, a calling, a person, and a relationship (85-87).

stances it is but not always. Yet of every divorce it can be said that it is a consequence of the disorder brought into our world by sin."[42]

The recognition of failure carries within itself the readiness to receive forgiveness; and on Christian terms, the readiness to receive forgiveness carries within itself the readiness to forgive. "Forgive us our debts, as we also have forgiven our debtors. . . . For if you forgive men when they sin against you, your heavenly Father will also forgive you. But if you do not forgive men their sins, your Father will not forgive your sins" (Matt. 6:12, 14-15). Such forgiveness, especially with respect to treachery and failure in the most intimate of human relationships, is not in human nature. It is only when God's forgiveness has been sought and received that it is possible as well as necessary and desirable to confer forgiveness on a former partner. Only then will healing begin to take place.

A third setting in which pastoral care of the divorced finds expression is where divorce is followed by remarriage. Once more, the only secure foundation on which this can rest is the moral. Remarriage undertaken to fill a void, as a cure for loneliness, or, worst of all, as the underlying intent of the divorce all along falls hopelessly short of the Christian idea of covenantal commitment and is almost certainly part of the reason the rate of failure for second marriages is as high as, if not higher than, the failure rate for first marriages.

Within a Christian framework anyone who remarries following divorce or enters into marriage with an intended spouse who has been divorced should be brought to a clear recognition of several spiritual truths. First, remarriage is not a right but a redemptive privilege. If the argument of this book has been sound—that lifelong marriage has always been God's design but that there is forgiveness where there has been failure to achieve it—then remarriage, as bound up with divine grace, is an undeserved gift.[43]

---

42. Small, *Remarriage and God's Renewing Grace*, 72.

43. Cf. Small, "If we say that the couple has a right to remarry, what kind of right do we mean? Surely not personal right, not a right inherent in the orders of creation, nor in Kingdom law. *Properly, it is not a right at all, but a privilege granted in God's provisional will.* But because all remarriage after divorce involves a breach of God's original design, it involves human sin as well. Although it may not involve willful sin or necessarily sin against a person, it is nonetheless sin against God's purpose in marriage, against his unconditional will. Yet it is forgivable for the penitent who applies for God's forgiving grace. God in turn is free to bless the penitent with the healing of a new marriage" (*Remarriage and God's Renewing Grace*, 71).

A further spiritual reality to be acknowledged is that there can be no remarriage without repentance and forgiveness. This has already been addressed and needs no further treatment here. Suffice it to quote the words of Derrick Sherwin Bailey regarding those who have divorced and for whom there is no realistic prospect of reconciliation:

> May one or both then contract a new marriage? Consider the position in terms of personal relation: a marriage which has broken down and disintegrated is no longer a union in "one flesh," or the love from which it alone derived validity and meaning is dead; the marriage is an empty shell, wholly devoid of inner significance, long before divorce reveals the true state of affairs. All this, however, does not in itself justify remarriage; for this, there must be penitence and forgiveness for the sin that caused the breakdown. The failure of love can destroy the *henosis* [oneness], and civil divorce may annul the marriage, but only repentance can sever the bond of guilt for their failure which still unites husband and wife to one another. . . . When relational failure (and divorce) occur, a union does not simply go out of existence: in some sense it continues as a bad, dead thing and can only be terminated by the penitence through which the sin of husband and wife is redeemed.[44]

Yet another spiritual reality to be faced is that there can be no remarriage within a Christian framework without meaningful commitment to Christian marriage as permanent and lifelong. The problem posed by such a requirement is obvious: How can one be sure that such a commitment is no more than empty words, particularly since it comes from one who has made that commitment before and broken it? The answer is that in the last analysis, one cannot be sure—though that is also true of first marriages. That, however, does not mean that the question should not be posed. On the contrary, it should very much be posed.

For one thing, the pastor who is to perform the ceremony is the custodian and trustee of the Christian view of marriage each time he or she conducts a marriage service. Through pastoral acquaintance with the couple pastors are best placed to assess the depth of their responses and will be acutely aware that in addition to responsibility to the couple they also have a responsibility to God, the Church, and society. At the same time, it does not follow that because vows have

---

44. Bailey, *Mystery of Love and Marriage,* 83-84.

been made and broken in the past, new vows will necessarily be broken in the future.[45] If this were so, it would put an end to all hope and possibility of redemption anywhere. Where repentance is real, it brings not only remission but also renewal. It is the task of responsible pastors whose calling lies precisely in the sphere of things spiritual both to raise this issue and satisfy themselves that those seeking remarriage within the Church are acting in a spirit of moral sensitivity and responsibility.[46]

Instruction in the Christian View of Marriage

Not the least important need in the Church today is for instruction in the Christian view of marriage. This is where the Church's most effective contribution to the problem lies. To concentrate energies upon bringing some kind of Christian resolution to the problem of divorce is necessary now and will remain so, but great as that need is, it consists essentially in effecting rescue and restoration after the damage has been done. What is needed is action that will prevent the damage in the first place.

---

45. Cf. Atkinson, "It is not clear why it is thought impossible to be sincere in penitence for the past, and at the same time hope for a new start in the future. Indeed, sometimes it is the recognition of the mistake, indeed sin, in making the first vows which is being expressed in the penitence for divorce" (*To Have and to Hold,* 190).

46. The question arises at this point as to whether, for the sake of its witness, the Church ought not to use a different ritual for remarriage than for first marriages. Such a ritual would both acknowledge past failure and at the same time proclaim God's grace in making a new life possible. (It is not unknown for divorced persons to request such a ritual.) Dr. John Stott quotes Professor Oliver O'Donovan of Oxford University as contending for some form of "institutional visibility" in this matter: "The primary question is how [the Church] may find *some* arrangement that will give adequate form both to its beliefs about the permanence of marriage and to its belief about the forgiveness of the penitent sinner." Stott continues, "It could express this ambivalence either by permitting the remarriage in church (emphasizing the gospel of redemption), while adding some kind of discipline (recognizing God's marriage ideal), or by refusing the remarriage in church (emphasizing the ideal), while adding some expression of acceptance (recognizing the gospel). I myself incline to the former" (Stott, *Decisive Issues Facing Christians Today,* 305). John Stott writes, of course, from the perspective of the Anglican Church in England. The question raised here has to do with the form of service used for remarriages performed in church or a church setting. This is not the place to pursue the matter. The question is discussed with some fullness by Atkinson, *To Have and to Hold,* 189-97 (though this, again, is against the background of the Anglican Church in England). A proposed Ritual for Remarriage (to be used where one or both parties have been divorced) may be found in Morgan, *Is There Life After Divorce in the Church?* 119-24.

The scale of the task should not be underestimated. Divorce is not simply *accepted* but *expected.* A large percentage of young people as yet unmarried *expect* to be divorced at least once. Divorce is simply regarded as a fact of life. Not only so but the shape of living today—its expectations, demands, and pressures—creates a predisposition *against* rather than *for* the permanence of the marriage relationship.

David Atkinson quotes J. Richard Udry for the view that the only thing likely to lower the divorce rate is a return to a rural, religious, nonindustrialized way of life where families function as economic production units. "Courts of reconciliation, waiting periods, high school and marriage courses—all of these things may help some, but none will help much. The kind of marriage Americans believe in simply has high divorce rates."[47] Sociologically, Udry may be right, in which case the challenge to the Church is immense, but the Church has a long history of proclaiming its faith in hostile climates, as well as of seeing people come to share its faith. It is this challenge that the Church must address now. At least two elements in the Church's response may be commented on.

First, the Church must put an end to its silence on the subject. In particular, the pulpit must put an end to its silence. Official declarations and legislative regulations have their value, but they remain largely unknown to the rank and file. The rank and file do hear the pulpit. The pulpit has allowed itself too much to be intimidated into silence, largely from the well-intentioned motive of not giving offense to the divorced and remarried within the congregation, but the Church has paid a terrible price for this silence. Since the pulpit has said nothing, hearers, particularly young people of marriageable age, have assumed that the Church has no position on this subject, and consequently they have taken their view of marriage from the only other place where they could get it, namely, from the society in which they live.

What is chiefly needed from the pulpit is not tirades against divorce and remarriage, though the biblical position on these matters should not be left unstated. What requires chiefly to be insisted upon is lifelong marriage as the setting in which human personhood finds its flowering and fulfillment; in which personal values are

---

47. Atkinson, *To Have and to Hold,* 182.

transvalued as they are shared; in a word, in the covenant faithfulness expressed for all time in Gen. 2:24.[48]

The same message is to be conveyed in the counseling or instruction of those planning to be married. Here the pressures upon the pastor are many and intense. The pastor knows well that the younger the couple, the greater the probability of divorce[49] and that the fewer shared interests, the harder the establishment of a common life, this being particularly the case with respect to a shared faith. But pastors have no weapons beyond their authority as ministers and their personal credibility with those to whom they give counsel. All of these things more than validate the conclusion of James Efird that "it is really not easy to get a divorce; what is wrong is that *it is too easy to get married* in the first place!"[50] It is simple enough to give armchair counsel to pastors about refusing to marry those unwilling to receive instruction on the Christian view of marriage; the least that can be said is that pastors should satisfy themselves that those whom they marry understand the Christian significance of the marriage rite.

Second, in its instruction regarding the meaning of Christian marriage, the Church should highlight the positive nature of the Christian view. Some reference has already been made to this with respect to marriage as a relation between persons. It is understandable that in an age of unprecedented marriage breakdown, the Church should have given most of its attention to marriage breakdown, particularly as a declension from the biblical pattern. The unfortunate by-product of this is that the Church has seemed in consequence to have more to say about what is *wrong* with marriage than about what is *right* with it. In particular it has gained the appearance of trying to cabin and confine marriage by forcing it into a rigid mold, regardless of whether it created joy or misery.

---

48. For a penetrating analysis and powerful statement of marriage in terms of personalistic norms, see Karol Wojtyla (Pope John Paul II), *Love and Responsibility,* ET H. T. Willetts (New York: Farrar, Straus, Giroux, 1994). However one might dissent from some of the Pope's conclusions, his exposition of marriage as relation between persons is profound, compelling, and biblical.

49. David Atkinson quotes Jack Dominian for the conclusion that "every study seems to confirm that age at marriage is important for ultimate stability. Those under twenty are specially vulnerable" (*To Have and to Hold,* 184).

50. James M. Efird, *Marriage and Divorce: What the Bible Says* (Nashville: Abingdon, 1985), 88-89.

In accenting the positive side of marriage, particularly in its aspect of lifelong faithfulness, it needs to be pointed out that Scripture is not forcing on marriage something that is alien to its nature. On the contrary, it belongs to the nature of love to be faithful. Love expresses itself spontaneously in declarations of abiding constancy, as though fidelity is part of its inner quality. For love to be broken is a betrayal of its real meaning.

Most of all, in Christian marriage is seen something of the nature of God himself. Gerald Coleman writes, "Marriage, then is a form by means of which God's eternal love and faithfulness, revealed in Jesus Christ, are made historically present."[51] This is because something of the love of Christ for the Church is visible in the exclusive and abiding relationship between husband and wife (Eph. 5:31-32). To participate in that love, even in partial measure, is life and joy indeed.

---

51. Coleman, *Divorce and Remarriage in the Catholic Church*, 17.

Appendix

Marriage and Divorce in the Early Church to the Time of Augustine

WHILE THE TEACHING of the Early Church lies beyond the strict compass of this book, it has a collateral bearing in witnessing to the earliest interpretation placed on the New Testament data. In seeking to understand that interpretation it is important to keep in mind factors that exercised a powerful influence in the Early Church's attempt to understand and apply the New Testament teaching. Among these were the following: (1) The insistence of current Jewish and Roman law that an adulterous wife *must* be divorced. This had been the case in Judaism since the abolition of the death penalty for adultery as is indicated in the Mishnah.[1] The case was similar in Roman law, following the promulgation of new marriage laws by Augustus between 18 B.C. and A.D. 9, the so-called *Julia Rogationes.* (2) The spread across the empire of a wave of asceticism in keeping with the tenets of stoicism as well as of a variety of philosophies and religious cults. This expressed itself in celibacy and a refusal to take a second wife after the death of the first.[2] Such views quickly took root in the Early Church, as the New Testament itself witnesses (1 Cor. 7:1; 1 Tim. 4:3), threatening the equilibrium of Christian doctrine.[3] (3) A rigoristic understanding of repentance and forgiveness, holding that there was

---

1. Ket. 3:4-5; Sot. 5:1. See also the discussion in Lövestam, "Divorce and Remarriage in the New Testament," 59.

2. For a brief account, see Pat E. Harrell, *Divorce and Remarriage in the Early Church* (Austin, Tex.: R. B. Sweet Co., 1967), 27-30.

3. Ibid., 164-65.

only one opportunity to repent of sins committed subsequent to baptism, and that some sins—notably murder, idolatry, and adultery—could be forgiven only on Judgment Day. Harrell claims that this was the prevailing view throughout the Church in the second and third centuries.[4] Against this background, we may summarize the teaching on marriage and divorce found in the Early Church. It is more varied than is sometimes recognized. Leaving aside minor differences, the following seem to have been the main positions held.

1. A marriage defiled by adultery *must* be ended, but no remarriage is permitted. This view is held by Hermas in *The Shepherd, Mandate* 4. Great importance attaches to this evidence, since it dates no later than 150 (possibly as early as 100) and originates in Rome.[5] The question under discussion is whether a husband, aware of his wife's adultery, becomes culpable if he continues to live with her. The answer given is that he does; therefore, "Let him put her away and let the husband remain by himself. But 'if he put his wife away and marry another he commits adultery himself.'"[6] In response to the further question whether a husband should receive back his wife if she repents, the answer is given: "It is necessary to receive the sinner who repents, but not often, for the servants of God have but one repentance. Therefore, for the sake of repentance the husband ought not to marry" (8; cf. 10). The baseline of Hermas's teaching is that divorce is disallowed and therefore remarriage is impossible: the final sentence of paragraph 6 is virtually a quotation of Matt. 19:9 without the exceptive clause. However, the focal concern of Hermas is with problems arising from that position, namely, cohabiting with an adulterous wife. His answer, for which there is no scriptural authority, is that separation is mandatory, and where there is repentance, there should be forgiveness but not too often. In Section III of *Mandate* 4, he elaborates the view that there is no second repentance. In Section IV, he rejects the view that second marriage following the death of a partner is sinful but affirms that remaining single is more pleasing to the Lord (1, 2).

A kindred position is held by Justin (c. 150). In his *First Apology for the Christians,* contending that the morals of Christians were loftier

---

4. Ibid., 183-89.

5. So G. H. Joyce, *Christian Marriage: An Historical and Doctrinal Study* (London: Sheed and Ward, 1948), 305; Heth and Wenham, *Jesus and Divorce,* 25.

6. *The Apostolic Fathers,* with an English translation by Kirsopp Lake, *Loeb Classical Library* (Cambridge, Mass.: Harvard University Press, 1992), 2:79.

than those of Roman citizens, he quotes what appears to be a combination of Matt. 5:32 and Luke 16:18, "Whoever marries a woman divorced from another man commits adultery" (chap. 15). No hint is given of any exception. In his *Second Apology* he cites the example of a pagan convert to Christianity who tried to reform her debauched husband and, failing, gave him a *repudium* (certificate of divorce) so that she would not be implicated in his wickedness (chap. 2). In chapter 15 of the *First Apology,* he takes a step beyond Hermas, condemning those who marry again after the death of a spouse.[7]

2. Christian marriage, as creating one flesh, disallows a second marriage for any reason, even following the death of a spouse. This seems to be the import of chapter 33 of the *Plea for the Christians* addressed to the Roman Emperors Marcus Aurelius and Commodus by the converted Athenian philosopher Athenagoras in A.D. 177. The Christian view of marriage, he writes, calls "either for a man to remain as he was brought into the world, or else to abide in one marriage and no more, for a second marriage is a fair-seeming adultery. 'Whosoever shall put away his wife,' Scripture says, 'and shall marry another, committeth adultery.' It does not allow him to divorce the one whose maidenhead he had, nor to bring in another wife beside her. One that robs himself of his first wife, even if she be dead, is a covert adulterer, thwarting the hand of God—for in the beginning God made one man and one woman—and destroying the unity of the flesh that was meant for the propagation of the race."[8] The passage has been variously interpreted, Crouzel holding that remarriage after divorce is alone in mind.[9] It is noteworthy that the passage sets out to show that the Christian belief is that people should be content with one marriage, and that is the note on which it ends. If the intervening material includes reference to remarriage following divorce—as where Athenagoras cites Matt. 19:9 minus the exceptive clause—that merely demonstrates that he regards remarriage in any circumstances as being non-Christian.

---

7. Greek *digamia* is regularly used in early Christian writings to denote successive marriage. It may be that this passage is a blanket condemnation of all forms of adultery, including remarriage after divorce. For discussion, see Henri Crouzel, *L'Église Primitive Face au Divorce* (Paris: Beauchesne, 1971), 53-54; Heth and Wenham, *Jesus and Divorce,* 27-28. For the text of Justin's *Apologies,* see *The Ante-Nicene Fathers,* vol. 1, ed. Alexander Roberts and James Donaldson (Buffalo, N.Y.: Christian Literature Publishing Company, 1886), 159-93.

8. "Embassy for the Christians," chap. 33, in Joseph Hugh Crehan, *Ancient Christian Writers* (Westminster, Md.: Newman Press, 1956), 23:74-75.

9. Crouzel, *L'Église Primitive Face au Divorce,* 56-60.

This view reaches its highest pitch with Tertullian, the brilliant North African lawyer and controversialist who, in his later years, separated himself from the orthodox Christian faith, becoming a Montanist. Tertullian's view became progressively more rigid as he moved from orthodoxy to Montanism. While all three of his works on the subject oppose second marriage, they do so with increasing virulence. In the *Ad Uxorem (To My Wife),* written between 200 and 206 before he became a Montanist, which takes the form of advice to his wife should he die before her, he begins by insisting on the spiritual character of the life of heaven. "No, when the future time arrives, we shall not resume the gratification of unseemly passion. It is not such worthless, filthy things that God promises to those who are his own."[10] He at once qualifies this: "Of course we do not reject the union of man and woman in marriage. It is an institution blessed by God for the reproduction of the human race . . . but only once may it be contracted."[11] At the same time, he does not forbid his wife to remarry in the event of his death. "You sin not in remarrying," he writes.[12] "When the Apostle writes that widows and virgins should *so continue,* his language is that of persuasion, since he says, 'I wish all to persevere according to my example.'"[13] As to divorce, this the Lord "absolutely forbids, except for adultery."[14] His next work, *An Exhortation to Chastity,* dates from the period 206-12 when he had become sympathetic to Montanism though not yet a member. In this work, he maintains essentially the same position as in the earlier work, though with additional arguments. In his third work, *On Monogamy,* written sometime after 212-13, his tone is much sharper. He admits one marriage, just as he admits one God.[15] "If a man is not to separate by divorce those whom God has joined together in marriage, it is equally true that man is not to unite in marriage those whom God has separated by death."[16] Christ "permits divorce for this one reason only, that the offense has already been committed which the prohibition of divorce is intended to prevent."[17] As to why he forbids marriage after

---

10. William P. Le Saint, ed., Tertullian, *Treatises on Marriage and Remarriage,* ACW (Westminster, Md.: Newman Press, 1951), 10.

11. Ibid., 11.

12. Ibid., 20.

13. Ibid., 24.

14. Ibid., 27.

15. Ibid., 70.

16. Ibid., 88.

17. Ibid., 90.

the death of a spouse when Paul assumes it as an acceptable possibility in Rom. 7:1-5, his reply is that it has been forbidden by the revelations given by the Paraclete to the Montanists: "The new law abrogated divorce . . . the new prophecy outlaws second marriage."[18] Passages in yet another of Tertullian's writings, *Against Marcion,* have sometimes been taken to mean that Tertullian understood Jesus to teach that divorce was permissible. Arguing against Marcion's contention that while Moses permitted divorce, Jesus forbade it, Tertullian writes, "I maintain, then, that there was a condition in the prohibition which He now made of divorce; the case supposed being, that a man put away his wife for the express purpose of marrying another. His words are: 'Whosoever putteth away his wife, and marrieth another, committeth adultery'—'put away,' that is, dismissed, that another wife may be obtained. . . . Permanent is the marriage which is not rightly dissolved; to marry, therefore, whilst matrimony is undissolved, is to commit adultery."[19]

Harrell comments, "The entire tenor of this passage is to suggest that divorce and remarriage are possible under proper conditions. These words of Tertullian provide an extreme difficulty for those who are committed to maintaining the impossibility of divorce with the correlative right to remarry."[20] On the surface this appears to be so. However, it overlooks the ad hominem element in Tertullian's argument, not to mention his lawyer's style of stating a position in unqualified form first, adding the qualifications later. In this instance the qualifying statement is this: "The Creator, however, except on account of adultery, does not put asunder what He himself joined together. . . . Thus you have Christ following spontaneously the tracks of the Creator everywhere, both in permitting divorce and in forbidding it. . . . He prohibits divorce when He will have the marriage inviolable; He permits divorce when the marriage is spotted with unfaithfulness."[21]

Still another representative of this position is Tertullian's great contemporary, Clement of Alexandria. At the same time, their views appear not to have been completely identical, partly because Clement was no Montanist and partly because Clement himself is

---

18. Ibid., 103.

19. *Against Marcion,* IV 34, in ANF, ed. Alexander Roberts and James Donaldson (Buffalo, N.Y.: Christian Literature Publishing Company, 1885), 3:404.

20. Harrell, *Divorce and Remarriage in the Early Church,* 179.

21. Ibid. For a close examination of these passages from *Against Marcion,* see Crouzel, *L'Église Primitive Face au Divorce,* 97-108.

not always consistent. His teaching on marriage is found in his vast work the *Stromateis*, or *Miscellanies*, which Oulton and Chadwick describe as "a baffling and enigmatic work."[22] In keeping with this, they characterize his attitude to marriage as "curiously confused."[23] In some measure, the confusion arose because he was fighting simultaneously on two fronts—against ascetics and against libertines —but it also arose because, though ostensibly defending the Christian view, his personal view was more ascetic than could readily be reconciled with it.

Clement's view of marriage may be summed up as follows: First, against the ascetics who branded marriage as fornication, Clement affirms that it is a divine institution, citing biblical passages that counsel marriage or assume its acceptability.[24] At the same time, however, he makes it clear that the sole purpose of marital relations is the procreation of children. This is the "middle position" that he stakes out between asceticism and libertinism.[25] In keeping with this, he insists that desire has no place in such marriage. "A man who marries for the sake of begetting children must practice continence, so that it is not desire he feels for his wife, whom he ought to love, and that he may beget children with a chaste and controlled will."[26] This places Clement at odds with Paul's advice in 1 Cor. 7:2, 5, 9, and he seems to try to have it both ways by agreeing that Paul is addressing those experiencing sexual desire but then understanding this to refer to the desire to have children.[27]

From all of this, it is not surprising to find that Clement is opposed to second marriages. Here again he finds himself at odds with Paul and therefore concedes that second marriage is permissible where burning with passion is the alternative; but he at once insists that such a person "does not fulfill the heightened perfection of the gospel ethic. He gains heavenly glory for himself if he remains as he is, and keeps undefiled the marriage yoke broken by death."[28]

As to divorce, Clement sees this as expressly forbidden by Scrip-

---

22. J. E. L. Oulton and Henry Chadwick, *Alexandrian Christianity,* in *Library of Christian Classics* (Philadelphia: Westminster Press, 1954), 19. This translation is used except where indicated otherwise.

23. Ibid., 33.

24. Ibid., 45-46, 56, 61-62.

25. Ibid., 73, 76.

26. Ibid., 67.

27. Ibid., 85.

28. Ibid., 78-79.

ture, except for fornication, adding further that Scripture "regards as fornication, the marriage of those separated while the other is alive."[29] The allusion is evidently to Matt. 5:32; 19:9. He adds the further argument against the remarriage of divorcés that it forecloses the possibility of reconciliation. And while affirming that the law commands that the adulteress be put to death, he goes on to say that the gospel, which is not at variance with the law, teaches that repentance can bring about "a regeneration of life; the old harlot being dead, and she who has been regenerated by repentance having come back again to life."[30]

3. While the indissolubility of marriage is the biblical ideal, divorce followed by remarriage may be permitted as an inferior choice. This view first emerges with Origen (ca. 185—254) in the course of a comment on Matt. 19:2-11 in his commentary on that Gospel. His comment is prompted by the permission granted by certain bishops to a woman to remarry although her husband was still alive. Further, it stands in a section in which, discussing Jesus' statement that Moses' divorce law was given to take account of hardness of heart, Origen suggests that in the new covenant also, some laws may be of the same character. The heart of his comment is as follows:

> But now contrary to what was written, some even of the rulers of the church have permitted a woman to marry, even when her husband was living, doing contrary to what was written, where it said, "A wife is bound for so long as her husband lives," and "Therefore a woman is called an adulteress if she be with another man while her husband lives." Yet they did not take the step altogether without reason. It would seem that they make this concession contrary though it is to the law established at the creation and contained in Scripture, as the lesser of two evils.[31]

This passage is remarkable on two counts. First, Origen states plainly, several times over, that remarriage of a woman whose husband is alive is "contrary to what was written," quoting Rom. 7:2-3,

---

29. ANF, II:379.

30. Ibid. The foregoing account of Clement's teaching, if accurate at all, makes very improbable the suggestion of Harrell (*Divorce and Remarriage in the Early Church,* 180) that *Stromateis III,* 50 envisages the possibility of remarriage following divorce for those unable to accept celibate life for the sake of the kingdom of heaven (Matt. 19:12). Clement clearly takes the passage to have this reference. But to infer, as Harrell does, that the words "not all can receive this saying . . . let him receive it who can receive it" imply that remarriage is an available option following divorce is to give the words a sense that is natural neither in Matthew nor in Clement. Cf. Crouzel, *L'Église Primitive Face au Divorce,* 73.

31. *Commentary on Matthew,* Book XIV, 23, ANF IX, 510.

including the words of verse 3 that such remarriage makes the woman an adulteress. Second, he justifies the episcopal action nonetheless on the grounds that it is the lesser of two evils. He does not define these evils, but the options implied in the circumstances would appear to be living together without benefit of marriage and living in a regularized relationship even if it fell short of the divine plan and order.

A similar principle appears to underlie the decrees of two Early Church councils. The Council of Elvira in Spain, held in 305-6, issued several canons regarding marriage, directed toward women, probably because Roman legislation passed in 293 permitted women to divorce their husbands simply by writing a certificate to that effect. Two of the canons read:

> Canon 8: Again, women who, without any preceding cause, leave their husbands and take up with other men, are not to receive communion even at the end.
>
> Canon 9: Further, a baptized woman who leaves her adulterous baptized husband and marries another, is forbidden to marry him; if she does, she shall not receive communion until the death of her former husband, unless by chance the pressure of illness demand that it be given.[32]

Two features are noteworthy. First, both canons mention the principle of the permanence of marriage. Women who, with reason or without it, divorce their husbands and marry again are banned ·from Communion. Second, the penance is less severe for the spouse of an adulterous husband. She may receive the sacrament even if her first husband is still alive, in the event that her life is threatened by illness. Thus, while the principle of the permanence of marriage is upheld, it is not applied in an inflexible way.

A similar position in principle was adopted by the Council of Arles in France, in the year 314. The relevant decree reads:

> As regards those who find their wives to be guilty of adultery, and who being Christian are, though young men, forbidden to marry, we decree that, so far as may be, counsel be given them not to take other wives, while their own, though guilty of adultery, are yet living.[33]

The decree has been understood in a variety of ways, which

---

32. Samuel Laeuchli, *Power and Sexuality, the Emergence of Canon Law at the Synod of Elvira* (Philadelphia: Temple University, 1972), Appendix, The Canons, 127.

33. Translation as in Joyce, *Christian Marriage,* 310, where the original Latin is also given.

need not be recited here. Several things seem clear. First, the base-line assumed is that remarriage is forbidden for Christians during the lifetime of their partner, even if that partner has committed adultery. Second, it is recognized that such a position will impose severe strain on young Christian men, to whom this canon is directed. Third, the canon urges that such individuals be given all possible counsel to abide by the Christian standard (Latin, "in quantum possit consilium iis detur"), but the implication is that this may prove ineffectual. No penalty is specified in such cases. Crouzel is almost certainly correct in seeing here a combination of a firm doctrinal position with a more indulgent practical attitude.[34]

4. Remarriage is permissible where a marriage has been defiled by adultery. Although several fathers are claimed to have held this position (notably Lactantius, who flourished about 310, and Hilary of Poitiers, who died 367), there is only one of whom the claim can be made with any credibility. This is Ambrosiaster, the name given to the unknown author of commentaries on Paul's Epistles written about 375 and originally attributed to Ambrose of Milan. The commentaries prescribe sharply different rules for men and women. The latter are denied the right to remarry, even if the husband were guilty of adultery. With husbands it is different. Commenting on the final clause of 1 Cor. 7:11, "Let not the husband put away his wife" (KJV), he writes:

> We must supply the words "save for the cause of fornication."
> And therefore the Apostle does not add, as in the case of the woman:
> "but if he depart let him remain unmarried," for a man may marry, if
> he has put away his offending wife; since the law does not bind him
> as it does the woman, for "the head of the woman is the man."[35]

In a later comment on 1 Cor. 7:15, Ambrosiaster interprets Paul's words referring to the desertion of a believer by an unbelieving spouse—"the brother or sister is not bound in these things"—to mean that the believer is free to remarry. Joyce dismisses all of this—notably the unequal treatment of the sexes—as a local accommodation to Roman practice.[36] Heth and Wenham emphasize the singularity of Ambrosiaster's views among early Christian writers,

---

34. Crouzel, *L'Église Primitive Face au Divorce*, 122.

35. Translation as in Joyce, *Christian Marriage*, 321-22, where the Latin text is also given, though the page reference to Migne is inaccurate. It should read, *Patrologia Latina* XVII, 230.

36. Joyce, *Christian Marriage*, 322.

stating particularly that in allowing divorcés to remarry he was "a stranger to the dominant Christian attitudes of the early church."[37] Even so, Crouzel is probably nearest the mark in concluding that all Ambrosiaster was attempting to do was to expound Scripture, and that his exposition reflects the prevailing practice of his time.[38]

5. Marriage not merely should not be dissolved but cannot be dissolved because the marriage bond is indelible. This view came to its clearest and fullest expression with Augustine (354—430). This is not to say that it cannot be found in essence earlier. Clearly it is present in principle in section 1 above, though the emphasis there falls on the *necessity* of ending a marriage relationship where adultery has intruded. The same is true of section 2, except that there *any* second marriage, even following the death of a spouse, is forbidden. In section 3 the baseline of the teaching of Scripture is taken to be the permanence of the marriage bond, even if exceptions are envisaged.

Moreover, some of Augustine's great contemporaries in the Church, Jerome and John Chrysostom, adopt the same position in principle, even if they do not set it in the same theological framework as Augustine. Thus Jerome (ca. 347—420) more than once paraphrases 1 Cor. 7:10 to show that a wife who has left her husband has only two options: to live alone or be reconciled to her husband.[39] He elaborates the point still more forcefully in another letter, written in response to an inquiry made by a priest, Amandus, on behalf of a parishioner who had divorced her husband for adultery and sexual vice and had been compelled against her will to make another marriage. Could she remain in communion with the Church without doing penance, even though her first husband was still alive? Jerome replied:

A husband may be an adulterer or a sodomite, he may be stained with every crime and may have been left by his wife because of his sins; yet he is still her husband and, so long as he lives, she may not marry another. . . . Therefore if your sister who, as she says, has been forced into a second union, wishes to receive the body of Christ and not to be accounted an adulteress, let her do penance; so far at least as from the time she begins to have no

---

37. Heth and Wenham, *Jesus and Divorce,* 38.

38. Crouzel, *L'Église Primitive Face au Divorce,* 22.

39. *Against Jovinian,* I 10, in *Nicene and Post-Nicene Fathers,* second series, ed. Philip Schaff and Henry Wace (Grand Rapids: Eerdmans, reprint, 1979), *St. Jerome, Letters and Select Works,* 6:353. Cf. Letter XLVIII, 5.

farther intercourse with that second husband who ought to be called not a husband but an adulterer.[40]

Chrysostom (ca. 347—407), bishop of Constantinople, speaks with the same voice. Many statements on the unbreakability of the marriage bond can be found in the homilies of which the following is typical:

> Indeed, just as when a woman who is married to one man has intercourse with another she commits adultery in consequence, so if a man who is married to one woman takes another wife, he has committed adultery.[41]

But perhaps most telling is the vivid passage from the work *De Libello Repudii (Concerning the Certificate of Divorce),* the second of three homilies on marriage. Expounding 1 Cor. 7:39, "A woman is bound to her husband as long as he lives," Chrysostom concludes:

> If then a man wishes to dismiss his wife or the wife wishes to leave her husband, let her remember this saying and that it represents Paul as present and pursuing her, crying out and saying: "The wife is bound by the law." Just as escaped slaves, even if they have left the house of their master, still carry their chain, so wives, even if they have left their husbands, have the law in the form of a chain which condemns them, accusing them of adultery, accusing those who take them, and saying: "Your husband is still living and what you have done is adultery."[42]

It is with Augustine that the understanding of marriage as indissoluble achieves coherent theological expression. He wrote on the subject as early as 390 and devoted an entire two-volume work to it as late as 419, *To Pollentius—On Adulterous Marriages.* The recurring note of this work is that while adultery is a sufficient ground (and indeed the only ground) for a husband to dismiss his wife or a wife to leave her husband, yet it does not break the marriage bond. Consequently, any subsequent marriage is adulterous. He gives voice to this view again and again.

> Both husband and wife have the same nature, each of them commits adultery, if one or the other enters into a second union,

---

40. NPNF, 6:110-11.

41. *Fathers of the Church,* St. John Chrysostom, *Commentary on St. John,* Homily 63, trans. Thomas Aquinez Goggan (Washington, D.C.: Catholic University of America Press, 1960), 41:188.

42. The Second "Homily on Marriage," *De libello repudii,* in Migne, *Patrologia Graeca* (Parisiis: Migne, 1856), 51:218-19 (my translation).

even though a union with an unfaithful spouse has been disrupted.[43]

In response to the claim that the offended party has the right of remarriage, he asserts:

> We likewise declare him to be an adulterer who puts away his wife without the cause of immorality and marries another; yet we do not therein defend from the taint of this sin the man who puts away his wife because of immorality and marries another. For while the one offense is greater than the other, we yet recognize both men to be adulterers.[44]

The exception stated in Matt. 5:32 and 19:9 is not one that breaks the marriage bond, thereby giving freedom to remarry. The unqualified statements in Mark and Luke rather give the fundamental principle.[45] The exceptive clauses in Matthew were rather given as a safeguard against the hardness of heart that would divorce for any and every reason (19:8).

> Therefore the Lord, to strengthen the rule that a wife should not lightly be put away, excepted only the case of fornication. All the rest of whatever annoyance might exist He orders to be courageously put up with in the interests of conjugal loyalty and chastity.[46]

Thus far, Augustine has said nothing that has not been said by his predecessors or contemporaries. He was clearly searching for some understanding that would stamp marriage with an unbreakable seal. This he found in viewing it as a sacrament. Hence in the treatise *On Marriage and Concupiscence,* written about the same time as *On Adulterous Marriages* (ca. 420), he compares marriage with the sacrament of baptism.

> It is . . . also a certain sacramental bond in marriage which is recommended to believers in wedlock. Accordingly it is enjoined by the apostle: "Husbands, love your wives, even as Christ also loved the Church." . . . Thus between the conjugal pair, as long as they live, the mystical bond has a permanent obligation, and can be cancelled neither by separation nor by union with another. . . . In like manner the soul of an apostate, which renounces as it were

43. I 8, as in *Fathers of the Church,* St. Augustine, *Treatises on Marriage and Other Subjects,* trans. Charles T. Wilcox (Washington, D.C.: Catholic University Press, 1955), 27:70.

44. I 9, as in *Fathers of the Church,* 72.

45. Ibid., I 9, 10.

46. "The Lord's Sermon on the Mount," Book I, 14, 39, in ACW (Westminster, Md.: Newman Press, 1948), 5:48.

its marriage union with Christ, does not, even though it has cast its faith away, lose the sacrament of its faith, which it received in the laver of regeneration. He retains, however, the sacrament after his apostasy, to the aggravation of his punishment, not for meriting the reward.[47]

To Augustine marriage is not merely permanent in the divine intention, it is indestructible and indelible in character and therefore remains untouched by divorce.

Augustine's view remained a guiding light to the Church for the next thousand years. It is worth noting, however, that he appears not to have been wholly satisfied with his resolution of the issue. Toward the end of his career, he wrote the two volumes of *Retractations,* a kind of collection of "second thoughts" about much of what he had written during the previous 40 years. Referring to his work *On Adulterous Marriages,* he wrote: "I wrote two books on adulterous marriages with the desire of solving, according to the Scriptures, to the best of my ability, a very difficult question. I do not know whether I have done this very clearly. On the contrary, I think that I did not reach a perfect solution of this question, although I have clarified many of its obscurities."[48] In *Retractations* I 18, he expresses a similar reservation about his interpretation of the exceptive clause in Matt. 5:32 (quoted above), saying:

> But the following question should be considered and examined again and again: what immorality the Lord means to be understood as that for which one may put away his wife—that which is condemned in licentious acts or that about which the following is said: "Thou destroyest everyone who is unfaithful to Thee," in which, certainly the former is included. . . . But what is to be understood by immorality and how it is to be limited, and whether, because of it, one may put away his wife is an almost obscure question. Yet there is no doubt that this is permitted because of the immorality committed in licentious acts.[49]

Indeed in a much earlier treatise, *On Faith and Works,* dating from about 413, he had written:

---

47. NPNF, St. Augustine, *Anti-Pelagian Writings* (Grand Rapids: Eerdmans, reprint, 1978), 5:268.

48. *Retractations* II, 83. ET *The Fathers of the Church. Saint Augustine, The Retractations,* trans. Mary Inez Bogan (Washington, D.C.: Catholic University of America Press, 1968), 247.

49. *Retractations* II, 82-83.

The man who leaves his wife because of adultery and marries another is not, it seems, as blameworthy as the man who for no reason leaves his wife and marries another. Nor is it clear from Scripture whether a man who has left his wife because of adultery, which he is certainly permitted to do, is himself an adulterer, if he marries again. And if he should, I do not think that he would commit a grave sin.[50]

Joyce declines to see more in these qualifications than an admission by Augustine that his exegesis may not have been absolutely correct, pointing out that Augustine never amends his view that marriage is indissoluble.[51] This is true. On the other hand, it is hard to believe that Augustine is making no more than a conventional disclaimer of infallibility, especially in view of his repeated statements of the difficulty of the subject. He appears rather to have harbored an inner hesitation about some aspect or aspects of his teaching, though he never gives any specific indication of what these might be.

Conclusion

Is there any unity of view in all of the evidence surveyed? At first sight this might appear unlikely in view of the wide diversity disclosed, ranging from obligatory divorce in cases of adultery but without the possibility of remarriage to the permissibility of divorce and remarriage in cases involving adultery, not to mention the intervening permutations. However, this wide disparity is diminished significantly by several considerations. To begin with, it is diminished by the factors listed at the beginning of this appendix as exerting a weighty influence upon the thinking of the Early Church on this subject. These include the insistence of current Jewish and Roman law that an adulterous wife must be divorced; the impact of stoic asceticism, which exalted celibacy and discouraged remarriage after the death of a spouse; and the tendency within the Church itself to a rigoristic understanding of repentance and forgiveness. Another consideration is the distribution of the evidence because, while the various views listed can all be documented from Early Church sources, they are by no means evenly supported either in all geographical areas of the Church or in all of the first five centuries.

No doubt it is dangerous and can be misleading to seek a "com-

---

50. St. Augustine, *On Faith and Works* (ACW, No. 48). Trans. and annotated by Gregory J. Lombardo (New York: Newman Press, 1988), 43.
51. Joyce, *Christian Marriage,* 319.

mon core," which may be no more than a lowest common denominator. Nor is it always possible to identify which factors may be operating in a given instance. However, it is at least worth attempting to see how far it is possible to isolate a common mentality in the Early Church, and if there was such, what it may tell us of the earliest understanding of the teaching of Jesus. When we do this at least three conclusions appear to be indicated.

1. The Early Church believed marriage to be permanent and lifelong. The various fathers did not all use the same language, and as we have seen, it is not until Augustine that the indissolubility of marriage is defended on the grounds that it is sacramental. Marriage was understood by them as a lifelong commitment that was not to be broken. It is shown for example by the sense they give to terms denoting divorce—a point easily overlooked by modern readers and fruitful of much misunderstanding. While they speak of "rupture" or "breach" or "dissolution" of marriage by adultery, they do not use these terms in the modern legal sense of the termination of marriage with the freedom to contract another. They rather mean the termination of married life but not the breaking of the marriage bond. Again, they interpret the exceptive clauses of Matt. 5:32 and 19:9 in terms of their basic understanding of marriage and so do not read them as providing exceptional grounds on which an existing marriage is ended and therefore a new one may be begun. The same may be said of the statement in 1 Cor. 7:15 that the believing spouse is not bound to maintain a marriage when an unbelieving spouse has deserted. The sole exception to all of these specifics is Ambrosiaster.

On the other hand, most of the views that go beyond the understanding of marriage as permanent embody—necessarily—the principle of permanence. This is the case where adultery is regarded as terminating a marriage but without permitting remarriage. The same principle underlies the view that remarriage is forbidden following the death of a spouse. These represent intensifications of the principle of permanence rather than breaches of it.

2. At the same time, and without repudiating the foregoing principle, there is significant evidence of allowances being made on pastoral grounds. We have seen how Origen was prepared to accept episcopal permission of remarriage, while the Councils of Elvira and Arles, though maintaining the principle, did not apply it rigidly. Augustine himself, while arguing strenuously in *On Faith and Works* that immorality must be renounced before baptism and questionable marriages avoided, nevertheless hesitates to say whether, in

cases where they have already been formed, they should constitute a permanent impediment to baptism.[52]

3. Divorce and remarriage were not regarded as unpardonable sins. This is implicit in some sense in the pastoral allowances just discussed, which were more than simply a condoning of wrong but rather adjustments of law to human situations so that the law did not become productive of greater evil. However, the recognition that there could be forgiveness for divorce and remarriage became explicit in the penitential system of the Church. Typical are the so-called Canons of Basil (330-79), bishop of Caesarea in Cappadocia. In truth, these are responses in a series of letters to questions asked by Amphilocius, bishop of Iconium. Prominent among these are questions of marriage, divorce, and remarriage and the varying penalties imposed for various sins. For example, Canon 21 of Epistle 199 reads:

> A married man committing lewdness with a single woman is severely punished as guilty of fornication, but we have no canon to treat such a man as an adulterer.[53]

The distinction between fornication and adultery was considerable. Canon 58 fixes the penalty for adultery at 15 years, while for fornication the penalty is fixed at 7 years in Canon 59. (The form of the punishment is exclusion from Communion.) The details of the penance are not of concern here. The point of moment is that remarriage was not treated as a sin demanding exclusion. That is not to say that it was not taken very seriously.

---

52. "However, there are some marriages which are certainly illicit, and whoever enters into them should not be admitted to baptism unless he amends and does penance. As for doubtful marriages, these we should try to prevent. For what advantage is there in marriages of this kind. But if some are already married in this way, then I am not so sure that we should admit such persons to baptism" (ACW, No. 48, 43).

53. NPNF, ed. Henry R. Percival (Grand Rapids: Eerdmans, reprint 1979), 14:606.

Select Bibliography

Adams, Jay E. *Divorce and Remarriage in the Bible*. Grand Rapids: Zondervan Publishing House, 1980.

Atkinson, David. *To Have and to Hold: The Marriage Covenant and the Discipline of Divorce*. Grand Rapids: Wm. B. Eerdmans Publishing Co., 1979.

Coleman, Gerald D. *Divorce and Remarriage in the Catholic Church*. New York: Paulist Press, 1988.

Collins, Raymond F. *Divorce in the New Testament*. Collegeville, Minn.: Liturgical Press, 1992.

Cornes, Andrew. *Divorce and Remarriage: Biblical Principles and Pastoral Practice*. Grand Rapids: Wm. B. Eerdmans Publishing Co., 1993.

Guenther, W., et al. "Marriage, Adultery, Bride, Bridegroom." In *New International Dictionary of New Testament Theology,* vol. 2., ed. Colin Brown. Grand Rapids: Zondervan Publishing House, 1977.

Hawthorne, G. F. "Marriage and Divorce, Adultery and Incest." In *Dictionary of Paul and His Letters,* ed. Gerald F. Hawthorne and Ralph P. Martin. Downers Grove, Ill.: InterVarsity Press, 1993.

Heth, W. A., and G. J. Wenham. *Jesus and Divorce*. Nashville: Thomas Nelson Publishers, 1985.

House, H. Wayne, ed. *Divorce and Remarriage: Four Christian Views*. Downers Grove, Ill.: InterVarsity Press, 1990.

Keener, Craig S. *And Marries Another: Divorce and Remarriage in the Teaching of the New Testament*. Peabody, Mass.: Hendrickson Publishers, 1991.

Laney, J. Carl. *The Divorce Myth: A Biblical Examination of Divorce and Remarriage*. Minneapolis: Bethany House Publishers, 1981.

Lövestam, E. "Divorce and Remarriage in the New Testament." In *Jewish Law Annual* 4, 1981.

Luck, William F. *Divorce and Remarriage: Recovering the Biblical View*. San Francisco: Harper and Row, 1987.

Marshall, I. H. "Divorce." In *New International Dictionary of New Testament Theology,* vol. 1, ed. Colin Brown. Grand Rapids: Zondervan Publishing House, 1975.

Richards, Larry. *Remarriage: A Healing Gift from God*. Waco, Tex.: Word Publishing, 1990.

Roberts, William P., ed. *Divorce and Remarriage: Religious and Psychological Perspectives*. Kansas City: Sheed and Ward, 1990.

Small, Dwight Hervey. *Remarriage: and God's Renewing Grace*. Grand Rapids: Baker Book House, 1986.

Stein, R. H. "Divorce." In *Dictionary of Jesus and the Gospels,* ed. Joel B. Green, Scot McKnight, and I. Howard Marshall. Downers Grove, Ill.: InterVarsity Press, 1992.

Stott, John R. W. "Marriage and Divorce." In *Decisive Issues Facing Christians Today.* Old Tappan, N.J.: Fleming H. Revell Company, 1990.

von Allmen, J. J. *Pauline Teaching on Marriage*. London: Faith Press, 1963.

Subject Index

211

Index of Modern Authors

Index of Ancient Authors

Scripture Index